Hold Still

Hold Still

A Memoir with Photographs

Sally Mann

LITTLE, BROWN AND COMPANY

NEW YORK   BOSTON   LONDON

Little, Brown and Company
Hachette Book Group
1290 Avenue of the Americas, New York, NY 10104
littlebrown.com

First Edition: May 2015

Little, Brown and Company is a division of Hachette Book Group, Inc. The Little, Brown name and logo are trademarks of Hachette Book Group, Inc.

The publisher is not responsible for websites (or their content) that are not owned by the publisher.

The Hachette Speakers Bureau provides a wide range of authors for speaking events. To find out more, go to hachettespeakersbureau.com or call (866) 376-6591.

The names and identifying characteristics of certain individuals have been changed, whether or not so noted in the text.

Excerpt from "Reality Demands" from *Poems New and Collected* by Wisława Szymborska. English translation copyright © 1998 by Harcourt, Inc. Reprinted by permission of Houghton Mifflin Harcourt Publishing Company. All rights reserved.

ISBN 978-0-316-24776-4

LCCN 2014959584

10 9 8 7 6 5 4 3

QG-T

Designed by Laura Lindgren

Printed in the United States of America

The steady eyes of the crow and the camera's candid eye
See as honestly as they know how, but they lie.

—W. H. Auden

Contents

The Meuse

We all have them: those boxes in storage, detritus left to us by our forebears. Mine were in the attic, and there were lots of them. Most were crumbling cardboard, held together by ancient twine of various types: the thick cotton kind sold for clotheslines wrapped once around and tied with an emphatic square knot; its weaker version, better suited for wrapping a packet of letters, and the shaggy blond string used for hay bales, the ends raveling.

I remember having seen some of the oldest boxes, those from my father's and mother's families, when I was a child. They had been stored in cabinets above the piles of rags where the dogs slept in the carport and had accumulated dander and dog hair from decades of boxers and Great Danes. Though decaying with age, the boxes bore unmistakable signs of craftsmanship, such as the elegant advertisements from the era stamped on the sides, or the delicate painting on the tin case my father used to ship artworks from "Pnom-Pehn" in the 1930s, which gave them a decorous, dignified air.

In our attic, they kept an increasingly disapproving vigil, it seemed to me, over the promiscuous sprawl of stuff that piled up around them as my husband, Larry, and I and our kids made our own histories: snapshots, of course, by the thousands, but also letters, science fair exhibits, entubed diplomas, the remains of a costume in which Jessie dressed up for Halloween as a blade of grass, snarly-haired dolls, the sawn-apart cast from Virginia's broken leg when she was six, paper dolls with outfits still carefully hooked over their shoulders, report cards, spangly tutus and soiled, hem-dangling pinafores, receipts, a box of broken candy cigarettes, bank statements, exhibition reviews, a trunk of dress-up ball gowns, tatty Easter baskets still bedded with a tangle of green plastic grass, two pairs of Lolita sunglasses, their plastic brittle and faded, and the section of Sheetrock cut from the kitchen of our old house on which the heights of the children were penciled each year.

And, of course, there was also in the attic the residue of my own unexamined past: the many variously sized boxes, secured with brittle masking tape, containing letters, journals, childhood drawings, and photographs. These had been left untouched for decades as I ignored Joan Didion's sage advice to remain on nodding terms, at least, with the people we used to be, lest they show up to settle accounts at some dark 4:00 a.m. of the soul.

The tape and twine on these boxes, where my family's past sleeps, might never have been cut nor their complicated secrets revealed if I hadn't gotten a letter early in July 2008 from John Stauffer, distinguished professor of English, American Studies, and African American Studies at Harvard, asking me to deliver the Massey Lectures in the History of American Civilization. After reading the letter, I cycled through the familiar antics of disbelief: forehead slapping, eye-rolling, exaggerated scrutiny of the envelope for an error . . . but, no. They wanted me, a photographer, to deliver the three scholarly lectures at Harvard beginning on my sixtieth birthday, three years down the road, in May 2011.

Rushing to my Day-Timer, I searched in vain for a conflict. In fact, I searched in vain for a calendar page that far in the future.

No way could I reasonably decline. Years earlier, my brilliant young friend Niall MacKenzie had been given to prefacing his ironically self-inflating forecasts with the line "Well, Sally, when they ask me to deliver the Massey Lectures . . ." I had heard this refrain so many times that the Masseys had come to represent for me the pinnacle of intellectual achievement. But I didn't think of myself as much of an intellectual, and I was certainly no academic. I wasn't even a writer. And what did I have to write about, even supposing I could?

I had acquired some acclaim and notoriety, as well as the irritating label "controversial," in the early 1990s with the publication of my third book of photographs, *Immediate Family*. In it were pictures I had made of my children, Emmett, Jessie, and Virginia, going about their lives, sometimes without clothing, on our farm tucked into the Virginia hills. Out of a conviction that my lens should remain open to the full scope of their childhood, and with willing, creative participation from everyone involved, I photographed their triumphs, confusion, harmony, and isolation, as well as the hardships that tend to befall children—bruises, vomit, bloody noses, wet beds—all of it. In a case of cosmically bad timing, the release of *Immediate Family* coincided with a moral panic about the depiction of children's bodies and a heated debate about government funding of the arts. (I had received grants from the National Endowment for the Arts and the National Endowment for the Humanities but not for the pictures of my children.) Much confusion, distraction, internal struggle, and, ultimately, fuel for new work emerged from this embattled period.

Would the Massey committee at Harvard expect me to justify my family pictures all these years later? I didn't mind doing that, but I hoped I could also focus on the work that came afterward, deeply personal explorations of the landscape of the American South, the nature of mortality (and the mortality of nature), intimate depictions of my husband, and the indelible marks that slavery left on the world surrounding me. With trepidation, I called John Stauffer, and his answer only made me more anxious: anything, speak about anything you want.

Oppressed by this indulgence and uncertain how to proceed, I went into a spasm of self-doubt and fear so incapacitating that it was nearly a year before I told Stauffer I'd do it. And then, as often happens to me, the self-doubt that had dammed up so much behind its seemingly impermeable wall allowed the first trickles of hope and optimism to seep out, and through the widening crack possibility flooded forth. Insecurity, for an artist, can ultimately be a gift, albeit an excruciating one.

I began looking for what I had to say where I usually find it: in what William Carlos Williams called "the local." I wonder if he would think my admittedly extreme interpretation—working at home, seldom leaving the spacious plenty of our farm—too *much* local. For Larry, it sometimes is: he once irritatedly clocked five weeks during which I didn't so much as go to the grocery store. But like a high-strung racehorse who needs extra weight in her saddle pad, I like a handicap and relish the aesthetic challenge posed by the limitations of the ordinary. Conversely, I get a little panicked when I have before me what the comic-strip character Pogo once referred to as "insurmountable opportunities." It is easier for me to take ten good pictures in an airplane bathroom than in the gardens at Versailles.

And so I turned to the boxes in my attic, starting with those that bore witness to my own youth. Who and what would I find in them?

My long preoccupation with the treachery of memory has convinced me that I have fewer and more imperfect recollections of childhood than most people. But having asked around over the years, I'm not so sure now that this is the case. Perhaps we are all like the poet Eric Ormsby, writing of his childhood home: We watch our past occlude, bleed away, the overflowing gardens erased, their sun-remembered walls crumbling into dust at our fingers' approach. And, just as Ormsby wrote, we all would "cry at the fierceness of that velocity / if our astonished eyes had time."

Whatever of my memories hadn't crumbled into dust must surely by now have been altered by the passage of time. I tend to agree with the theory that if you want to keep a memory pristine, you must not call upon it too often, for each time it is revisited, you alter it irrevocably, remembering not the original impression left by experience but the last time you recalled it. With tiny differences creeping in at each cycle, the exercise of our memory does not bring us closer to the past but draws us farther away.

I had learned over time to meekly accept whatever betrayals memory pulled over on me, allowing my mind to polish its own beautiful lie. In distorting the information it's supposed to be keeping safe, the brain, to its credit, will often bow to some instinctive aesthetic wisdom, imparting to our life's events a coherence, logic, and symbolic elegance that's not present or not so obvious in the improbable, disheveled sloppiness of what we've actually been through. Elegance and logic aside, though, in researching and writing this book, I knew that a tarted-up form of reminiscence wouldn't do, no matter how aesthetically adroit or merciful. I needed the truth, or, as a friend once said, "something close to it." That something would be memory's truth, which is to scientific, objective truth as a pearl is to a piece of sand. But it was all I had.

So, before I scissored the ancestral boxes, I opened my own to check my erratic remembrance against the artifacts they held, and in doing so encountered the malignant twin to imperfect memory: the treachery of photography. As far back as 1901 Émile Zola telegraphed the threat of this relatively new medium, remarking that you cannot claim to have really seen something until you have photographed it. What Zola perhaps also knew or intuited was that once photographed, whatever you had "really seen" would never be seen by the eye of memory again. It would forever be cut from the continuum of being, a mere sliver, a slight, translucent paring from the fat life of time; elegiac, one-dimensional, immediately assuming the amber quality of nostalgia: an instantaneous memento mori. Photography would seem to preserve our past and make it invulnerable to the distortions of repeated memorial superimpositions, but I think that is a fallacy: photographs supplant and corrupt the past, all the while creating their own memories. As I held my childhood pictures in my hands, in the tenderness of my "remembering," I also knew that with each photograph I was forgetting.

I closed my boxes and turned to those of earlier generations. They had come to my attic in stages—first from Larry's parents and grandparents and then from my father and mother—and they had not been opened since the deaths that necessitated boxing up a life. In them was all that remained in the world of these people, their entire lives crammed into boxes that would barely hold a twelve-pack.

When an animal, a rabbit, say, beds down in a protecting fencerow, the weight and warmth of his curled body leaves a mirroring mark upon the ground. The grasses often appear to have been woven into a birdlike nest, and perhaps were indeed caught and pulled around by the delicate claws as he turned in a circle before subsiding into rest. This soft bowl in the grasses, this body-formed evidence of hare, has a name, an obsolete but beautiful word: *meuse*. (Enticingly close to Muse, daughter of Memory, and source of inspiration.) Each of us leaves evidence on the earth that in various ways bears our form, but when I gently press my hand into the rabbit's downy, rounded meuse it makes me wonder: will all the marks I have left on the world someday be tied up in a box?

Cutting the strings on the first family carton, my mother's, I wondered what I would find, what layers of unknown family history. Would the wellsprings of my work as an artist—the fascination with family, with the southern landscape, with death—be in these boxes? What ghosts of long-dead, unknown family members were in them, keeping what secrets?

I will confess that in the interest of narrative I secretly hoped I'd find a payload of southern gothic: deceit and scandal, alcoholism, domestic abuse, car crashes, bogeymen, clandestine affairs, dearly loved and disputed family land, abandonments, blow jobs, suicides, hidden addictions, the tragically early death of a beautiful bride, racial complications, vast sums of money made and lost, the return of a prodigal son, and maybe even bloody murder.

If any of this stuff lay hidden in my family history, I had the distinct sense I'd find it in those twine-bound boxes in the attic. And I did: all of it and more.

PART I

Family Ties:
The Importance of Place

1

The Sight of My Eye

Until my early twenties, I kept handwritten journals. As I filled each one, I would pile it on top of the others under my desk and discard the bottom one. The first to go, I remember, was a small, pink child's journal with "My Precious Thoughts" in cursive gold lettering on the cover, those thoughts safeguarded by a pitifully ineffectual brass lock.

When I was eighteen, in the winter prior to my June wedding, I relinquished my room to my mother, who had huffily left her marital bed when Tara, a Great Dane, moved into it with my father. Cleaning out my stuff, I pulled out the journals accumulated so far and bundled them into a box I labeled "Journals, 1968–."

Ripping the desiccated masking tape off that box some forty years later, I wasn't surprised to find that the first entry in the earliest journal was a paean to the formative Virginia landscape of my youth. It begins:

> It has been a mild summer, with more rain than most. We work hard
> and grow tired. The evening is cool as we watch the night slide in and
> hear each sound in the still blue hour. The silver poplar shimmers
> and every so often the pond ripples with fish. The mountains grow
> deep. They are darker than the night.

Judging by the unembellished declarative sentences in those first paragraphs, it's a safe bet I was reading Hemingway that summer, somewhere around my seventeenth. But read down a few more lines and I come over all Faulknerian, soaring into rhapsodic description:

We reach the top pasture and you are ahead and spread your arms wide. I run to catch up and it opens to me. There is no word for this; nothing can contain it or give it address. There are no boundaries, no states. The mountains are long and forever and they give the names, they give the belief in the names. The mountains give the name of blue, the name of change and mist and hour and light and noise of wind, they are the name of my name, the hand of my hand and the sight of my eye.

I have loved Rockbridge County, Virginia, surely since the moment my birth-bleary eyes caught sight of it. Not only is it abundant with the kind of obvious, everyday beauty that even a mewling babe can appreciate, but it also boasts the world-class drama of the Natural Bridge of Virginia, surveyed by George Washington and long vaunted (incorrectly, as it turned out) on local billboards as one of the Seven Natural Wonders of the World. Like any true native, I didn't bother to investigate our local tourist draw until well into my thirties, and when I did I was chagrined, blown away by its airy audacity.

After checking out the Natural Bridge, visitors looking for a dose of the Ye Olde will usually make a stop in history-rich Lexington, the county seat (pop. 7,000), where I grew up. Plenty of interesting people have been born or passed time in Lexington, the artist Cy Twombly being among the more notable, but also Cyrus McCormick, inventor of the reaper; Gen. George Marshall; Tom Wolfe; Arnold Toynbee; Alben Barkley, vice president under Truman, who not only passed through here but passed away here, being declared dead on the dais in midspeech by my own physician father; and Patsy Cline, who lived just down the creek from our old house in town.

The young novelist Carson McCullers, burdened by the meteoric success of *The Heart Is a Lonely Hunter* and recovering in Lexington, was once hauled out of a bathtub at a mutual friend's house, fully clothed, drenched, and drunk, by my mother. Thinking about it now, it's probably a good thing that my mother is not around to receive the unwelcome news that her oft-told stories about Edward Albee writing *Who's Afraid of Virginia Woolf?* while in Lexington are likely apocryphal. Not only that, but she said he did so in a cottage on the grounds of my childhood home, Boxerwood, while visiting its occupant James Boatwright. I'm pretty sure her assertion that the Albee characters George and Martha had been based on a local faculty couple famous for their bickering and alcohol consumption is incorrect, too, but that probably wouldn't stop her even now from deliciously persevering with it. Besides, it's still believable to me, for I well remember the sounds of the drinking and bickering during Boatwright's late-night literary parties at the cottage drifting down to my open bedroom windows during the early sixties.

The eye-filling Reynolds Price visited Boatwright often (as did, at various times, Eudora Welty, Mary McCarthy, and W. H. Auden), and on the night I attended my first prom at age fourteen, he and Boatwright emerged from the screen porch to drunkenly toast me, calling me Sally Dubonnet, a term I find baffling even today, as their gin rickeys sloshed over the glasses.

What brings both luminaries and regular visitors to Lexington are often the two handsome old colleges, Washington and Lee University and Virginia Military Institute, which coexist uncomfortably cheek by jowl, as well as the homes and burial places of Stonewall Jackson and Robert E. Lee. The remains of those defeated generals' horses, Little Sorrel and Traveller, are also here, one at VMI, the other at W&L.

When I was growing up, Traveller's bleached skeleton was displayed on a plinth in an academic building at W&L, pinned together somewhat worryingly by wire and desecrated with the hastily carved initials of students. Just a few blocks north from Traveller at neighboring VMI, the nearly hairless hide of the deboned Little Sorrel was displayed in the museum. I was told that a local guide once explained to his clutch of credulous tourists that the skeleton was Little Sorrel as a mature horse and the stuffed hide was Little Sorrel when he was just a young colt.

The Shenandoah Valley attracts many visitors; some come for its history, especially its Civil War history, but even more for its undeniable physical beauty. It is said that as the radical abolitionist John Brown stood on the elevated scaffold in his last minutes, he gazed out at our lovely valley in wonderment. Eyewitnesses reported that before the hangman covered his head, John Brown turned to the sheriff and expressed with windy eloquence his admiration for the landscape before him. The sheriff responded laconically but with unambiguous agreement, "Yup, none like it," and signaled the hangman to pull, pdq, the white hood over Brown's valley-struck eyes.

John Brown was gazing south from the northernmost, and widest, part of the valley, but had he been standing on the scaffold in our part, some 150 miles south, his wonderment and fustian would have been tenfold. Everyone's is, even without the scaffold and the imminent hood. Had Brown been in Rockbridge County, he would have begged the hangman for one more minute to experience the geologic comfort of the Blue Ridge and Allegheny mountain ranges as they come together out of the soft blue distance.

This effect is especially apparent as you drive down the valley on I-81, the north-south interstate that parallels I-95 to the east. As you approach Rockbridge, the two mountain ranges begin to converge, forming a modest geographic waist for the buxom valley. By the time you cross the county line, neither of them is more than a ten-minute drive in either direction.

If that weren't enough extravagant beauty for one medium-sized county, then shortly after crossing into Rockbridge you are presented with the eye-popping sight of three additional mountains: Jump, House, and Hogback. Responding to Paleozoic pressure, this anomalous trio erupted like wayward molars smack in the central palate of the valley, each positioning itself with classical balance, as though negotiating for maximum admiration. When they come into view at mile marker 198.6, occasionally radiant with celestial frippery, you will stomp down on the accelerator in search of the next exit, which happens to be the one for Lexington.

I had the good fortune to be born in that town. In fact, even better, I was born in the austere brick home of Stonewall Jackson himself, which was then the local hospital. Due to overcrowding, I bunked in a bureau drawer (maybe Jackson's own?) for the first few days of my life. And when I was a stripling I rode my own little sorrel, an Arabian named Khalifa, out across the Rockbridge countryside just as Jackson did. I could ride all day at a light hand gallop through farm after farm, hopping over fences oppressed with honeysuckle and stopping only for water. Much of that landscape is now ruined with development, roadways, and unjumpable fencing, but the mysteries and revelations of this singular place, just as I observed in my earliest journal entries, have been the begetter and breathing animus of my artistic soul.

2

All the Pretty Horses

Except for a stretch in the middle of my life, horses have been either a fervent dream, as these childhood drawings attest,

or a happily realized fervent passion. To write about how important place is to me, especially in my life with Larry Mann and in my photographs, I have to address how essential horses have been to it as well. Larry and I had three often cash-strapped decades when we had no horses in our lives, between our marriage in 1970 and our move thirty years later to our farm. But all that time my buried horse-passion lay still rooted within me, an etiolated sprout waiting to break greenly forth at the first opportunity.

And when at last that opportunity came in the spring of 1998 and Larry and I acquired our family farm from my older brothers, Chris and Bob, I bought the first horse I could find. With the purchase of that spavined old (re-)starter mount, my dormant obsession burst into full, extravagant leaf.

I've been said to be temperamentally drawn to extremes, in good ways and bad, and part of what I love about the kind of riding I do is the extreme physicality of it. Appropriately called "endurance riding," the sport entails competitions of thirty, fifty, and one hundred miles, going as fast as you safely can and almost exclusively on tough little Arabian horses just like Khalifa.

The landscape through which we race is usually so remote it is just the horse and me for dozens of fast and sometimes treacherous miles, an elemental, mindless fusion of desire and abandon. Sometimes we are running alone in the lead, and at those times I can't deny the observation of the writer Melissa Pierson that nothing may be fiercer in nature or society than a woman gripped by a passion to win. Nothing, that is, except a mare so possessed.

And in those moments I am wowed by the subtle but unambiguous communication between our two species, a possibility scoffed at by those unfortunates who haven't experienced it, but as real and intoxicating as the smell of the sweating horse beneath me. That physical and mental bond—the trail ahead framed between my eager horse's pricked ears, and the ground flying under her pounding hooves—can reset my brain the way nothing else does and, in doing so, lavishly cross-pollinates my artistic life.

This riding rapture, so essential to my mind and body, would never have been possible, and my slumbering horse passion would have remained buried and unrealized, were it not for our farm. And not just that: without the farm, many of the other important things in my life—my marriage to Larry, the family photographs, the southern landscapes—might never have happened either.

On our fortieth wedding anniversary, in June 2010, I received this email from our younger daughter, Virginia:

> Although you have said you don't want to make a big fuss about this, I think you are both proud of what you have achieved today: it is a testament to love, to a commitment to equality, patience, selflessness and, of course, the farm.

How odd it is that a piece of land should figure so prominently into her concept of our marriage, and yet how perceptive and accurate that observation is. Even before Larry and I met, in December 1969, our farm had been the setting for an Arthurian pageant of predestination, set in the aftermath of an epic flood.

In August 1969, Hurricane Camille rolled into Pass Christian, Mississippi, where she hit with Category 5 intensity, then made her way northeast and crossed the Appalachian Mountains into the Shenandoah Valley. Picking up moisture from heavy rains in the previous days, Camille dumped a staggering twenty-seven inches of rain in three hours onto the mountain streams that drain into the Maury River, the dozy midsized waterway that loops around our farm.

Our cabin on the Maury, built well above any existing flood line, was clobbered by a wall of water carrying logs, parts of buildings, cars, and detritus of every imaginable kind. The water reached the roofline, but a large hickory prevented the cabin from joining its brethren headed a hundred and fifty miles downstream to Richmond. As the flooding diminished, leaving angry snakes, a poignantly solitary baby shoe, tattered clothing, splintered wood, and nearly a foot of sand on its floor, the cabin subsided more or less where it had been before.

My parents wearily began shoveling out the sandy gunk, noting the many treasures washed away by the floodwaters. Most vexing was the loss of the large entry stone, concave like an old bar of soap, that had memorably required several men to put it in place at the cabin's 1962 christening. Believing such a rock could not have been swept far, my father eventually located it under a mound of debris and shoveled it free. But he needed some help to move it back to the doorway, so he called my W&L boyfriend, who offered to come with his strong friend, Larry Mann. The three of them rode out to the farm on a fall afternoon in my father's green Jeep.

Apparently, the rock's smooth surface made it difficult to grip and several times it nearly mashed their toes. After one particularly close call, Larry asked the other two to stand back and, in a moment I imagine as bathed in a focused beam of mote-flecked sun streaming through the tree canopy, hoisted the rock onto his back.

My father and boyfriend surely stood openmouthed . . . no, indeed, in my mythically heroic replay, I am sure they knelt, shielding their eyes as they gazed up at the epic vision of luminous Larry Mann replacing the threshold stone.

But in prosaic truth, lusterless Larry staggered to the cabin with the stone barely atop his back and unceremoniously dumped it in reasonable proximity to the door, panting with the effort. Still, even without the imagined heroism, my boyfriend said that when he glanced over at my father he was startled to see him looking at Larry with a bright gleam of acquisitiveness in his eye. Certainly it was more than just satisfaction at having the stone back in place. My boyfriend said he knew right then that the result of this portent-laden moment was that Larry Mann would be marrying my father's daughter.

And here is where the horses come back in. One of the tenuous links that my childhood had with Larry's was that we both rode and loved horses. Without this link, my father's marital hopes for his daughter might never have been realized. But, like so much of his childhood, Larry's riding experience was a world apart from mine.

⌐───⌐

There's a certain horse culture to which I yearned to belong when I was young—the culture of grooms, bespoke boots, imported horses, boozy hunt breakfasts, scarlet shadbellies, and grouchy, thick-bodied German instructors biting down on their cigars. This was Larry's horse world.

Mine, more passionate and far less structured, revolved around a Roman-nosed plug and her companion, a bright chestnut Arabian yearling given to my father, a country doctor, in return for a kitchen-table delivery. The former was misnamed Fleet and we named the colt Khalifa Ibn Sina Demoka Zubara Al-Khor, which classed him up a little. There were no grooms to clean the boggy lean-to that housed this unlikely pair, I rode without a helmet in Keds sneakers and untucked blouses with Peter Pan collars, and I never had a real lesson.

At first I didn't even have a saddle, as my parents assumed that if they made it miserable enough, this "horse-crazy" phase would pass. But I stuck with it, riding that old mare bareback, her withers so high and bony they could serve as a clitoridectomy tool. After six months of this, I decided that the nicely rounded back of the little Arabian colt looked awfully appealing.

So, one day I climbed up on the eighteen-month-old youngster who hadn't had the first moment of training, and off we rode, a rope halter my only means of control. As one might imagine, Khalifa taught me the only thing I ever really needed to know about riding, and perhaps about life: to stay balanced. Never mind the heels down, the pinky finger outside the rein, or mounting from the left. This little red colt taught me how to ride like a Comanche.

And that's what we did, flying hell-bent-for-leather across the nearby golf course, which my socialist-minded parents had taught me to disdain, sailing over barbed-wire fences and, when the heat softened the asphalt, racing startled drivers on flat stretches of the road. I rode Khalifa every day and, in a preview of my later miscreant teenage behavior, would set my alarm to ring under the pillow and climb out the window to ride under the wild, fat moon.

My parents, despite my obvious joy in riding, still refused to support it. I understand their indifference, or perhaps it was something stronger—disapproval. They were intellectuals; they hung out with artists and academics, not horse people. The thought of my proper Bostonian, *New Yorker*–reading mother resting her spectator pump on a muddied rail and chatting up a neatsfoot-oil-smelling horse mother is almost impossible for me to conjure. So antithetic is that notion that even then, when I suffered their indifference most painfully, I didn't particularly resent it.

It would suit this narrative if I were to tell you that my mean and insensitive parents sent me to boarding school in the snowy north to separate me from my true love, Khalifa. But the truth is this: my confused and concerned parents sent me to the snowy north (that part is still true) because my reckless behavior on horseback had morphed into reckless behavior in other areas. The biggest threat to a young equestrienne is not the forbidden bourbon from the flask on the hunt field or a foot caught in the stirrup of a runaway horse. It is, of course, boys.

My first horse chapter ended badly. When I left for boarding school, my father shuffled Khalifa and Fleet out to the farm where they apparently harried the cattle belonging to a tenant. This cowpoke called our house one night and, with a bumpkin persuasion that could charm a snake into a lawn mower, convinced my father to give the horses to him for riding. Within a week he sent the old mare to be killed at the meat market. When we discovered this, I went in search of my fine little sorrel Khalifa, tracking his dwindling fortunes as he went from one horse trader to the next in *Black Beauty*–like abasement, before ending up, like the mare, as dog food.

3

The Bending Arc

As many people have remarked, I am lucky to have found Larry Mann when I did. Whether I was born this way or my personality was formed by circumstance, I don't think anyone would call me an easy person to deal with, and by the time our paths crossed, the hormones of the teen years had only made things worse.

I had been a near-feral child, raised not by wolves but by the twelve boxer dogs my father kept around Boxerwood, the honeysuckle-strangled and darkly mysterious thirty-acre property where I grew up. The story of my intractability has been told and retold to me all my life by my elders, usually accompanied by a friendly little cheek pinch and a sympathetic glance over at my mother. Recently, in tracking down stories about Virginia Carter, the black woman who worked for my family for nearly fifty years, I visited Jane Alexander, a ninety-six-year-old who repeated to me, in a soft voice with a bobby-pin twang to it, the now familiar tale of my refusal to wear a stitch of clothing until I was five. Family snapshots seem to bear this out.

I know that my mother tried to raise me properly, but I made her cross as two sticks, so she turned the day-to-day care of her stroppy, unruly child over to Virginia, known to everyone as Gee-Gee, a name given her by my eldest brother, Bob. Jane Alexander reminded me about the beautiful, often handmade dresses that Gee-Gee would lovingly press for me, in hopes that they would soften my resolve to live as a dog. I have them still, pristine and barely worn.

If my early years sound a bit like those legends of wolf-teat sucklers, I guess they were. But, all the same, when I compare the lives of children today, monitored, protected, medicated, and overscheduled, to my own unsupervised, dirty, boring childhood, I believe I had the better deal. I grew into the person I am today, for better or worse, on those lifeless summer afternoons having doggy adventures that took me far from home, where no one had looked for me or missed me in the least.

Looking back, though, it could be that my parents were a bit on the less-than-diligent side, even for the times. Once, when I was with my mother in the dry-goods section of Leggett's department store, we saw the distinctive going-to-town hat worn by Mrs. Hinton bobbing above the bolts of cloth. She was the mother of my brother Bob's best friend, Billy Hinton. When she saw my mother she brightened and said, "Oh, Billy just received a postcard from Bob. Apparently he loves his new school!"

My mother, rubbing some velveteen between forefinger and thumb, responded distractedly, "Oh, that's good, we hoped he had gotten there okay."

Turns out that ten days before, my parents had packed a steamer trunk full of warm clothes for my fifteen-year-old brother and driven him to the Lynchburg, Virginia, train station. After eight hours on the Lynchburg train, he had to change stations in New York. My parents told him to carry his trunk from Penn Station to Grand Central and to locate the overnight train to a town near the Putney School, the Vermont boarding school he was to attend. Then they left him and apparently never wondered if those connections had worked for the boy, who had not traveled alone before, or even if he had made it to Putney at all. They had heard nothing since dropping him off and had never called the school to check.

My mother told that story countless times, laughing gaily at her recollection of Mrs. Hinton's shock.

The assumption back then, in the palmy, postwar Eisenhower years in America, was that everything was fine now—and that was true, for the most part. I think my parents were fairly untroubled by child-rearing issues, except for the constant battles over clothing their stubborn hoyden; my father called me "Jaybird" because I was that naked. But eventually even that was solved by the arrival, in 1956, of Mr. Coffey's carpentry crew, there to build a cottage for my grandmother Jessie on the property. My mother proposed a deal: if I wanted to hang out with the carpenters, I had to wear clothes of some sort. I was so lonely I took it.

Even though I finally agreed to wear clothing, I had some difficulty working out the details, as my mother's exasperated journal entries report.

> Sally is in a towering rage in her room because I won't let her go to play school with tattered and dirty under pants – instead of the clean ones – her turn to create a ruckus, I'm firm and calm at present, but I'm about to blow-up myself.

Despite being kicked out several times for not wearing *any* underwear, never mind tattered and dirty, a few mornings a week I began to attend Mrs. Lackman's preschool, where I worked on my socialization skills. By springtime, I had managed to make some human friends whose parents drove them out to my house for a birthday party presided over by Gee-Gee.

By the time I began real school, I was almost normal: I no longer spent my days poking at snapping turtles in the pond, or hiding out with my grubby blanket in my honeysuckle caves, or following my unneutered beagle on his amorous adventures down the paved road, from which, when I was hungry, I would pull stringy hot tar to chew like gum. I now wore crinolines, little white socks, and gauzy dresses.

I joined the Brownies

and the Episcopal Church choir.

But look closely: if you study the choir picture, something is still not quite tamed in the child pictured there.

And what is this? What is in those Brownie eyes?

If you had to judge by my average test scores, I suppose it's not raw intelligence you see in them. I was always a pretty bad test taker, especially so where math was concerned.

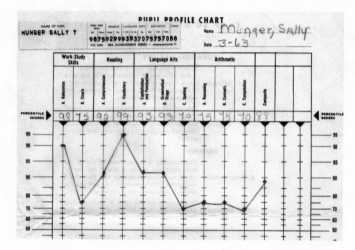

Still, I had enough gray matter in the brainpan and was a diligent and hard worker once I got fired up. As I went through school I discovered I was also competitive, on the honor roll all the way until high school:

(Note my father's whimsically varied signatures. I lined up eight years of report cards, all signed by him, and all signed in a different way. He was a busy man, a practicing medical doctor: how did he manage to keep this silly conceit going?)

In those years and the horse years that followed (the pre–driver's license years), I had as halcyon a life as any rural girl, despite the obstacles my horse-insensitive parents placed in my way. My natural, unquenchable rebellious streak played out on horseback, and, as I am still engaging in irresponsible, high-speed horse behavior, who am I, now in my sixties, to condemn that high-flying wild child?

Not so easily forgiven is the girl who dismounted for the last time from her exhausted horse and, learner's permit in pocket, peeled out of the driveway, double clutching and burning rubber. This is a chapter we'll cut short: the bleached hair and blue eye shadow, tight pants with what little tatas I had pushing up out of my tank top above them, the many boy-friends, the precocious sexual behavior, the high school intrigues, the vul-gar, sassy mouth, the very deliberate anti-intellectualism and provocation.

My poor parents. What else could they do but adopt the posture of benign obliviousness that had served them so well in the past? They gave me rules, of course, but at every turn they must have despaired of ever enforcing them. The law, or at least the superintendent of schools, Mr. Tardy, stepped in at one point to whack me for my irresponsible driving, and my father embraced his efforts with what I thought of at the time as unseemly prosecutorial zeal.

ROCKBRIDGE COUNTY SCHOOLS
LEXINGTON, VIRGINIA

. KAY, DIVISION SUPERINTENDENT

Dr. Robert S. Munger   December 18, 1967
Ross Road Extended
Lexington, Virginia

Dear Dr. Munger:

Your daughter, Sally, violated one of the first safe driving rules that she learned when she failed to stop for a standing school bus discharging students. This was on the Thursday afternoon before she went away to school. She nearly struck your neighbor's son as witnessed by the child's father and by the bus driver. This violation was called to our attention too late for legal action at the time. Consequently, Superintendent Floyd S. Kay suggested that she be warned instead.

Anticipating your daughter's presence in the community during the vacation period, we suggest that she be reminded of her responsibility as a driver and that a second offense may result in the privilege of driving being taken from her.

With best wishes for a pleasant and safe Holiday, I am

                         Sincerely yours,

                         Harry J. Tardy
                         Harry J. Tardy
                         General Superv.

I remember this event as if it were yesterday—hell, better than I remember yesterday. We lived at the top of a big hill on Ross Road, and I had been allowed the car to run afternoon errands (who knows what trouble I was really getting into). On the way home, when I got to the hill, I found myself lugging along behind the exhaust-spewing school bus. I knew that bus well, Rockbridge County #54, and knew it was mostly filled with country children often smelling of urine, their teeth rotten, one of them subject to epileptic fits in the aisle of the bus, painfully arcing and frothing until she subsided into a pool of pee, while the bus driver indifferently flicked his eyes up to the mirror and the rest of us exchanged helpless, anxious glances. I had ridden that bus for years and wanted to send it and its occupants the message that I was on my own now, in my own car. When the hill leveled off and the bus began to brake at our neighbor's house, I downshifted hard into second gear and gunned the car past the bus, not even glancing to see if the folding doors on the far side had been opened to let the three Feddeman children out.

Turns your blood to ice, doesn't it? It certainly did my father's, who wrote back to Mr. Tardy, as he says, within minutes. And that was a Tuesday, a full office day with a waiting room overflowing with patients; he was plenty pissed. I'm sure he punished the hell out of me, but I don't remember it in the way I remember being the asshole who pushed that accelerator.

December I9, I967

Mr. Harry J. Tardy
Rockbridge County Schools
Lexington, Va.

Dear Sir:

Thank you for your letter which I received a few minutes ago. I am grateful to you for this information; and, of course, I am very sorry that Sally could not have been prosecuted. She is now "grounded" until we talk further with her and devise an appropriate punishment for this violation.

Again thanks, and with best wishes for a pleasant Christmas.

Sincerely yours,

Robert S. Munger, M. D.

cc: Mr. Floyd Key
Court House Square
Lexington, Va.

On the weekends I would head off with my date in his Chevelle or El Camino, my hair rat's-nested and lacquered into ringlets atop my heavily made-up face, eyelashes curled and matted with mascara, heavy black lines drawn across and well past my eyelid in a Cher-like Cleopatra imitation, lips shiny with cheap lipstick, Jungle Gardenia flowering at my throat, on my wrists, and between my A-cup breasts, which did their best to swell out of a padded bra.

I would generally heave in pretty close to my absolute curfew so as not to enrage my punctilious father unduly and find my parents serenely sitting on the couch in the living room. My mother, with her stockinged legs tucked beneath her, would be wreathed in blue cigarette smoke, deep in the *New York Times* or *Harper's*. My father, a well-sharpened yellow pencil in hand, would be reading with pointy intensity some scholarly paper or plant catalog from the Far East and wouldn't deign to raise his eyes. Stripping off her reading glasses, my mother would squint through the smoke at me with vague confusion, as though an unexpected stranger had just appeared.

Weaving slightly, I would stand not in front of them but off to the side, as if eager to head down the hall to my bedroom to get some last-minute studying done. My hair, trailing bobby pins, would be matted and tendriled against my hickey-spotted neck, and the skirt of my dress would be wrinkled, the taupe toes of pantyhose peeking out from my purse. My swollen lips were now a natural, chapped red, and my cheeks blushed with beard burn. Peering over the angry marks on either side of her nose left by her glasses, my mother, studying the stone fireplace four feet behind me, would ask casually: "Oh, did you have a nice time, dear?"

Really, what choice did they have but to send me away to school? My brothers, nine and seven years older than me, were hectoring them to send me to Putney, which they'd both attended and loved. Even I knew, on some level, that I needed to get out of the high school world whose horizon stopped at cheerleader tryouts and drag races on the bypass.

Ray Goodlatte, the admissions director at Putney, must have waived a few of their policies to get me in. In a pattern that has remained constant all my life, my verbal scores were in the ninety-ninth percentile but, oh god, were my math scores abysmal; and my high school grades were only so-so, not always on the honor roll anymore. Most of the kids at Putney were sophisticated children of urban intellectuals with good scores and good grades, fewer than 20 percent from below the Mason-Dixon Line.

Not one would have known, as I did, what a whomping a four-on-the-floor GTO could give a Barracuda in the quarter-mile on the bypass.

So in September of 1967 my mother packed me and my brass-cornered trunk, the same one that my brother Bob had lugged from station to station in New York, into her powder-blue Rambler station wagon and we set off for Vermont.

Sally — off to Putney

Halfway there, the car blew a head gasket and died, so we rented a much newer car. In it, as we pulled up to White Cottage, my new dorm, I unknowingly enjoyed the last moment of personal confidence that I was to feel for a long time.

The first week, I raised my hand in Hepper Caldwell's history class and asked what a Jew was. Hepper (we were allowed to call our teachers by their first names), though startled, refrained from making fun of me, but no such luck from the rest of the class, many of whom were Jews. I was the most ridiculed minority of all: a dumb cracker, with a trunk full of very uncool reversible wrap-around skirts my mother had sewn herself, Clarks desert boots with crepe soles from Talbots, and variably sized pink foam hair rollers. Nobody at Putney had hydrogen peroxide blond hair teased into a beehive, nobody at Putney wore makeup, and nobody at Putney listened to the Righteous Brothers or wore her boyfriend's letter sweater and heavy class ring, its band wrapped with dirty adhesive tape.

In fact, hardly anybody at Putney even had boyfriends and girlfriends. I was suddenly living in another country where my currency was worthless, where all my hard-earned stock was downgraded. I tried to interest a few of the more likely boyfriend prospects in my wheelbarrow loads of devalued charm and sexual allure, but was met with perplexity and occasionally humiliating disdain.

Confused, but not defeated, I began to mint a new currency based on qualities valued at Putney: creativity, intellect, artistic ability, scholarship, political awareness, and, most important, cool emotional reserve.

Through it all, trying to sort out a whole new life, I ached for home. I missed the embrace of the gentle, ancient Blue Ridge and the easy sufferance of the gracious Shenandoah Valley. I missed Virginia, where sentimentality was not a character flaw, where the elegiac, mournful mood of the magnolia twilight quickened my poetry with a passion that, even read in the hot light of the next day, was forgiven, where the kindness of strangers was expected and not just a literary trope, where memory and romance were the coin of the realm. There I was, desolate with longing, in rawboned, doubt-inducing, unpoetic, chapped-cheeked, passionless Vermont.

The letters I wrote to my parents from that time, cringe-inducing and excruciating to reread, show a clear progression. First come uncertainty and loneliness, but in bouncy teenybopper talk, punctuated with what we now call emoticons, hearts and flowers drawn in the margins. But as months go by, the tenor of those letters changes, and they begin to explore existential questions about the nature of man, the nature of revolution, much discussed at Putney, and the "Negro problem," as the white problem was termed at the time.

By the time I went home for Christmas break, I had largely sorted myself out. The official reports from my teachers and counselors were all good . . .

What an effervescent girl! Sally is terribly refreshing to be around and her liveliness is quite catching. She has a marvelous way of teasing without being at all malicious. These qualities combined with an energetic application in regard to her work clearly shows that Sally is developing steadily. Her academic work presents no visible problems with the exception of her Math course. Sally is coasting along doing nothing terribly outstanding in Math. She is very aware of this and knows that she will with some outside help do satisfactory work. She feels that Math is and always will be irrelevant to her and I think is approaching it with a "just one more year" attitude. I think that it bothers her a bit since she feels compelled to do well in her academic work. History is very relevant to her now and is

and my brothers and parents were relieved.

I had set the course for what proved to be the rest of my life.

Writing came first. I was frequently the poet on duty when the Muse of Verse, likely distracted by other errands, released some of her weaker lines, but that didn't stop my passion for it. Beginning in that first year at Putney, I could be found, way after lights-out, crouched in the closet earnestly composing long, verbally dense poetic meditations, almost always in some way relating to the South.

These are the last lands: My blood and heritage.
The seasons, the sky and the soil are within me . . .

I have asked of the sky
And it gives me the reply of the cyclic ages—
Blistering sun and the cool blink of nightfall . . .
It offers its knowledge on the flat palm of morning,
For what has not been drawn into its black fist at nighttime?

I return to these lands for the last time.
Languid days of mottled light and sycamore
and nights of thick, sweet violet.
With this sky, this soil, these seasons,
with the Southlands I was born
and with them I grew, and now
I return to them
and to the past which composes them.
I am called by the frail and intangible thread of . . .

. . . and so on. You get the drift.

Early on I tried my hand at the traditional arts—painting, woodcuts, pottery, and etchings.

But in none of them was there a glimmer of talent.

Bill Hunt, my Putney art teacher, had this to say about my artistic practices:

Sally Munger
SUBJECT *Art* TEACHER *Bill Hunt*

It's not that you waste time because you don't, but rather that you fuss too much over a work. Everyday is a crisis of some sort. I expect the problem lies in preconceiving the final result to perfection. In short, you're too rigid.

Your art history work however was excellent... the best in the class.

ly Munger
NG ACTIVITIES
ACTIVITY *Graphics* HEAD *Bill Hunt*

woodcut. You created some fine prints, but they could have been better if you could control your emotions as you work. You get easily frustrated if things don't go as you expect.

So, so true, Bill.

And then came photography.

Here is a paragraph from the sprawling, excited letter I wrote to my parents from Putney in April 1969 after I developed my first roll of film, which had been shot on spring break in Rockbridge County with an old Leica III my father had given me.

I have just returned triumphant from the darkroom. The best photographer in the school helped me develop my film and both he and I

35

were absolutely ecstatic with the results. A lot of the pictures were of patterns of boards, textures of peeling paint on walls and some vines and old farm machinery. But their composition and depth and focus were all really good. I am absolutely frantic with . . . happiness and pride. . . . It's all rather unbelievable and perhaps a total fluke, but really <u>very exciting</u> anyway. <u>God!!</u>

This is the contact sheet of the exposures that survived from that first roll.

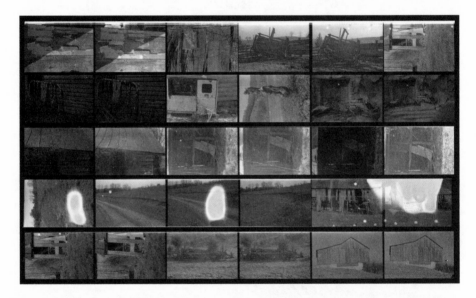

Maybe I was high that night, or maybe my expectations were low, but either way, from this vantage point, it's hard to see what all the commotion was about. All the same, I shouldn't make fun here of the loopily excited girl who wrote that letter after developing her first roll of film.

Because I am still that girl when it comes to developing film. There is nothing better than the thrill of holding a great negative, wet with fixer, up to the light. And, here's the important thing: it doesn't even have to be a great negative. You get the same thrill with any negative; with art, as someone once said, most of what you have to do is show up. The hardest part is setting the camera on the tripod, or making the decision to bring the camera out of the car, or just raising the camera to your face, believing, by those actions, that whatever you find before you, *whatever you find there*, is going to be good.

And, when you get whatever you get, even if it's a fluky product of that slipping-glimpser vision that de Kooning celebrated, you have made *something*. Maybe you've made something mediocre—there's plenty of that in any artist's cabinets—but something mediocre is better than nothing, and often the near-misses, as I call them, are the beckoning hands that bring you to perfection just around the blind corner.

So, there I was, age seventeen, holding my dripping negatives to the lightbulb, and voicing to my parents in exuberant prose my roiled-up feelings. Maybe I didn't know it at the time, but I had found the twin artistic passions that were to consume my life. And, in characteristic fashion, I threw myself into them with a fervor that, from this remove, seems almost comical. I existed in a welter of creativity—sleepless, anxious, self-doubting, pressing for both perfection and impiety, like some ungodly cross between a hummingbird and a bulldozer.

Not so different, really, from the way I am now.

My writing instructor, Ray Goodlatte (the same admissions officer who allowed me to squeak into Putney in the first place), prophesied greatness for me in a nearly illegible Putney report:

> You are launched on a lifetime writer's project. I feel privileged to have seen your work in progress. Your splendid critical intelligence qualifies you, as maker, to receive a high order of gift. . . . You are a person by whom language will live. I shall look forward to reading you.

It would seem that having discovered my True Calling(s), writing and photography, and enjoying some academic success, I might tone down the cussedness and rebellious behavior that had defined my life thus far.

But no, not really.

I smoked, I drank, I skipped classes, I snuck out, I took drugs, I stole quarts of ice cream for my dorm by breaking into the kitchen storerooms,

I made out with my boyfriends in the library basement, I hitchhiked into town and down I-91, and when caught, I weaseled out of all of it.

Cathy Carlisle   1/29/68
Sally Munger

From Weekend Duty Report *

    "Cathy Carlisle and Sally Munger and two

        unidentified others walking toward Putney

        during Sunday meeting."

If true - why?

                                              Ben

My attitude sucked about the farmwork required at the school.

WORK JOB REPORT

Name: *Sally Munger*   Work Crew: *Lawns & Grounds*

Date: *June 10, 1969*

Quality of work:	☐ Satisfactory	Unsatisfactory ☒
Quantity of work:	☐ Sufficient	Insufficient ☒
Supervision needed:	☐ Some direction	Constant direction ☒
Punctuality:	☐ On time	Often late ☒
Care of Tools:	☒ Adequate (*Never used any*)	Careless ☐
Cooperation:	☒ Works well with others	Distracts ☐

Comment on the following where appropriate —

Shows interest in work — *None*

Attitude — *Lousy*

Resourcefulness — *None*

Cooperation with head — *Sometimes*

Good example for others — *Definently not*

Shows improvement — *Never*

Other Comments — *Good luck next year!*

There is no need to switch on the fog machine of ambiguity around these facts: I was still a problem child.

I got in big, real-world trouble a few times, the kind of trouble that I was barely able to flirt my way out of. Once, while visiting my boyfriend at Columbia, I shoplifted a blouse in Macy's. I did it in the crudest kind of way, just as I had tucked those quarts of ice cream under my winter cape. Of course, I was immediately apprehended and taken down to the basement, where my dramatic memory has me passing a series of Hollywood-worthy interrogation rooms, painted a celadon color just a bit too far on the olive side, whose lone wooden tables were illuminated by a single bulb dangling from the ceiling. Past those I was apparently led, trembling, to a small, cluttered office. The head of security, an ex–New York cop, stared at me with lowered lids, a cigarette burning in the ashtray.

He'd clearly seen my type before and he let me know, with a snort of derision, what he thought of us. Eyes averted, in a soft southern voice with a goodly amount of throb in it, I tried the "But I'm just a poor Appalachian girl . . ." routine and he interrupted me by finishing my sentence: ". . . who just happens to go to one of the most expensive private boarding schools on the East Coast." I fell to pieces like a dollar watch; I was fucked. I wasn't scared in the least of this ex-cop, or of the New York legal system. No, I was terrified that this talking piece of dry ice was going to pick up the phone and call my no-gray-ever, all black or white, absolutely moral, never-an-inch-of-wiggle-room-for-equivocations-or-excuses, King of Perfect Rectitude and Repercussions, *father*.

The ex-cop knew that, of course, and played with me for a while, a well-fed and uninterested cat with a mouse. Then, with a surprisingly avuncular, weary little smile, he stood up, stubbed out his cigarette, and walked me back to the main entrance, keeping his eye on me as I went through the revolving door and out onto the street.

The next time I got into bad trouble, of the full-tilt terror with teeth variety, was when I was given a credit card number said to be that of Dow Chemical, on which to charge my long-distance phone calls to my boy-friend in New York. Of course all of us antiwar radicals hated Dow, so, the way I saw it, it was fine to be charging my calls to their number. After all, Dow Chemical was burning babies alive with flaming jelly. How bad were a few little phone calls within the scope of that evil?

And besides, they were never going to catch me.

```
Sally Munger                                    June 5, 1969


        I have just received two telephone calls from a
Mrs. Mann, Telephone Company, Sacramento, California

        916-482-4188

regarding a phone call which you made on May 7th to Jon
Crary in New York (59 minutes cost $9.85).

First, she said a wrong Telephone Credit Card number was
given, then when she called the number from which the
call was placed, 387-5893, asking for the girl who made
the call, she talked with a girl who said her name was
"Jane Anderson".  I told her we had no student by that
name and she said she would again call the 387-5893
number.  She then called me back with the information
that she had found out that the girl's name is "Sally
Munger".  This time I said "yes", we do have a student
by that name.

Now, Mrs. Mann says this is a very serious offense,
giving a wrong credit card number and also an incorrect
name.  To straighen this matter out, she asks that you
call her at the above number either this afternoon or
tomorrow.
                                        Ruth
                                        Business Office
```

Of course, it's only now, finding this letter stuffed into the pages of my journal, that I note the irony in the name of the telephone operator.

So, my parents, with ostentatious righteousness, paid up and punished the snot out of me, again. For two weeks when I got home after graduation they worked me like a rented mule, making me haul thorny brush and all uphill, too.

I even got in trouble at Putney with photography, and right about the same time as that phone call, a week or so before graduation. Having loaded my second-ever roll of film into the Leica on a beautiful sunny afternoon, I headed off with my friends Kit and (let's call him) Calvin to a stand of pines adjoining the school. There they stripped down and let me photograph them in a series of completely harmless nude poses. I shot only twenty-four images, eight of which were of Kit lying alone in the grove, my attempt to imitate one of my favorite images, that of an incandescent bare-naked child in a forest clearing by Wynn Bullock in *The Family of Man*. Afterward they dressed and we settled down to the real business of rolling cigarettes and drinking gaggingly sweet sherry out of a clay jar I had made in pottery class.

With the same dumb naïveté to which I am unfortunately still susceptible, I never considered the images anything other than a sweet meditation on the figure. And, indeed, that is all they were. Both Kit and Calvin were strikingly beautiful; sunlight dappled the pine-needled forest floor, and I was keen to expand upon the successes of my first roll of film. Nothing in the pictures suggests that anything of a sexual nature had taken place.

So, you might wonder why I'm not showing you the contact sheet of this photo shoot, as I had originally intended. That's an interesting question.

And the answer, as ever, hinges on the power, interpretative lability, and multifarious hazards of photography itself. In preparing this book for publication, I contacted Kit and Calvin about using the pictures. Kit, now a semiretired medical doctor, responded with alacrity, saying she was honored. Not so easy with Calvin, who was at first delighted to hear from an old school chum but then had second thoughts. He wrote that he was no longer a happy-go-lucky youth, and that he was now working "in a corporation with political colleagues," and that "the photos could suggest that teenaged sex has or is about to take place."

So, respecting Calvin's fear of being mistaken for someone who might have had teenaged sex forty-five years ago, I won't show you the tender and unambiguously nonsexual pictures I decided to print up that spring at Putney. Images can have consequences.

They had consequences then: within thirty-six hours there I was sitting, not for the first time, before furrow-browed Ben Rockwell, the headmaster. I wasn't surprised to discover that it had been the photography teacher, Ed Shore, who had turned me in. He had submitted this report on my work a few weeks before:

Oversensitive and insecure, I felt it to be lackluster and somehow read "appealing from an artistic point of view" as a pejorative.

Shore turned me in for inappropriate subject matter but also probably for sexual misconduct, of which I was guilty in a general sense, but it was a charge I resisted vehemently in the case of this perfectly innocent afternoon.

With the force of that conviction I oiled with charm and denials the choppy administrative waters and despite the now-familiar threat of expulsion ultimately took my seat, to the strains of Bach's *Magnificat*, in the graduation procession.

Many times on my account that bending arc of the moral universe has allowed me a bypass in its route toward justice, maybe because I was flat lucky or maybe because, if you want to think cosmically, some redeeming attributes justified the detour. Difficult I was, conniving I was, without a doubt rebellious I was, but six months after squeaking out of Putney the universe gave me a pass on all of those things, bringing me face-to-face with Larry Mann.

Those who say I am lucky to have found him are right.

4

The Family of Mann

After Putney and a wayward summer writing poetry and taking pictures in Mexico, I enrolled at Bennington College, figuring it would be pretty much the same as Putney, forty-eight miles away. I wasn't any fonder of being way up north, but it was a known quantity, as opposed to Sarah Lawrence or Barnard, schools that I decided were too urban for me.

Flying the familiar route on Piedmont Airlines to tiny Weyers Cave airport, I arrived home for Christmas in 1969 and finally met Larry, three months after our destiny, unbeknownst to us, had been sealed on the afternoon he moved the epic stone. The farmhouse where my Lexington boyfriend lived had an odd layout, and one night as I slouched in a satanically bad mood on the edge of his bed, Larry walked through the room to the shared bathroom. I had no idea who he was, he did not so much as glance in my direction, but my eyes followed him with a warm, glittering interest. We were married six months later.

Everything about Larry's past, not just his horse history, was the opposite of mine. Where I had that laissez-faire, semi-neglected, rural upbringing, he had a suburban New Canaan, Connecticut, childhood of parental pressure, social climbing, and embarrassing excess. As a toddler he was dressed in starched sailor suits, brass-buttoned, double-breasted jackets, and bow ties.

Just by way of comparison, at roughly the same time, this is what I was doing.

By the time I met him at twenty-one, he owned five custom tuxedos: white ones, everyday ones (apparently there is such a thing as an everyday tuxedo), and a black one with tails. His starchy tuxedo shirts hung in his closet like expectant armor, and blue boxes with engraved cuff links shared his dresser drawers with freakishly uncool madras cummerbunds.

Since the age of fourteen he had been instructed to hand out embossed Tiffany calling cards. His sterling silver hairbrushes were monogrammed, and it wasn't just them. Everything was monogrammed: the Brooks Brothers shirts, his sheets, towels, even the most diminutive washcloths. And of high quality, too. This one is still serving me as a darkroom towel some fifty years later.

Since the time he could stand up to pee, he had been given dance and etiquette instruction, and then came private piano, tennis, swimming, skiing, and art lessons. To appear to have been born into the upper classes, Larry had to memorize Emily Post right down to the footnotes. He knew how much to tip the washroom attendant at the opera, when to pick up the fish fork, how to cut in on the dance floor. His diction was perfect.

The rules were smacked into him by his mother, Rose Marie. She was a commanding woman, tall enough to hold her own against Larry's six-foot-five father, and she had glossy black hair that in middle age sprouted a striking white forelock.

Formidable enough right there, but by the time she was getting down to the serious work of beating on Larry she was quite hefty. She hadn't started out that way; in fact most of the pictures we have of her in her youth show a beautiful and slender young woman. But she bore a torment within her. She had been born in 1925 to a young, unmarried Little Rock woman and put up for adoption at birth. That in itself should not be a problem, but for some reason her adoptive mother passed her on a few years later, like a hand-me-down dress, to her younger sister.

Just guessing, but I'd say that might make her want to light into someone with an oversized wooden spoon, as she did with Larry. And maybe the fact that after she moved to Chicago and fell in love with the jazz that she heard there, her priggish young medical student boyfriend, Warren Mann, insisted that she throw away all her 78 rpm jazz records, reminders of those good times, and attend to the business of being a doctor's wife—that also might make one want to bring out the spoon.

But which of the two newlyweds was more dedicated to improving their social status is hard to say. They both appeared to be scrambling up the ladder in tandem and with a similar and relentless desire for a higher rung. Warren was a young shrink on the rise, and during the years when Larry was still small enough to be smacked around, Dr. Mann was enjoying a stimulating and prosperous practice with some highly placed Greenwich and New Canaan socialites under his care. Rose Marie was, even for a socially conscious town like New Canaan, stunningly class-conscious and all too aware of her humble and murky origins.

Whatever the reason for her fury, she vented it so often upon Larry that when I first met him he would still flinch at a sudden movement of my hand toward his face. If he inadvertently allowed his forearm to stray from its proper position at the family dinner table, his mother would stab it with her fork. To this day, there are tine marks in that cherry-veneer dining table testifying to the quickness of Larry's reflexes.

Gangly, solitary, over-mannered, mistreated at home, Larry was painfully aware of what his parents were doing, their obvious ambitions for him, their manipulations and control. He describes himself during this time of his life as a prisoner, and like all prisoners, he contrived subtle ways to preserve some independence. For a time he was allowed to go to school and return on his own, but his mother insisted on dressing him in Lord Fauntleroy–like outfits. Trying to fit in at school, he would switch them out at the end of the driveway for cooler clothes he kept stowed in a bag under a bush, reversing the process at the end of the day.

In general, when he was not in school or at after-school lessons, he was confined to the home, where he could be protected from the influences of the common world. But the fatal mistake in that strategy was that, alone in his room, he found the prisoner's treasured sliver of daylight, the soft tapping at the walls, the hidden hacksaw: he found books.

Along with a purchase of the *Encyclopaedia Britannica* his parents had also bought, as library ornaments, the fifty-four *Great Books of the Western World*. They never suspected the subversive potential behind all that gleaming leather and gold. Larry read damn near every one of them, methodically moving along the shelf: Homer, Sophocles, Plato, Aristotle, Chaucer, Shakespeare, Milton, Locke, Hegel, Melville, Tolstoy, Kierkegaard, Nietzsche, Dickens, Twain, and Heidegger. These great minds cracked open the door and gave him a peek at his legal future, although at the time, of course, he didn't recognize it as such. He became a philosophy major in college and eventually, through a program started by Thomas Jefferson encouraging self-disciplined but impoverished Virginians to become lawyers in that state, he "read the law" for three years to become an attorney.

As though he were practicing for the long hours in his future with dense law books, Larry would read alone as the afternoon sun leveled its rays through the gap in his curtains and the sounds of the children playing outside diminished. He would be so lost in reading that he would miss the call from his mother to change to the more formal dinner clothes that were expected at every evening meal. In the exhilarating world of ideas, he found himself free for the first time in his life, teaching himself in the process to be content alone, to read carefully and to reason, and most of all, to watch and listen.

You'd never know it by looking at the parents' allocation of resources and time, but there were two sons in the Mann family, Larry and Chad, two years younger.

The Manns had chosen to concentrate their efforts on Larry, probably because of his exceptional good looks, tractability, and general social ease. Directly inside the front door of their home was a large, gilt-framed painting of Larry the equestrian executed in the fawning style of an ancien régime court artist. Nowhere in the house was there any sign that there was another child in the family, no pictures or trophies or framed diplomas. Chad also came in for physical abuse by his mother, but he surmises that because he wore glasses he didn't get the hard facial slaps that sent Larry to school with his ears ringing and reddened, and instead got just the spoon and the brush. Except for the beatings, Chad was basically ignored, which in a way was a blessing.

The Manns zeroed in on the horse world as the best place to show off their handsome son and to make contacts with the right kind of people. Every afternoon after school, Larry was picked up by his mother in a Mustang convertible, her bouffant covered by an Hermès scarf, and driven to Ox Ridge Hunt Club for intensive lessons in dressage and jumping by their top instructors. In fact, he loved horses and riding, even ring work and the fancy horse shows. Like me, he found time on a horse transcendent and healing in some way, but especially in the less structured disciplines, playing polo, fox hunting, or occasionally just galloping on the cinder paths that lined the fields.

While his mother drank martinis at the club bar, Larry hung out with the forbidden groom underclass and realized, all the more clearly, the trap into which he had been born. But even into his late teens he remained pliant, escorting the daughters of the rich to balls at the Ritz while, with the avidity of a Spanish conqueror seeking Inca gold, his mother scoured the hunt clubs and society pages for just the right wealthy daughter-in-law.

The girl Larry brought home in spring 1970 was far from meeting any of their criteria.

"She goes to *Bennington??*" they had asked incredulously, responding to the news of our romance as if he had found me in a leper colony outside Baton Rouge. Implacably, Larry said yes. Bending to his unexpected defiance, they offered a grudging invitation for me to visit. When Larry and I arrived over Easter, his mother placed a Lilly Pulitzer outfit on the bed in my room as an alternative to my 501s and Frye boots. I decided right there that she was a ring-tailed yard bitch. The feeling was clearly mutual.

At the midday Easter dinner, when we announced we were going to get married in six weeks, his parents and grandparents burst into tears and left the table. We looked over at Chad, who raised an eyebrow and smiled, then, spooning mint jelly onto his plate, continued eating. We did the same and, that night, Larry crossed from his bedroom to mine and we made noisy love before leaving at dawn. We found out later that after that week his parents made an appointment with their lawyer to cut Larry out of their will.

Their disapproval only increased our determination and the perverse pleasure we took in our unacceptable love. The preparations for the wedding were easy: we bought two simple gold rings at Ed Levin's shop in Bennington and I designed a demure cotton dress that I had a local seamstress stitch up. My father dusted off his Linhof and shot a few pictures, one of which Larry's parents grudgingly put in the New Canaan newspaper.

The one that didn't make it into the paper is the real portrait, capturing the fey, Golightly feeling of the weeks before the wedding and, not incidentally, the Great Dane Tara in the background, the dog that had run my mother out of her marriage bed. My mother salved her injured feelings by purchasing the biggest Zenith that Mr. Schewel had in his showroom and moving it into my old bedroom, in defiance of my father's rip-snorting disdain for and prohibition of television in our home. My brother Chris and I date the moment when a TV was allowed in the house as the end to the family dynamic as we knew it, and the beginning of a corresponding decline in our mother's intellectual acuity.

Meanwhile, Larry's parents ostentatiously refused to come to the wedding, making a point of starting every phone conversation with, "Don't think for a minute that we're coming for your wedding." Certainly they sensed our see-if-we-care shrugged shoulders as we replied, "It's okay, don't."

So they did. Two days before the June twentieth wedding they announced they'd come but only, in their exact words, "tanked up on Miltown." I dreaded to see the bagful of spiders they would surely pull over our heads but, sedated, they were the picture of probity and forced good cheer. At dinner the night before the wedding, they made a show of announcing that they were giving us a car as a wedding present, and around the table was rejoicing—and relief. It seemed that they had made peace with the marriage and would finally embrace our union, as disappointing as it was to them.

The wedding was held a little after dawn in my parents' garden. It was modest; only our two families and a few friends attended—there couldn't have been more than two dozen people, tops. We had some difficulty finding someone to marry us because there was no mention of "God the Father" or "the Holy Spirit" in our handwritten vows. We solved it by reading aloud the E. E. Cummings poem "i thank You God for most this amazing day," that first line satisfying the God requirement, and, as for the Holy Spirit, we figured Cummings had it covered in "the leaping greenly spirits of trees." The almost childlike lack of punctuation and capitalization that characterizes Cummings's poetry and his affirmation of the natural "which is infinite which is yes" somehow caught the innocent spirit of those barefoot nuptials, our green optimism, and the wingding gaiety of the day.

Another sure proof of the divine presence was that the man who married us, David Sprunt, looked like the brilliant offspring of a coupling among God himself, Judge Parker from the funny papers, and Atticus Finch.

A small reception followed and, for a moment at least, Larry's parents, there on the left with Chad, deigned to step into the picture with their new in-laws, whose heedlessness of status, unconventional tastes, and political liberalism they despised.

It was a near-perfect day from our point of view: low-key, modest, and relaxed. And cheap, as my delighted mother would report afterward: the most expensive part of the whole thing was the wheel of Brie.

We honeymooned at the cabin on the Maury, of course.

The wedding may have been cheap, but my parents were generous with their gift to us, a check for $1,000. Right away, we deposited it in our newly opened joint account, and it comprised every cent we had. We were nineteen and twenty-two, and for us this was a fortune. Now I look back at that endearingly optimistic, cash-flush young couple with the rueful headshake of an old marital veteran, many cash-flow wars behind her.

We still needed the promised car and a few months after the wedding found one that would suit our needs: a used front-wheel-drive Saab station wagon. With the taxes, it topped out at $990. Perfect! We called Larry's parents, told them about our choice, and they said airily, "Just go ahead and pay for it and we'll pay you back."

Of course we should have known what was going to happen next, so eager still were his parents to sabotage the marriage, but when it did, we were knocked flat with the disaster it meant to our young lives together. I have not forgotten the cruelty in his mother's voice when we called to see when they could repay us. Mockingly, she began the predictable sentence with something like, "Oh, please, did you really expect we'd . . ."

Despite this treachery and its damning financial consequences for the start of our marriage—a ten-dollar bank balance being all that remained from our wedding present—we toughed it out. Larry's parents continued to do everything they could to undermine our relationship, such as giving us expensive carving sets for Falstaffian cuts of meat that we could not afford, knowing full well we were eating out of a twenty-five-pound bag of soybeans that also served as a beanbag chair in our basement apartment.

Through those rough years we clung to each other tenaciously: I sure wasn't going to give them the satisfaction of seeing us come apart. We were flat broke, always, and my parents, for reasons I have never quite figured out, did not offer to help, paying only my tuition and a small food and housing allowance. But now, in retrospect, I believe that made us stronger. Not that any of it was fun. Not at all.

After we had been married seven years, late on the night of July 21, 1977, Larry's mother rose from bed and stepped over her underwear lying on the floor, its crusty yellow crotch facing upwards. She walked to the closet across the room and pulled out a Stevens single-barrel 410 shotgun and a box of shells. Returning to her side of the bed, she sat next to her husband, who was covered up to his chin with a light summer blanket, sleeping on his back, his left foot casually crossed over his right. Breaking open the gun, she loaded one shell and clicked shut the breech. Then she pressed the muzzle tight against the back of his head between the ear and the midline and blew his brains out the other side.

We've wondered whether he registered the lock of the breech or if his eyes foggily flicked open at the cold touch of the barrel against his head. And we've speculated on how long she sat there afterwards, ears ringing with the blast, the air pinkly misted with blood. The pillow and sheets were a ruin of tissue and bone, and a dark stream was running from her husband's right nostril. Except for the slightly elevated left eyelid revealing a sliver of dull eye, the crime-scene photos show that his face was intact and looked to be that of a handsome deep sleeper, an incongruously debonair Superman curl of black hair drifting across his forehead.

Here's the thing, buried in the police report, that I thought strange: after she fired the gun, Larry's mother picked up the ejected shell casing and carried it, still warm, across the room to the trash can. As if, in that scene of murderous disorder, one spent shell casing was just too much mess.

Who knows how long it took her to reload the gun with the second shell, and adjust the two pillows behind her head so her upper torso was slightly elevated. Placing the stock between her legs, she fed the gun barrel up into her mouth. When she pulled the trigger with her left forefinger, the wad of the shell exited ferociously from her forehead.

The air conditioner continued to run for three days until a friend who had come to the unlocked front door heard the barking of the frantic, starving German shepherds who had the run of the downstairs. He called the police, who somehow pushed the dogs into the kitchen and went upstairs to find the bodies.

When we arrived at the house the next day, nothing except the bodies and bedclothes had been moved. On the living room rug were several weeks of unopened mail, each day in its own pile, and dog shit smeared by frantic paws. The curtains were all closed tight, just as they had been for weeks. Upstairs, the underwear, somehow for me the most disquieting thing, was still untouched on the floor. Was it a testament to her suicidal state of mind that she hadn't reached out with her big toe on the way to the closet to flick them over into the corner? Or was it her final Fuck You to leave them there?

The contents of the bathroom said Fuck You, too, fuck the New Canaan society she so wanted but couldn't get into, fuck the country club, and fuck her husband's medical reputation. It was awash with prescription drug bottles, many empty, the mirrored medicine cabinet door hanging ajar. A deep, multishelved bathroom closet and a closet outside in the hall each held a cornucopia of prescription drug bottles, way more than any two people could use in a lifetime.

And Fuck You, she said, in leaving behind a peculiar letter in the pages of a book next to her bed. This frustratingly cryptic piece of evidence, overlooked or ignored by the New Canaan police, indicated that there was more to Larry's parents' death than we knew. On the blood-flecked front of the envelope, in confident feminine handwriting, was "Rose Marie." On the back flap: "Leave answer under garbage can—? & I will pick up if not understood on phone."

The text:

Rose Marie—

Today I took $ 1500 out of my safety deposit—then I was concerned how to get it in check form from my family and not me—So, as you thought, I will give it to Mr. Glazer Monday in cash form, saying my family had sent me a check for $1600 instead of $1500 so I had cashed it.

1) Is this what you suggest?

I am concerned about the rest of the money in the safety deposit box–that it could possibly be examined—

2) Do you think I should take it out in the morning?

3) Perhaps get a certified check at the P.O. or money order and mail to Tommy?

4) Or should I get a check just from the bank for the sum? Giving them the cash? I would rather do this if you think this would be alright—

I have the 4 questions written down so you can answer yes or no . . . or else leave a note and I will pick up early Saturday morning.

The letter is not signed.

At the time, when I asked Rose Marie's friends, nobody recognized the names Tommy or Mr. Glazer or the handwriting, and there was no safety deposit box that we could find in Rose Marie's name. I guessed that she was somehow involved in selling drugs, but no one in the New Canaan police department seemed inclined to investigate, and Larry and I were overwhelmed as it was.

In fact, we were so overwhelmed that we were unable even to do the most straightforward, obvious things. For example, as strange as it seems to me now, it never crossed my mind to take pictures. I almost certainly had my camera with me at the cabin on that Sunday afternoon when a friend brought the news to us as we took turns rope-swinging into the river. But when we dashed out of town the next morning, I didn't think to tuck that camera in my bag. An image of that darkened, shit-smeared living room, or the underwear or the drug-filled closet, would have told the whole story of their addiction. What kind of dumbass photographer does that make me?

Despite having read the letter, we didn't quite pin down the drug thing then, either. We spent that first day walking through the house and doing some of the police paperwork down at the station. Our friend Robbie Goolrick arrived from New York and took one look at the contents of the bathroom and the closet and went in search of a box big enough to contain all the drugs. In the laundry room he discovered that a new washer had recently been delivered and the box had been set aside for the trash man. He brought it to the bathroom and nearly filled it with drug bottles and sample packs.

By evening, we were more than ready for some drugs ourselves, but maybe not for the fancy cocktail party that friends of Larry's parents held in our honor. The living rooms of the house were filled with animated, well-dressed strangers, and we stood somewhat dazed, strong drinks in our hands. After a time, one of the guests who had been in the Manns' house with the police furtively gestured for us to follow her into a back room.

In an agitated whisper she confessed that she and her husband had seen the extent of the drug archive in the bathroom and the adjoining hall closet. They knew they shouldn't have, she whispered, glancing out the door and into the living room, where the sound of cocktail chatter reassured her, but as a favor to the memory of Rose Marie and Warren, they had removed as much of the incriminating drug evidence as they could carry.

Startled, since we had seen the washer box damn near full two hours before, we thanked her and drifted back into the crowd. A medical examiner who had worked the case was also at the party and, mimicking the hostess's secretive maneuvers, he too pulled us aside. Sotto voce he told us that, while the police were otherwise occupied, he had slipped into the bathroom and pocketed some rather serious drugs, which, had they been found, would have reflected badly on Larry's parents.

Again we stared in amazement and he, mistaking it for the expected gratitude, patted each of us on the arm in that "Don't mention it—it's the least I can do" kind of way and turned back to the party.

As if to reassure ourselves that we were not imagining things, when we got back to the house that night we checked the bathroom: Sure enough, the box was filled with bottles of Valium, Dermid, Miltown, Seconal, Darvon, Percodan, Librium, Dalmane, Tranxene, and Placidyl, some in extra-large size, and punctuated with syringes preloaded with Adrenalin and Valium.

Okay, then.

So what the hell were the reputation-destroying drugs that the helpful friends had removed? And why on earth did they have so many drugs anyway, the prescriptions written not just by Dr. Mann but by other doctors as well, and written to people other than the Manns?

Thirty-five years later, and still asking those questions, I picked up the phone and called the Records Department of the New Canaan police. I requested the Mann murder-suicide file, and at the time, I didn't think it strange when the officer reported that it was easy to get since the file was on the desk in the next room. When the copies of it arrived they included several curious pieces of information, among them an anonymous letter sent to the chief of police a few days after the deaths. The handwritten letter stated that the police were too stupid to get the facts right and here they are: Dr. Mann was having an affair with one of his patients, a divorced woman in Greenwich, and when he asked Rose Marie for a divorce she killed him. Since it was not the same handwriting as the letter by the bedside I presumed the infidelity wasn't tangled up with the drug business.

This affair made some sense to me, though, as the final indignity for Rose Marie. Murder-suicides committed by women, especially with a shotgun, are rare, and I always figured that she was in a state of extreme agitation and rage, her apparent sangfroid in carrying out the deed notwithstanding. She had dedicated her adult life to climbing the social ladder but knew they would never be among the landed gentry to which she aspired. They were deeply in debt, and a risky drug operation designed to make a little more money could well explain an unstable state of mind. But why that night, three days before her fifty-first birthday, and a week before a big party they'd been planning? A jealous rage began to make sense to me.

In addition to the anonymous letter, within the file was mention of the numerous, usually empty, drug bottles found by the police although, perhaps to protect the reputation of the Manns, the quantities of drugs found in the house were not mentioned. Two notations in particular caught my eye. One was that an empty bottle of Placidyl had been found that had been prescribed only six days before by a Dr. Schwimmer. When asked by a detective about this July 15 prescription, Dr. Schwimmer denied writing it, suggesting that Dr. Mann must have somehow renewed a prescription written previously.

The other odd thing was that the police found a bottle of Dalmane prescribed to a Deanna Pritty filled less than a month earlier. It struck me as curious that in the Manns' bathroom would be prescriptions written to other people.

Continuing my detective work, I placed a phone call to one of the friends who had been in the house when the police found the bodies, a soft-voiced, tack-sharp octogenarian now living in Florida. I asked her first about the letter by the bedside, and whether she knew anything about a safety deposit box, a Mr. Glazer, or someone named Tommy who appeared to be handling the money transactions with Rose Marie. She was as mystified as I was, but said she had also suspected that some shady drug business was going on.

I asked her what had happened to the drugs that she and her husband had taken from the house. She told me that they had enlisted a police detective to help get the really bad ones out. The detective had often driven the Manns to the airport in his off-duty hours. Like everyone else, he wanted to protect their reputation and the reputation of the other doctors whose names were on the prescription labels. The staggering amount of drugs found in the hall closet and the fact that some prescriptions were written to other people were bound to have concerned the detective as well.

The husband wanted to take the drugs out on a boat into Long Island Sound and dump them, but the police detective nixed that idea. Instead they contacted a third friend, who worked at a pharmaceutical company and arranged to have them destroyed there.

Hanging up, I thought, okay, that's what happened to some of the drugs, whatever they were, but how did the Manns get that many prescription drugs in the first place? And what about that anonymous letter to the police about the Greenwich woman, the patient with whom Dr. Mann was allegedly in love?

Remembering the empty bottle with the prescription for Dalmane written to Mrs. Pritty, I began a search for her and, after a bit of sleuthing, found her still in Connecticut, in what she referred to as "a shitty nursing home." Yes, she's a character, eighty-four years old and I think still in love with Warren Mann.

So the last piece to the puzzle, or almost the last piece, anyway.

The charmingly candid Mrs. Pritty told me that when she heard about the murder of the man who had been her psychiatrist for six years, a man who, she said—and this was couched carefully—was "inappropriately fond" of her, her grief was so great an ambulance had to take her to the hospital, where she stayed for several days. She was quick to say that there was no sexual aspect to the relationship, but I didn't find that entirely convincing. If you think about it, why would anyone admit adultery to a stranger who calls up out of the blue on a Sunday afternoon almost forty years later? I wouldn't and don't blame her for not.

The final puzzle piece slotted in when I asked her about the prescription for Dalmane found in the bathroom. "Oh," she said, "that's the thing Dr. Mann was famous for—he refused to give any of his patients drug prescriptions. He just never did."

My theory?

Dr. Mann was writing prescriptions for his patients, and he, Rose Marie, or the bedside letter writer was picking them up from the drugstore and bringing them home to the hall closet. He was able in those lax regulatory days, as Dr. Schwimmer confirmed, to renew prescriptions written by other doctors, and he collected the drug samples that were lavishly handed out back then by pharmaceutical companies. Those drugs that the Manns did not use themselves—and judging by their pungent stew of neuroses they were using plenty of them—I think they sold, hoping to work their way out of the debt their social-climbing lifestyle had caused them to accumulate.

So when he came home and told Rose Marie he wanted a divorce, where would that leave her? Really, are you surprised that she did what she did?

<hr>

We hired a bagpiper to play at the funeral and when it was over, our friend Robbie approached him to settle up. The man, plainly embarrassed, confessed to Robbie that for the last two parties at which he had played for Larry's parents, with whom he had posed for pictures beforehand,

he had never received payment, despite repeated requests. Mortified by proxy, Robbie quickly wrote him a check.

This distressing pattern became the norm as we sifted through their financial affairs. Despite the appearance of wealth, the Babylonian lifestyle, the big house, the horses, the country clubs, the parties, travel to Europe in the summer and Florida in the winter, despite the drug business, the Manns died deeply in debt. Their mortgage insurance barely covered it.

After disposing of everything in the house, as a gesture of absurd hope, Larry and I brought home from New Canaan the custom tack, the saddles, bridles, boots, and horse blankets. We kept them around for several years but we each knew, struggling as we were and living in town, that we would never put them to use. Eventually we sold them.

We never voiced it but we were reasonably sure that our riding lives, the only slim sickle of intersection between our two childhood orbits, were over. And, indeed, for twenty-one years, until we bought the farm in 1998, the closest I came to a horse was pressing my face into the steaming necks of the carriage horses, with their madeleine-powerful horse scent, that carry tourists on the streets of Lexington.

5

The Remove

In the summer of 1973, four years before the deaths of Larry's parents, he and I returned to Rockbridge County for good. This was our third year of marriage, following my sophomore year at Bennington and junior year studying abroad, where we held each other close, broke and lonely, throughout our travels from Great Britain to Greece.

Lying on the empty beaches of Paros, the remote Greek island where we washed up that spring, we stared out at the storied Aegean while homesickness sucked our starving hearts right out of our chests. Even after all we had seen in our year of travel, Rockbridge County was still the most beautiful place we knew.

We were certainly not alone in this opinion. Travelers on I-81 frequently pull off at the Lexington exit to get fuel, and, while gassing up, gaze in wonder at the landscape. Then not a few of them restart their cars and head directly to the realtor's office. It is a testament to the allure of the area that the artist Cy Twombly, who lived and traveled in some of the world's most beautiful places, chose to live half the year in Lexington, his hometown.

In writing about Cy's work, the late critic David Sylvester cited Paul Klee's depiction of artistic creation, which he said was analogous to a tree's growth. Nourishing sap from the roots flows through the tree's trunk (the artist) and enriches the crown of growth (his resulting work of art). While the crown does not exactly reflect the roots, existing in a completely different element, it nevertheless forms a mass equal to them, just as a great oak is said to require the same amount of space below ground as above.

Sylvester implies that Cy's early experience in Lexington, like the root system of that oak, quietly but essentially informed and enriched the crown of his art throughout his life. Cy seemed to concur, saying to Sylvester in a 2000 interview:

> Where I'm from, the central valley of Virginia, is not one of the most exciting landscapes in the world, but it's one of the most beautiful. It's very beautiful because it has everything. It has mountains, there are streams, there are fields, beautiful trees. And architecture sits very well in it. . . .
>
> I've found when you get old you must return to certain things in the beginning, or things you have a sentiment for or something. Because your life closes up in so many ways or doesn't become as flexible or exciting or whatever you want to call it. You tend to be nostalgic.

The phrase "Twombly returns to Lexington" recurs, choruslike, throughout Nicholas Cullinan's detailed chronology of Cy's life in the last pages of *Cycles and Seasons*, the Tate Modern's catalog for its Twombly show of 2008. In fact, there is hardly a year of his life that he did not visit and, for many years, live and work in Lexington.

And he got a lot of work done here. For example, the epic saga of the fifty-two-foot-long painting *Untitled (Say Goodbye, Catullus, to the Shores of Asia Minor)*, now at the Cy Twombly Museum in Houston, came to a triumphant conclusion in a warehouse across the street from our old house on the industrial side of town. The tripartite painting was begun in Rome, but remained unfinished for twenty-two years until it was shipped to Cy in Lexington in 1994.

I can remember many afternoons walking to pick up the kids from school and seeing the tall, slightly stooped, densely overcoated and stocking-capped figure of Cy making his way down from his home on nearby Barclay Lane to the warehouse. It was probably the only place in all of Lexington big enough to house such an enormous painting, but he had to share the space with the table saws, paint cans, sawhorses, and wood shavings belonging to a local contractor.

One Easter weekend, Cy unknowingly got a little help with the final panel of the piece from a seventeen-year-old carpenter named Josh Campbell who had come to the warehouse to prime some siding laid out on sawhorses next to the painting. Halfway through the job, Josh was surprised to see Cy, about whom he knew nothing, ducking in through the far door with some sort of army satchel over his shoulder, prepared to work. Recapping his paint cans, Josh offered to leave, noting the greater magnitude of the job left for Cy to do on his project.

Ever the gentleman, Cy demurred and insisted that Josh keep on priming the boards, saying he would be back later. After he left, Josh, who himself worked by the job, glanced at the great expanse of canvas, much of it as yet unpainted, and thought he could help the poor guy out, since it was obvious he still had a long way to go on it.

Setting down his big paintbrush, he picked up one of Cy's small brushes and set to it, helpfully adding some paint to the third panel, which at the time had, as he put it, just a few big balls on it. He signed his efforts in tiny letters: JMC.

Once the big canvas was finished and shipped off to the Gagosian Gallery for its New York debut, the JMC now largely obscured, Cy rented a small glass-fronted storefront in downtown Chitlin' Switch, as he affectionately called Lexington. It was on Nelson Street, one of the four streets that compose the town's elemental hash-sign layout. An unlikely setting for a studio, being right on the street, it gave the lie to Cy's general proclivity to live and work "in a palace . . . but in a bad neighborhood," as a friend had once remarked. This place was no palace; it was a dive, but in a good neighborhood, within walking distance of his house and, notably, next to a restaurant with treacly pecan pie.

I photographed in that studio on many occasions, in part because of the coquettish quality of the light peeking through the tightly shuttered plate-glass windows, and in so doing documented, almost by accident, the artistic extremes of Cy's productive last years; the mind-storming rapture of the canvases contrasted with the calm intelligence of the sculptures. He seemed able to get a lot of work done in that funky place, as he remarked to his friend Sir Nicholas Serota, director of the Tate gallery:

> My favorite [cycle] is Sesostris. . . . I started them in [Gaeta] years
> ago. They were five or six years on the wall and then I took them to
> Virginia and finished them there. I finished a lot of things there.

How, I don't know. The lights were buzzing greenish fluorescents, the temperature control capricious, the drop ceiling low, and the noise level high; but all the same, he got it done.

When I first began photographing in his studio, I remembered how Alfred Stieglitz, by making the altogether too-perfect images of Brancusi's sculptures, provoked Brancusi to grab up his own camera and overexpose, blur, and generally screw up his way to photographic sublimity.

Likewise, casually shooting with his dime-store Polaroid in the same space where I had Stieglitzly labored with my 8 × 10 inch view camera, Cy made affecting images of his own work, especially the sculptures.

In doing so, he brought me around to a Brancusi-like freedom of interpretation, and over the years my work in his studio changed from documentary to evocative.

In the earliest work, I simply wanted to record how Cy laid out his workspace.

The studio then was uncluttered enough to pass through from front to back.

In just a few years, jam-packed with sculpture, paintings, books, and junk from the Antique Mall, that same pristine space was barely traversable, joyful in its excess and misrule, flicking a casual bird to the compulsives among us.

When Cy reciprocated by photographing in my studio late in 2007, he zeroed right in on the small areas of Cy-like disarray and made good use of them with his Polaroid, which in his hands made profound even the most mundane of junk heaps.

Junk heaps in general he loved, and come springtime we would drive through the countryside around Lexington, stopping at the yard sales that sprang up along the roads like unnaturally fluorescent new vegetation.

So it might seem odd that Cy would also love the highly regimented dress parades at VMI, but he did. Each Friday afternoon the entire corps of cadets forms up in pressed white pants sashed with maroon and topped with bronze-buttoned gray coatees. Low on their brows, they wear an anachronistic shako dress hat sprouting a waggling phalluslike pom-pom, which the cadets call a "donkey dick." Cy delighted in the pomp, the donkey dicks, the crenellated barracks in the background looking like a Mexican War theme park, the melancholic wheeze of the bagpipes and, oddly enough, the orderliness of the proceedings.

It's not so odd when you think about it. Growing up as he did under the influence of the chivalric code and the lore of doomed military culture, it is no surprise that he responded to those parades or that we see an occasional martial strain in his work (*Lepanto, Fifty Days at Iliam*). I believe many diverse elements influenced Cy as he grew up here and that they came to be reflected in his art: the blaze of southern light on Lexington's columned buildings, its cultural grace and languor, the region's literary heritage, its pervasive sense of faded grandeur and venerated historical myth. As he put it once in a local interview, "It all came from here. All those columns . . . there are many, many things I never would have done if I'd been born somewhere else."

The VMI parades were best in the spring, by which time the corps had mastered the steps, and Cy almost never missed them. He loved the spring in Virginia, the way I do, with a hectic rapture at the beauty of it all. On pretty days, he would sometimes ask to be driven to the Walmart store, built on a commanding hilltop, where he would sit out on the benches by the exit doors and watch the spectacle of shoppers and the sun rays sweeping across the Blue Ridge Mountains in the distance. The light and mountains, the breezes and the green of the mayapples, the warmth of the sun finally soaking into the earth and into his sometimes painful bones—being in Virginia gave him great sensual joy.

It gives joy to many of us, irrespective of the old bones, or of the generation. The experience of growing up here is timeless and universal in certain ways: Cy's childhood experiences were remarkably similar to my own, despite the two dozen years that separated us. Like most southern white children of a certain economic and social class, we were both reared by black women whom we adored. I would wager that the woman who cared for Cy, whose name was Lula Bell Watts, gave him the same childhood experience of imperishable and bounteous love that I received from Gee-Gee.

Lula was only about thirteen when she went to work for the Twombly family, and Cy at that time was a toddler. So, unlike Gee-Gee and me, they were relatively close in age, and much later in his life when Cy was in town, he and his driver, Butch, would frequently take Lula out for a spin in the country. Lula, then in her eighties, still dished out her kick-ass lessons in proper manners, turning from the front seat, pinching a cigarette between her thumb and forefinger, and scolding Cy like a backseat child.

It's hard to imagine that Cy would need a manners tune-up from Lula, as he, much like my southern father, was exquisitely courtly, cultivated, and courteous. As Cy put it to Serota:

> It's very funny, but when I grew up you always had to say, "Yes Ma'am" and "Yes Sir." And you were never to talk about yourself. Once I said to my mother, "You would be happy if I just kept well dressed and [had] good manners," and she said, "What else is there?"

Cy grew up on tree-shaded Edmondson Avenue, just off Main Street and around the corner from Mrs. Lackman's preschool. My parents, who moved to Lexington when Cy was fourteen, must have met him soon after they arrived, because this delicate little sweetie of a sculpture, dated 1946, was given to them by Cy, a senior at Lexington High School, when he came to dinner at their house on Washington Street.

After they moved to Boxerwood in 1951, it found a home in the clutter of the living room bookcase and was soon thereafter joined by one of Cy's house-paint-and-pencil paintings, bought in 1955 for $150 while he was living in Lexington and teaching at a nearby women's college, Southern Seminary.

Other people in Lexington also bought Cy's work, including the reclusive Jack Roberson, who used to sit outside his unpainted, Boo Radleyesque house on Jefferson Street and offer blow jobs to the W&L students on their way back to the frat houses. I ran into Jack one Friday afternoon in the early nineties at the Stonewall Jackson Thrift Shop, located across from the bank in the basement of the seedy Robert E. Lee Hotel. He was struggling down the thinly carpeted ramp that led to the thrift shop with two brown paper bags, the big kind with handles, one in each hand. The bags were stuffed to capacity and apparently heavy, judging by the difficulty Jack was having even on a downhill slope.

When he achieved the basement floor he pushed his way between the racks of jersey wrap dresses and shoulder-padded blazers and set the bags, their contents covered with newspaper, next to the checkout counter. Having gotten everyone's attention, he wiped his brow in exaggerated Jack fashion and addressed his audience in a voice, alarmingly high-pitched at the best of times, but now beginning to trespass upon the dog-howling range. The damn fucking bank, he announced, had to choose this particular day to take a holiday and now he was going to have to spend the entire fucking weekend at home with ALL THIS CASH MONEY he'd gotten for selling that Cy Twombly painting he had kept behind his sofa for forty fucking years.

Only in an honest little town like Lexington would Jack Roberson be able finally to deposit that money, both bagfuls, early Monday morning.

It's a naïve little town, too. When Cy's mother, his last living parent, died in the late 1980s, his sister called Cy and asked him to come and get his stuff out of the attic so they could sell the house. Apparently Cy didn't realize the urgency of the request, or maybe he just blew it off, but everything in the attic was eventually gathered up and handed over to a local auctioneer.

The resultant Twombly auction was held one Saturday afternoon in spring 1988, at the Bustleburg baseball field behind the Rt. 252 Dumpsters, about three miles past our farm. It's a desolate little patch of land, the bases barely visible in the scrub, an abandoned-looking cinder block building behind the torn and sagging netting at home plate. In that building the residue of Cy's young life was spread out on long folding tables: boxes of papers, toys, and juvenilia of all kinds, as well as later stuff: paintings, photographs, and sculpture. There were two roughly foot-square gouaches from the late 1940s, one of which was an unusual orange color, but in bad shape. The other was in good condition and an antique dealer responded to the call of the auctioneer by raising his hand. He bid a dollar.

Nobody else bid, but a friend of mine, observing the proceedings, felt it was disrespectful for a painting to go for a dollar. So he raised his hand and ran the price up to thirty-four dollars, forcing the dealer to cough up thirty-five for the painting. When a half-dozen Rauschenberg boxes came up for bid, painted and adorned with feathers and bones, "weird, magical things," my friend said, the crowd laughed out loud at them. Naturally nobody bid, so he bought one for fifty cents, another for a dollar, and then for a few more dollars he picked up a cache of subtle still-life photographs from Black Mountain College by both Cy and Rauschenberg, some of them of Twombly paintings that had been destroyed. (Several of these photographs my friend recently made available to the Virginia Museum of Fine Arts. This is fitting since it was VMFA Professional Fellowships [1951 and 1953] that funded Cy's travels to Black Mountain and Italy.)

For years after the Bustleburg sale, Cy went from one local antique store to another, then broadened his search over the mountains into the Piedmont, asking after any sightings of a little painting he had done in his childhood which was special to him, and a toy he had loved, a sailboat. Both sold at the auction.

The warehouse in which Cy completed the fifty-two-foot-long painting was one of those charmless metal affairs that spring up practically overnight in industrial parts of town, but from our house we couldn't see it unless we walked up the driveway to the road. We had bought our little plot of marginal city land back in 1975 with the hope of putting up a blacksmith shop for Larry, who had become interested in metal sculpture in college and was sharpening plows, welding farm implements, and forging hand-wrought chandeliers for a living. Or something less than a living.

Smithy Has Helper:

Young Blood In Old

At a time when n
communities have l
losing their a
blacksmith shops, :
seems unique in
functional surviving
Not too many y
every village and to
own smith and th
shops ranging fr
specializing in mec
wrought iron wor
farriers who shoe
The oldest shops
nearly all types
employing tin
mechanics, wagon
and farriers as we
master smith wl
usually do almost
with a piece of iror
With the trans
revolution and the a
wide variety of met
smithies were force
their doors. Addin
problems was the i
difficulty of findi
helpers who were
in their kind of wc
meant that mos
traditional skills die
master smith.
One of the main
of the smithy has
farmer. This is p
primary reasc

WITH Manly Brown is his helper Larry Mann, who hopes to carry on a long and honored tradition here.

While Larry worked with ninth-generation blacksmith Manly Brown, I had a somewhat more lucrative position as the photographer for Washington and Lee University. It required only a 35 mm Nikon, but that didn't prevent me from trotting out my white Samsonite suitcase and setting up my 5 × 7 inch view camera to the complete bemusement of the sports teams I was there to document.

At least we had a paycheck coming in, and when that raggedy scrap of dirt-cheap city land came on the market we thought we could afford it. It was in an ugly part of town, forbiddingly steep, overgrown and trash-strewn. The whole town thought we were crazy. In fact, the man who sold it to us, the owner of a local taxi service, told us after the ink had dried on the contract that he thought we were crazy, too.

It lay below the old railroad line and abandoned rail station that served Lexington until the 1940s, at which point the track was used only for freight and finally torn up in the sixties. Something about the place must have seemed so bleak and unredeemable, even back then, that conductors and train crew felt it perfectly appropriate to toss onto this pathetic patch of scrub the trains' accumulated refuse: crockery, empty bottles, bent silverware, clothing, iceboxes, satchels, broken push-brooms, umbrellas, and curling leather boots in which we expected to find the skeletal feet of a dead hobo.

The Lexington residents followed suit with their trash. Since the late 1800s our land had been the unofficial city dump, its steep hillsides a cascade of more modern trash atop the train trash, and the flat bottomland mounded with dozens of honeysuckle-covered ex-taxis, paradise trees grown up through the windshields, snakes coiled in the seat springs.

We had nothing except energy and hope, and set to clearing and hauling a century of garbage from the land, hacking down the trash trees and scything through the multiflora thickets. We made a few pleasant discoveries: hidden behind all the overgrowth was an undernourished creek augmented midway by a watercress-rich spring (which in turn was fed by the hillside of garbage, but we chose not to think about that). We toiled for a year to reveal a view of the creek and to clear the spring, sweating and itching with nettle stings, slicing our soles each morning on the shards of glass that emerged from the ground like some particularly malevolent nocturnal plant form.

I had a vision of how I wanted to live. In 1969 my parents and I had visited Helen and Scott Nearing on their subsistence farm in Maine and I had made a heavily underscored mental note that this was exactly what I wanted for myself: a life of simplicity, pluck, seclusion, and soul-satisfying, ecological, sweat-of-the-brow, we'll-vote-with-our-lives self-sufficiency. Seven years later, Larry and I were giving it a go.

By 1977 we were digging by hand the footers for an impossibly peril-
ous cliff dwelling, and then for the next half decade we scavenged building materials for it, learning as we went. By the time Cy moved back to
Lexington in 1993, the resultant spindly, hand-built, Rube Goldberg–like
passive solar house had bulked up with a succession of shed-roofed add-
ons, living areas cantilevered out over the abyss and labyrinthine porches,
covered with vines. A commercial pilot we know once remarked that from
the air our house resembled those shantytowns on the edge of the Mexico
City dump, and we were not offended. It was a totally cool Big Sur–ish
house: impractical, whimsical, not to code in any respect, the kind of place
that stopped passersby in their tracks and lured them, cautious and curious, past the basilisk sculptures to our slab-wood front door.

Cy, too, would wander down from the warehouse to that door, calling
out in his distinctive, hesitant voice, "Sally? Are you receiving?" We both
liked to sit out on the wisteria-covered back deck overlooking the creek,
especially on those sultry summer nights when the fog rose from the
bottomland and wisped among the racemes of white bloom.

One such night found a group of us with Cy and Nicola, his gentle, erudite companion, sitting after a late dinner on that porch, the newspaper-covered table nacreous with oyster shells, bottles of wine darkening the center. I mentioned my past fascination with Ezra Pound, an American who, like Cy, had found Italy his place "for starting things" and about whom I had written my master's thesis. At this, Cy, sitting to my right at the head of the table, leaned over to me with the look of a confidence about to be divulged, so I pressed close.

When Cy was about to tell a story or make a naughty quip he would cover his mouth in a schoolchild's way, fingertips lightly touching his primly pursed lips, while above them the eyes were alight and impish. I watched memory veil those eyes as he spoke of a time in the late 1960s when he and Nicola had been invited to the Spoleto Festival by its founder, Gian Carlo Menotti. That evening a Russian pianist was performing, and Menotti honored Cy and Nicola by seating them in his private balcony in the Opera Theatre. As they took their seats they were startled to see behind them Ezra Pound and Olga Rudge, one of the three women with whom Pound had simultaneous relationships. Cy described Pound as having an aura, a mystical appearance, and as being somehow set apart from regular people. Nicola wrote me later that Pound "acted . . . extremely shy like only a northern blond child could be. He hardly looked at us and in a side way."

Telling me of this in the humid summer night, Cy emphasized how rare it was to see the reclusive poet, who seldom appeared in public in those later years. Pound had been driven mad (or perhaps more mad) by his wartime incarceration in Pisa for treason. It was there, locked up like an animal in a 6 x 6½ foot wire cage, that he began writing on a piece of toilet paper the uneven but brilliant *Pisan Cantos*. (Interestingly, housed in the cage next to him was Emmett Till's father, Louis, until he was hanged "for murder and rape with trimmings," as Pound put it.) After Pound began to show clear signs of a mental breakdown, he was shipped from Pisa back to the United States and confined to the "bughouse" at St. Elizabeths Hospital in Washington, D.C. A decade after his release in 1958, Pound stopped speaking altogether. Much was made of his self-imposed silence, and it has always been reported that not a single word ever passed his lips once he began it.

Except, to their amazement, Cy and Nicola heard Pound speak to Olga. They both described it as the whispering of a deeply wounded and suspicious man, but also of a man fading out of this life. Cy said he would have loved to exchange just one word with this intransigent, mysterious, wrong-headed, brilliant man. Instead he and Nicola somehow maintained a posture of intense interest in the music played before them, arching backwards in their seats, hoping to hear the thoughts of a genius.

Imagine that—on my peckerwood porch, late in the humid, cloyingly fragrant Virginia night, Cy, in a Pound-like whisper, tells a story I found marvelous in the many improbable threads it wove together: that he had seen, had *heard* Ezra Pound, the author of the lines written on my father's memorial stone, with whom I held a long fascination, and that within this tale was another of my long-held fascinations, Emmett Till. And of course that the storyteller was Cy, the local hero, come back to sit in the dungheap-turned-garden that was our home, the prodigal returning to Lexington.

⸻

Cy often walked the streets of Lexington, and I would occasionally go with him. Strolling along on the uneven brick sidewalks, he had a remarkably deferential physical presence for such a big man. He would step aside and nod decorously to the old "widder" women, who had long outlived their husbands. Lexington's streets have changed little since the war, and of course I mean *The War*, the only one that counts here. In certain charming ways (and others less so), much of the town dozed off in 1865 and it hasn't ever quite awakened.

A friend of my mother's tells a story about a house just over the hill from our farm, commandeered in 1864 by the Union army to be General Hunter's headquarters during his raid on Lexington. When I was young it belonged to a man with the unlikely name of Torkle McCorkle. My mother's friend visited Torkle's house and after examining some of the books in the library, he wrote:

> I did not find a single title published later than 1862 ... a mixture of melancholy and guilt assailed me. The library, the house, the grounds, were as General Hunter found them when he rode down the Valley toward Lynchburg. Time could be stopped, I thought, and by other hands than those of God.

He's right: time, if not stopped, is certainly slowed in Lexington, and that may have been what most charmed Cy; it certainly charms me. Even the pace of art-making, like most everything else, is leisurely, especially in summer. Evening, once the temperature drops, is the best time to work; often, late at night, driving through the shuttered town, I'd see light seeping from the venetian blinds of Cy's studio.

One of the theories about why so few successful practitioners of the plastic arts come from the South holds that the heat stultifies us. There is some truth to this, though it may also be time-related; I believe we in the South have a different sense of time and its exigencies. In fact, in Cy's case, I think growing up in the American South made his transition to Italy easier. Cy himself once remarked, "Virginia is a good start for Italy. . . . Virginia made me very southern in a way. They say that they are not creative in the South, but it's a . . . rare mentality."

The British historian John Keegan appears to have agreed with Cy's assertion. After traveling through America, Keegan reported:

> The thing about the South is that it retains for Europeans a trace of cultural familiarity, as the rest of the country does not. . . . I have often tried to analyze why I should have a sense, however slight, of being at home in Dixie. Class system, yes; history, yes; but more important, I suspect, is the lingering aftermath of defeat. Europe is a continent of defeated nations. . . . America has never known the tread of occupation, the return of beaten men. The South is the exception.

Its warrior spirit, which supplies the armed forces with a dispropor-
tionate flow of recruits, is a denial of the decision of 1865. The famous
femininity of its women—not a myth, not to European men at least,
who find them feminine as other American women are not—is a
quality that comes from grandmothers who found a strength their
men had lost, learnt to comfort, helped to forget, and never, never
said the unsayable thing. Pain is a dimension of old civilizations. The
South has it. The rest of the United States does not.

Shelby Foote, astute observer of his own southern culture, expanded upon
this sentiment:

> I remembered what my father had said about the South bearing
> within itself the seeds of defeat. . . . We were sick from an old malady,
> he said: incurable romanticism and misplaced chivalry . . . too much
> Walter Scott and Dumas read too seriously. We were in love with the
> past, he said; in love with death.

Mr. Foote was perhaps being a little extreme, exaggeration being
another southern characteristic. It's not that we southerners are exactly in
love with death, but there is no question that, given our history, we're on
a first-name basis with it. And such familiarity often lends southern art a
tinge of sorrow, of finitude and mourning. Think of the blues, for example, or early jazz; think of Faulkner, Welty, O'Connor, and others; think of
the titanic triad of Rauschenberg, Johns, and Twombly in the visual arts.
Cy was talking to me about them once, the three painters, and he said
that if a book were ever written about them, it should be called *Dickheads
from Dixie*.

That was classic Cy: oddly self-effacing, with a kind of negligent grace
about him. He made his rare gift, that genius, all the more seductive by
the casual way he possessed it: with a whiff of mischief, an ambivalent
intensity, and a charming insouciance. People mistakenly thought him
shy, which he wasn't really, and innocent, which he wasn't, either. Okay,

in some ways he was innocent, but for sure he wasn't naïve, and neither was his art. A friend once quipped that naïveté in art is like the digit zero in math; its value depends on what it's attached to. In Cy's case, it was attached to a honking big number.

He could be wickedly funny. I once watched as a quartet of worshipful, white-gloved young art handlers from New York untacked his paintings from the studio walls and laid them on pristine white cloths on the floor. Worth a king's ransom and headed to some major museum, they were rolled up and reverently placed in a temperature- and humidity-controlled truck. As soon as the doors were shut and triple-locked, Cy, exaggerating a hand-dusting maneuver, his eyes dancing with devilry, announced: "Well, I'm glad to get that shit out of here." He laughed to see the white gloves rush to the shocked faces.

Putting aside that self-deprecating assessment, nobody disputes that Cy produced some of the greatest art of this and the last century—and he made much of it right here in Virginia, not in spite of the place but because of it.

Choosing to work outside the art world's urban centers, as both he and I have done, is difficult, at least it certainly has been for me. More than any artist I know, Cy managed this classical remove, embracing James Joyce's artistic intent, summed up in three words at the end of *A Portrait of the Artist as a Young Man:* "silence, exile, cunning."

Cy did not use those exact words but, in speaking to Serota, remarked:

You know, I don't follow too much what people say. I live in Gaeta or in Lexington and I just have all the time to myself. I don't have to worry; I had years and years during which no one could care less, so I was very well protected.

This strategy worked well for Cy, and I believe it allowed him an uncommon freedom of lyric expression, especially evident in his photographs, with their soft, dreamlike quality. They edge close to the deadly minefields of sentiment, that most disputed artistic territory, but Cy always managed to stroll elegantly and imperviously through that dangerous landscape, putting elegiac feeling into these pictures—and screw anyone who didn't like it.

His photographs are hazy and casually indifferent to detail—this is not an eidetic memory; this is the way our minds recall and our hearts remember. They have a misty kind of luminosity, perhaps the mists of time or the forgiving scrim of recall.

He made these pictures not with a sharp Proustian vision but with an eye veiled by the famously thick, characteristically humid southern air. Cy tapped into some flow of ancient memory: with his distracted mien, fragmented speech, and works of rapturous mythic energy, he seemed to have been born out of time. Perhaps he was. Our part of the South, remote, beautiful, and patinaed with the past, allows us such a remove, the distance of another time.

I miss him now each spring and fall, the seasons when he would alight in our valley, and I miss him for lots of reasons, but especially because of his irreverence, his confidence in his (and my) art, and how comfortable he was working outside the urban art world. I miss our afternoons at the kitchen table over his favorite meal: tart apples, fried on the woodstove in the cast-iron skillet with bacon fat, salt, cinnamon, and brown sugar. We would chat about stuff, not always art, but at the mention of some piece of criticism or a highbrow article, Cy and I, both of us with sensitive bullshit meters when it comes to artspeak, would roll our eyes.

When Cy spoke about art, he often used the language of the passions, language I understand, once referring to our daughter Jessie's style of painting as "fierce." He understood the quirky ways we outliers have of measuring the strength of our work, remarking that his strongest paintings were usually those not sold by the end of the opening. My affinity for Cy and his approach to art, and my deep affection for him, gave me confidence that I could stay in this place I love, and make my work here.

It's not easy working in the South. Playing on a southern pronunciation of "Beaux-Arts," H. L. Mencken once dismissed the South as "the Sahara of the Bozart," and he had a point. Urban museums have little interest in artists who live down here or those who don't live in a city. We lack a collector base, and enjoy little support or artistic fellowship. As my friend Billy Dunlap remarked the other day, the rest of the world seems to love us only when we act like characters out of a Tennessee Williams play.

Cy would have loved that quip, and I miss not being able to tell him, to hear his snort of merriment. I miss his almost childlike glee at the most elementary human gaffes. Every time we would leave his house and catch a glimpse of the neighboring Reid White house behind the trees, one or the other of us would repeat our favorite line from a story my mother used to tell about the occupant of that house, Mrs. Breasted White. That's what I swear I remember her saying: "Mrs. Breasted White." But now, writing that name, it somehow seems highly improbable.

Anyway, we'd say the punch line, sometimes in unison, and then we would both howl with laughter, as if we had just heard it for the first time. Here's how the story goes:

Mrs. White was, of course, a member of the Lexington Garden Club (and the way "garden" is pronounced by these ladies is "ghee-yad-en"), and her specialty was roses. Every year its local members would compete to assemble the most exuberant floral display, to be judged by someone from a classier garden club, like, say, the one in Lynchburg. This competition would be followed by refreshments: small triangles of buttered white bread with edges trimmed and tomato aspic quivering on iceberg lettuce leaves, all washed down by the daily staple of those elegant Lexington ladies who insisted they didn't drink: restorative sherry (18 percent alcohol).

One year, Mrs. Breasted White's entry was a gorgeous arrangement of yellow roses whose particular qualities she endorsed in spidery cursive on a card placed nearby. Oh, how I miss our laughter, as Cy and I would recite the inscription in unison: *Good in bed, better against a wall!*

6

Our Farm—And the Photographs I Took There

I recently flew down the Shenandoah Valley on my way home from New York. As we began our descent into Roanoke I easily picked out my own sweetly unassertive Maury River, which heads southeast about two-thirds of the way down the valley. For its entire forty-three miles it flows through Rockbridge County, during which it goes fairly efficiently about the riverine business of dumping itself into the mighty James. But about midway through its course, the Maury seems to pursue one extravagantly wasteful detour: the big, languid loop with which it almost encircles our farm.

Even from 15,000 feet this anomaly is easily seen, resembling the shape of a boot, with the hint of an unsubstantial heel at its nether end as the river straightens out again, heading single-mindedly toward the James at Glasgow.

This beautiful river, and the cool of its overhanging sycamores, brought my father to the offices of a local veterinarian one Friday afternoon in 1960. Daddy was looking for a couple of acres on which to build a cabin for a family retreat, and the vet had a farm on the Maury. They had come to an understanding by phone about a stretch of bottomland and agreed to settle the deal after their respective office hours that afternoon.

Later that same evening, as my mother dressed for cocktails, turning in her full skirt before the mirror attached to the back of their bedroom door, Daddy announced that he had just purchased not the expected two acres on the river but three hundred and sixty-five. He spoke nonchalantly as he leaned over to buff his shoes, sitting on the miniature chintz-covered chair reserved for this purpose. In midturn, her skirts hissing to a stand-still, my mother froze before the mirror, her startlingly teal-colored eyes staring at the reflection of the man unconcernedly putting the last swipes down on his brown Stride Rites.

I wonder if most marriages of that time, fulcrum-based as they always have been, were as lopsided as this one, or whether my parents' was so lopsided because of the weight of my father's personality on the marital seesaw. He certainly didn't cause the asymmetry by displays of physical strength, anger, or unkindness. To the contrary, he moved quietly, his sinewy physical power concealed by the blocky way he dressed. Maintaining an air of distraction as though in profound thought, he seldom spoke, and, when he did, it was with a mannerly, almost tender gentleness. How is it, then, that we were all so intimidated and awed by him?

My mother, helplessly astride her insubstantial end of the seesaw, lacked the personal confidence and gravitas necessary for spousal balance with such a partner. Announcements to her of unilateral faits accomplis from the weighted side of the board, such as the purchase of the farm, were among the ways that my father further lightened her end, whether he meant to or not. What did he know about taking care of a large property with barns, tenant houses, pastures, forest trails, a rusting sawmill and fencing to maintain—and with what resources? He was, as we say about the novice farmer, all hat and no cattle, all hawk and no spit. But, as so often happened, this whimsical purchase was his decision alone. My father had never laid eyes on the farm he had just bought, writing without hesitation a personal check that Friday afternoon for the $75 an acre that the vet had spontaneously thrown out as a price, saying, "Oh hell, Bob, never mind the two acres. Why don't you just take the whole thing?"

And so, the next day, Saturday morning, my parents drove out Route 39 to look at their sudden new farm. With trepidation, they turned off the pavement onto dusty Copper Road, at the end of which was a drooping gate. Unlocking it, they passed into land so rich in beauty and perfect in proportion that by the time they unwrapped the wax paper from their sandwiches, sitting opposite the cliffs on the sunny beach where later they built their cabin, they were speechless with relief and happiness.

Stunned as well (it turns out) was the vet's wife when she found out that her husband, without consultation, had sold the very farm their sons were depending on for their future livelihood. I wonder if that shocking news was delivered to his wife with the same nonchalance that Daddy delivered his, but the vet heeded his wife's distress and wasted no time in calling my father to back out of the deal.

Having seen what he had purchased, my father was not about to give it back. But, as a way to minimize the farming family's disruption, he allowed their son to farm it for another forty years. Our family's contact with the farm was generally limited to holidays, and the memories we made there were correspondingly intense. We cut our Christmas trees from the edges of the forest and spent summer weekends at the cabin, a simple structure my father and brothers began building in 1961.

But, without anyone from our family living there, the farm went downhill. The pastures were a tangle of devil's shoelace and stickweed, with a few gallant saplings trying to make a go of it in the played-out soil. All the barns were rickety, with unpainted and leaky roofs, the tenant houses unlivable, the fences trampled by hungry cattle, and the roads impassable with ruts. In spite of the superficially terrible shape it was in, the land still had what my mother called "good bones"—beautifully undulating pastures, partly the result of our sinkhole-prone karst geology, extensive, cliff-protected river frontage, mountain views, old-growth forests, and a sense of deep privacy and sanctuary. My father deeded the farm to my two brothers and me in the 1980s, but, of the three of us, I was the one with the closest proximity, the greatest ability to maintain it, and arguably the strongest feelings about it.

And boy, were they strong. My feelings were of the most vital, the sine qua non, the fight to the death, the lie down in front of the bulldozers, forgo all food and water, but never, ever lose the farm variety. I had loved that farm since the day we got it. At age twelve I galloped bareback through pastures mined with groundhog holes, swimming Khalifa in the river to escape the flies, and fishing until it was too dark even to see the pale albino carp floating in the shallows.

What momentous family event did we not celebrate on the farm, what birthday, holiday, anniversary? There is no sinkhole into which we have not poked our walking sticks, no time-stretched initials carved in smooth beech bark that we have not traced with our wondering fingers, no deer trails unfollowed, no cliff from which we haven't dislodged medium-sized stones to make large-sized holes in our waiting canoe below, no deeply romantic swimming holes unsounded. The farm is a constant for all of us, glowing steadily in the unreliable, teasingly labile shadow of memory.

⌕

After I was sent to boarding school I wrote heartbroken love poems to the farm. Among my first curling, yellowed contact sheets of 35 mm images are dozens of pictures taken there.

When I began photographing with my 5 × 7 inch view camera, of course I hauled it out to the pastures, the woods, and the cabin.

Heartbreakingly, when I went to my storage box to pull the negatives of these images, the emulsion of every one was reticulate with cracks. They had been destroyed by vinegar syndrome, which afflicts certain "safety films" introduced early in the twentieth century to replace flammable nitrate film, the film on which my father made his images. Here's what they all look like now.

My manifest farm passion did not put me in a good bargaining position when I approached my two brothers to buy out their parts of the mutually owned property. They, reasonably enough, thought of it as their patrimony, sum remained in my mother's account after my father's death in 1988. The farm was basically all that was left for the three of us.

Of the predictably biblical, epic, and divisive negotiations involved in establishing a value for the farm, the less said the better. Only a gorgeous piece of good land can provoke that kind of piercing despair and dispute. Failed loves, complicated family relationships, broken hearts, errant children, lost lives—nothing so engages a southern heart as a good piece of family land.

But, having agreed on a price many decimals removed from the now mythical, fairy-tale-sounding $75 an acre my father paid, in early 1998 Larry and I walked into the local Farm Credit office and asked to borrow 100 percent of the purchase price for a farm upon which we were immediately going to place a conservation easement, thereby lowering the value by 30 percent.

The loan officer looked skeptical. I explained winningly that we would surely be able to make the mortgage payments with the sales of as-yet-untaken images of the Deep South, a trip on which I would be embarking the afternoon of the closing. Bless his heart, taking a look at my camera, portable darkroom, provisions, and maps in the Suburban parked outside his office, and infected with my confidence, he said okay. We had the loan.

We celebrated that night at the cabin, the repository of so many memories, but before I pulled out the next morning to head south, I made sure the cattle-running tenant was notified to take his stock off the farm and never come back, remembering my two horses, Fleet and Khalifa, he sold to be slaughtered.

Featured in so many of my photographs, the cabin perches at the very apex of the Maury River's exceptional oxbow around our farm. Emerging from the woods into the clearing where the cabin sits, the first-time visitor must crank back the noggin as the amazed eyes begin their long climb up the multicolored, New Mexico–looking cliff face towering over the river.

Scraggly arborvitae cling tenuously to it, or hang by their last roots—the same trees, in fact, that appear in a glass negative taken at this site in the 1860s by a returning Civil War veteran, Michael Miley.

Back in my early twenties, I had discovered some 7,500 Miley glass-plate negatives stored in an attic on the Washington and Lee campus. I knew Miley had photographed Robert E. Lee in retirement here, but the negatives I found included none of those relatively famous images. Instead I found pictures of familiar local places, many all but unchanged in the intervening century, among them several of the stretch of river where the cabin is now. This dark pool was a popular swimming hole in the 1800s, and it is easy to imagine that Lee himself swam there or, even more likely, Stonewall Jackson.

As I held those dusty Miley plates to the light, in the same careful way I now hold my own glass negatives, I found myself weirdly shifting between the centuries. In that same time-warpy way, the view we see now from the cabin deck has remained virtually unchanged for 150 years: the arborvitae pictured as a sapling in front of the cave opening in the Miley image almost certainly is the fallen, bleached tree trunk off to the left in this modern photo.

The grandson of a county native recently gave me a written account that describes a camp in the late 1800s where the cabin is now. Its name, the Covenanter Camp, would have pleased Stonewall Jackson, alluding to the religious and military history of the Scotch-Irish Presbyterians who first settled the area. The camp director, indeed, was a grizzled Confederate veteran who ran the place on rigid military lines. Surprisingly, it was coed, with twenty-five girls and seventy boys at the two-week session. A tent city was erected with a central "Main Street" dividing boys from girls, and a large cook tent anchored the operation.

Apparently, scheduled activities were few. Mostly the kids swam and raced and threw horseshoes, and once, for sport, in the absence of a pig, they greased and chased a kid named Tricky Johenning. Until the large beach along the river at the camp was literally sold out from under them to a man in need of sand to make brick mortar, the Covenanter Camp prospered and the kids played tirelessly on the beach and in the river.

Nearly a century later, so did our three children, Emmett, Jessie, and Virginia, not nearly as well covered up and making do with a smaller beach, but enough of one to serve the purpose for sand burials, castles, and sunbathing. On that beach and by that same river I began taking the family pictures, consisting of at least two hundred final images, some sixty of which were published in 1992 in *Immediate Family*. These pictures cannot be understood without the context of the farm and the cabin on the river—the intrinsic timelessness of the place and the privacy it afforded us.

7

Hold Still

On June 4, 1993, eight years into taking the pictures of my children, I wrote this to my friend Maria Hambourg:

So, I have come to a quiet moment before my daily walk to meet the girls after school (surveillance and protection of children still in force) and I face the blue screen, trying to reconstruct what has happened since we sat at your dinner table.

I'm stronger now, though I haven't taken any new pictures, which is where my strength has usually come from. I am still afraid for the children, the boogeyman kind of fear that may not leave me until they have outgrown their present skins. And I'm still afraid that the good pictures won't come, as usual.

This year, though, the good pictures of the kids might not come. The fear may scare them off. My conviction and belief in the work was so unshakably strong for so many years, and my passion for making it was so undeniable. Now, it is no longer the same: I am frightened of the pictures, I am reluctant to push the limits. I suspect this work is dying its natural death: I sense fertile ground as I bury it, though, and a new kind of wisdom that comes with the acceptance of the limits I wanted to push for so long.

The phenomenon of the last year spun me around and now leaves me wobbling, like a spent top, towards stasis. I am grateful for the peace that has finally begun to settle again in our lives: the phone calls are fewer, the list of sold prints within a year of being completed: I have the sense that I am getting control again. And I'm oh so much smarter now: I've had my 15 minutes and never has the sweet tedium of my life looked better.

The family pictures changed all our lives in ways we never could have predicted, in ways that affect us still. Their genesis was in simple exploration, at times of a documentary nature, at others conceptual or aesthetic and, in the best pictures, all at once. But the simplicity of intention and vision with which I began became complicated over time, by narrative, by defiance, by the natural evolution of an aesthetic, by doubt, and, yes, by fear.

Those pictures, rooted in our family's domestic routines and our little postage stamp of native soil, had the unlikely effect of delivering the kind of overnight international celebrity that so many people, including many threadbare artists, desire. Clichés tell us that fame is a prize that burns the winner. The clichés are often right. As Adam Gopnik once remarked, when we hit pay dirt, we often find quicksand beneath it.

The wobbling-top analogy I used with Maria isn't far off the mark; this brush with celebrity spun me near senseless. My refuge then, as it had been since childhood, was the farm, where within the sweet insularity of its boundaries I still find my equilibrium.

Never had I needed that equilibrium, the soothing balm of perfect proportion and beauty that I find on the farm, more than I did then. Most people who know me well, and even those who don't but know my work, will eventually use the word "fearless" to describe who they think I am. Maybe it's deserved, to a degree; certainly my horse-racing life qualifies, and sometimes, perhaps, my artistic life. But that mettle, the recklessness, self-possession, and hauteur—I know where that comes from.

My father was a renegade Texan with an excellent northern education, an atheist, and an intellectual. He kept packs of big dogs, bought art (Kandinsky and Matisse in the 1930s, Twombly in the fifties) and drove fast foreign cars. As a southern family in the 1950s and sixties, we were simply different and we knew it.

Other families had crèches at Christmas, but our living room had this decoration, to my mother's feigned mortification.

With Man Ray–like obsession, my father collected stuff and made singular art pieces late in the night in his workroom, even once replacing an uninspired floral arrangement on the dining room table with this, a petrified dog turd.

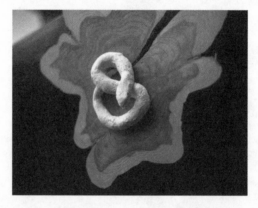

On the morning that his gardens were open to the Virginia State Garden Tour (you remember how to pronounce garden, don't you?), he put this sculpture on one of the back trails at the base of a big oak. When my mother came upon it with her group of white-gloved ladies trilling with nervous laughter, she rued the day she'd fallen for that irreverent wag.

He called it *Portnoy's Triple Complaint*, and after someone sent Philip Roth a photograph of it, Roth wrote back:

I react with wonder and awe. None of us should complain, of course; art reminds us of that. Dr. Munger is a brave man to have such a thing in his garden. I would be tarred and feathered and thrown out of my town if I dared. Luckily people forgive me my books.

But, while bodacious and impious, my father was also compassionate. He believed in socialized medicine, stating often that medical care is like education: everyone should have access to it. When the community doctors met and agreed to raise the rates for an office visit to seven dollars, Daddy lowered his to five. My mother, who at first kept his books, despaired of his refusal to charge those who could not afford to pay.

She once saw a patient who had not paid for the last several babies my father had delivered by lantern light at his remote home. The man was leaving the liquor store with an armload of bourbon as she was going in.

Indignantly she confronted my father about it at dinner that night and he responded flatly, "If you owed the doctor as much as that man owes me, you would want a drink, too."

He had strongly held beliefs and was brave about asserting them. And he made us kids be brave, too, facing the little-understood challenges of civil rights, integration, and separation of church and state. During the early 1960s the schools we attended had daily Bible study and I was the only grade-school child who had to leave the classroom and sit outside the principal's office while others studied Scripture. I can still remember the burning humiliation of having the younger students going single-file to lunch pointing and making fun of me. Never had I wanted more to be just like everyone else. But my father wouldn't yield, and year after year I masked my mortification with indifferent cockiness.

Our family had no wood-sided station wagon, no country club membership, no television, no church, and no colonial house in the new subdivision. We read the *New York Times* and used the sports pages to line the parakeet's cage. I think my father came to believe long ago what Rhett Butler told Scarlett: reputation is something people with character can do without.

Character and character building (other words, I guess, for sucking it up) were a big deal in our family. I have wondered whether my parents were right to expect me to suffer for a concept about which I lacked the maturity to form an opinion. Of course the fact that this parallels the situation of my own children, snickered at by their classmates for being in unconventional pictures, hasn't escaped my notice. I think the lessons I learned from my father, as painful as they occasionally were, made me the character I am. I don't regret them, especially as we could retreat to the farm, where who we were seemed normal.

Even now, when I look at the arc of my work, those pictures taken on the farm and at the cabin seem more balanced, less culturally influenced and more universal, than those taken anywhere else—like this little honey of an image made years before I'd even identified my children as possible subjects.

Why it took me so long to find the abundant and untapped artistic wealth within family life, I don't know. I took a few pictures with the 8 × 10 inch camera when Emmett was a baby, but for years I shot the underappreciated and extraordinary domestic scenes of any mother's life with the point-and-shoot.

Like this one of my preemie Jessie, born in 1981, hardly bigger than the spoon with which I stirred my tea:

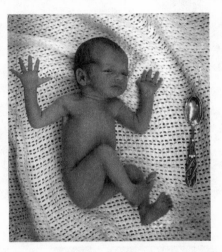

And her miraculous survival after countless bouts of pneumonia: Where was my camera then?

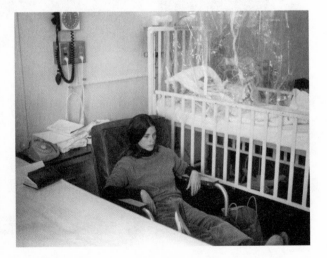

I missed so many opportunities, now tantalizingly fading away in the scrapbooks:

The puking,

the pets:

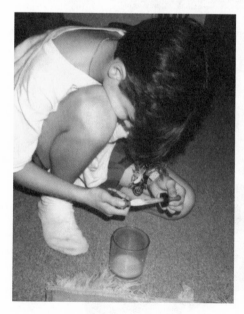

. . . and the toilet training, the never-ending toilet training.

Maybe at first I didn't see those things as art because, with young babies in the house, you remove your "photography eyes," as Linda Connor once called the sensibility that allows ecstatic vision. Maybe it was because the miraculous quotidian (oxymoronic as that phrase may seem) that is part of child rearing must often, for species survival, veil the intensely seeing eye.

I know for sure that the intensely seeing eye was different from the one I used to quarter thousands of school-lunch apples and braid miles of hair through my decades of motherhood. I had to promote this form of special vision and place myself, with deliberate foresight, on a collision course with felicitous, gift-giving Chance. I described this state in a 1987 letter:

I am working, every day, . . . on new photographs. This body of work, family pictures, is beginning to take on a life of its own. Seldom, but memorably, there are times when my vision, even my hand, seems guided by, well, let's say a muse. There is at that time an almost mystical rightness about the image: about the way the light is enfolding, the way the [kids'] eyes have taken on an almost frightening intensity, the way there is a sudden, almost outer-space-like, quiet.

These moments nurture me through the reemergence into the quotidian . . . through the bill paying and the laundry and the shopping for soccer shoes, although I am finding that I am becoming increasingly distant, like I am somehow living full time in those moments.

And again to Maria Hambourg in April 1989:

Good photographs are gifts. . . . Taken for granted they don't come. I set the camera up and . . . suspend myself in that familiar space about a foot above the ground where good photographs come. I wait there, breath suppressed, in that trance, that state of suspended animation, the moment before the frisson. . . .

It has always worked before and the moment when it starts to come is unlike anything else: when it falls so perfectly into place and Jessie cocks her hip and doesn't move out of the 1 inch of focus I have: when the wind blows up just the right little tracery in the water behind the alligator. That moment possesses such a feeling of transcendence: it's the ecstatic time: better than sex. The parallels are all too obvious and can only be understood, I maintain, by a woman.

But it wasn't really until 1985 that I put on my photography eyes, and began to see the potential for serious imagery within the family. I began, as I often do, with a promising near miss, using the 8 × 10 view camera to photograph Virginia's birth.

I had delivered both Emmett and Jessie without any drugs at all, damn near the hardest things I have ever done in my life. It was especially painful with the first child, Emmett, a relative porker at over six pounds, but easier with Jessie, who weighed in at only four pounds and change. Both were fairly fast deliveries, but with intense and unrelenting contractions that I barely managed with Lamaze breathing, Larry at my side. I figured I could do it one more time, and why not try a picture?

Two weeks before Virginia's due date, I took my 8 × 10 to the birthing room and set it up, pressing into service as my stand-in a bewildered candy striper who lay on the bed in what we assumed would be my posture at delivery. I focused on her hands demurely pressing her skirt down between her legs, which were elevated in steel stirrups the way we gave birth back then. Leaving the camera bellows at exactly that extension, I removed the camera from the tripod, and bent over my balance-destroying belly to make grease-pencil circles on the floor where the tripod legs were. Then I packed up, carried the equipment to the car, and went home to wait it out.

I didn't have long; my water broke in the early morning a week before my due date. I made the kids' lunches, walked them to school as usual, and Larry went off to work. The pre-focused camera, tripod, and film were waiting in the car, so I drove to the hospital, hauling my leaking bulk, plus the equipment, down the corridors to the OB floor. More accustomed to seeing a woman in labor carrying a floral overnight bag, the nurse on duty jumped up to help me in.

I was uncomfortable and it took more time than it should for me to get the camera set up on the black marks, insert the film holder, and do a quick light-meter reading, taking into account the wall of sun-filled glass into which I would be shooting. At noon my redheaded nurse, Mrs. Fix, was supposed to leave for her thirty-minute lunch break, but she eyed me, lying under the view camera, blowing and glassy-eyed with pain, and announced that she was calling Larry and the doctor right then. To hell with lunch.

Larry got there first. I was in labor delirium by then, breathing fiercely and speechless with hard contractions. At 12:30 I saw Dr. Harralson's white coat come flapping up the hill outside the windows and suddenly the room was filled with activity. Trying not to push, I signaled Larry to take the black slide out of the film holder and cock the shutter at the pre-set speed. He knew not to let the camera move an iota in that process, which is harder than you might think with shaking hands.

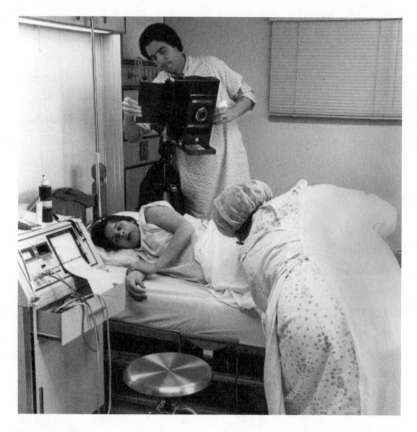

At 12:37 the baby crowned and I reached up to the camera, thinking, "Dammit, Lois Conner gave me a shutter release and if ever there was a time for one, this is it. How could I have forgotten it?"

But it wasn't camera shake from my fitful finger on the shutter that made the resulting image not all that interesting. I had correctly figured that Dr. Harralson's body would block the light from the windows so I'd have to use a slower shutter speed. Anticipating the likely light levels, I had calculated the aperture at f/4.5, wide-open, for a fifth of a second, and I was right.

But at such a slow speed, the barreling baby was blurred as she slid out.

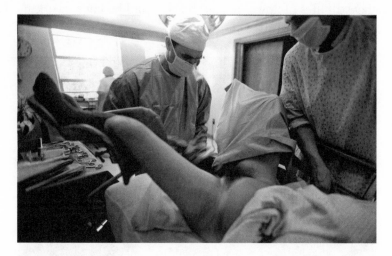

The picture was a dud.

But . . . maybe not a total loss. Perhaps, in hindsight, it was the birth of the family pictures, breathing life into the notion that photographs, and sometimes good ones, could be made everywhere, even in the most seemingly commonplace or fraught moments. A few months later, I took what I think of as my first good family picture. It was of Jessie's face, swollen with hives from insect bites, to which she is especially sensitive. This was the one I started with, when she showed up that afternoon:

Looking at this picture now, I realize it is a just continuation of the soft, gauzy still lifes of flower petals and chiffon I had been working on for years, except this one had a kid in it.

I had done some earlier abstracts of Emmett with the same idea, chiffon, flowers,

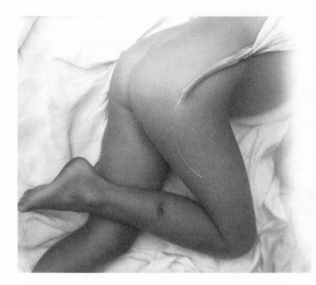

but, in the chiffony picture of Jessie, I sensed a new direction. I don't know if I'm all that different from other people, but for me great artistic leaps forward are not accompanied by thunderclaps of recognition. In truth, they aren't even usually great leaps. They are tentative toe testings accompanied by an ever-present whisper of doubt.

Despite that whisper, I went ahead and took another picture of Jessie that day, which I called "Damaged Child."

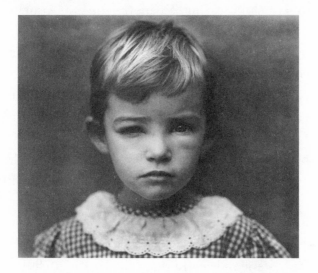

As soon as I printed it, I noticed its kinship with the familiar Dorothea Lange picture "Damaged Child, Shacktown."

In both, the girls have a look of battered defiance. Just in case anyone could miss it, I made sure that the title drove the comparison home.

As strange as it sounds, I found something comforting about this disturbing picture. Looking at the still-damp contact print, and then looking at Jessie, completely recovered and twirling around the house in her pink tutu, I realized the image inoculated me to a possible reality that I might not henceforth have to suffer. Maybe this could be an escape from the manifold terrors of child rearing, an apotropaic protection: stare them straight in the face but at a remove—on paper, in a photograph.

With the camera, I began to take on disease and accidents of every kind, magnifying common impetigo into leprosy, skin wrinkles into whip marks, simple bruises into hemorrhagic fever. Even when a scary situation turned out benign, I replayed it for the camera with the worst possible outcome, as if to put the quietus on its ever reoccurring.

Once at about age five, Jessie took a mind to hop across the creek on the big rocks with which we'd dammed it, and walk the half mile or so to Emmett's school. I was a pretty vigilant mother and had glanced out the window to see her, just a moment before, playing with her doll Maria on the tire swing, but suddenly I looked down at the bottomland and . . . no Jessie. Being the hysteric and fatalist that I am, I went into full panic mode, calling and running up and down the creek banks. By this time, Jessie was long gone, carefully looking both ways as she carried Maria across the nearby street on her way to Waddell School. I called the neighbors and my friends, and pretty soon we had a group of searchers fanning out into the woods. I stuck to the creek edge, certain I'd see a flash of gingham, of white sock and patent leather Mary Janes in the water.

Before long, the school secretary showed up with a beaming Jessie, and I sank into the bone-deep exhaustion of relief. The next day I set up the camera, cajoled seven-year-old Emmett into putting on a dress, and made this picture, almost too awful to look at, even now. I called it "The Day Jessie Got Lost" and I prayed it would protect us from any such sight, ever.

In fact, it didn't.

A short time later, on a hot afternoon in early September 1987, I walked to the road at the top of our driveway to meet Emmett, who was on his way home from playing with a friend. That crossing was then especially busy because of nearby construction, and I always went up there to help the kids get across. An idling bulldozer blocked my sightline, but I spotted Emmett as he approached the road where a flagman was holding back oncoming traffic. Emmett paused on the other side of the street by the bulldozer.

The noise it was making was such that I couldn't yell to him to wait, so instead I held up my hand, palm forward, in the universal "stop" sign. Not schooled in international hand gestures, Emmett mistook it for a "come to me in a hurry" sign and did just that. A second before he sprang forward, the flagman signaled the impatiently waiting cars to come ahead. The first car in the queue was a 1970s Chevelle, a heavy, powerful car driven by a seventeen-year-old who was only too willing to oblige the flagman's command. He didn't exactly gun it, but he wasn't going to miss the opportunity to show the workmen lining both sides of the road what his car could do.

The poor kid couldn't possibly have braked to avoid Emmett, who had leapt out from his side of the road, his happy eyes on mine. The car, going about thirty-five miles per hour, caught him midleap. Emmett's head slammed into the hood and he was catapulted more than forty feet, where he lay crumpled and bleeding in the middle of the road.

Of course nobody had cell phones then, but even if they had, everyone who witnessed this seemed frozen in place. I screamed for someone to call the rescue squad, and no one moved, so I ran back down to the house and did it myself, worrying that while I was gone another car might hit Emmett. Then I ran back up the driveway and down along the forty-seven feet of skid marks to the splayed figure in the road.

I have said many times that the image of Emmett lying there is burned in my mind, but that is not true. In fact, I can't tell you what he was wearing without consulting the photographs I took later in the hospital or even exactly how he had fallen. I remember lying in the sticky tar, I remember seeing the figures of the workmen in their hard hats standing on the hill above us, silent like a herd of curious bovines, and I remember knowing not to move the body. I also remember that I thought about photography in the eleven minutes it took for the first-aid crew to arrive.

When they did, Emmett was semiconscious, and when he was asked what his name was he spelled it out in a steady voice: E-M-M-E-T-T.

A glimmer of hope.

A few days after the accident came a knock on my door. Several of the workmen were standing there, yellow hard hats tucked under their elbows, one with a rose wrapped in cellophane from a convenience store. They stammered out their condolences and I then realized that they thought Emmett was dead from the minute they saw him hit. How could he not have been? That was why they never moved.

I thought he was dead, too. Seeing the Chevelle a few days later only reinforced the miracle of his survival. The still-shaken kid who had hit him drove the car over to our house and to demonstate the toughness of its metal suggested that Larry hit the hood as hard as he could. So Larry summoned up all his blacksmithing muscles and slammed his fist into the hood. Nothing.

Where Emmett had hit was a stomach-turning, head-sized dent.

After having made that dent and been catapulted down the road, Emmett, other than some vomiting and general pain, was found to be unharmed and was released from the hospital after just a few days. It is generally thought that what saved his life was that he was in midleap, airborne when he was hit, but who knows? To me, and I am sure to all of those who saw it, it is still inexplicable.

So in those eleven minutes, what was it about photography that I was thinking? Here's what I wrote to a friend a month later, in October 1987:

But now, the real image of Emmett lying in a pool of blood has come to make the family pictures seem, ummm, trivial to me.

I lay there certain that his life was ebbing from his unconscious form and thought about . . . the real meaning of photographing my children. About whether I actually could have brought myself to photograph what is now so horribly burned into my mind. About what kind of photographer I really am . . . who exhorts her students to "photograph what is important to you, what is closest to you, photograph the great events of your life, and let your photography live with your reality" but who is paralyzed by that very reality. I actually wondered as I lay there, with my dying son, (or so I thought) if I could even hold a camera up. And, of course, there was no way. I am just not that kind of photographer.

I thought during that eleven-minute eternity that the world of motherhood is a far more complex thing than you and I ever imagined when we plunged so willingly into it, and that the fear and . . . joy I have encountered have staggered me.

How I love those children.

And how much I fear for them. And how real those fears can become, in just an instant. Right before my eyes, even, my horrified eyes. And, what's worse is that I had imagined that scene, imagined it countless, terrible times and shaken myself out of it.

That is what those photographs were and now, of course, I am afraid of them. Afraid that by photographing my fears I might be closer to actually seeing them, not the other way round. Irrational, I know, but Emmett's accident has turned a woman who lived on the edge into one who slips periodically into the depths and is only retrieved by a thread.

So, I have reached some sort of emotional impasse, I suppose, with these pictures. These last few weeks the new ones are suffused with the late summer light and they are gentler, more Southern, perhaps. I know all this will pass and that the image of him will stop arising, unbidden, to my mind and that the photographs will work themselves out. But it often is quite hard to reconcile one's work with one's life, isn't it?

I had tried to exorcise the trauma of the experience by following my own commandment to "photograph what is important, what is closest to you, photograph the great events of your life." I had taken my view camera into the hospital the night of the accident, but got nothing special there.

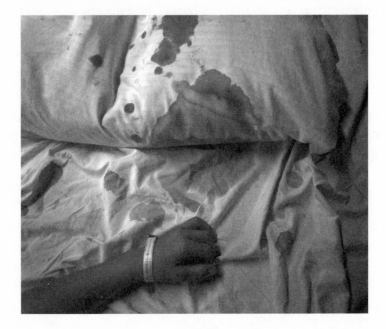

Then, a few weeks later I tried to make a photograph of the way Emmett looked when he was hit, or the way I felt he looked.

No go.

Emmett was completely recovered within a week, but I was still grievously wounded. I couldn't shake from my memory the image of his sunlit, smiling face as he sprang toward me. And each time it came to me, I would suffer the sickening realization of the inevitable, the unstoppable that played out in that interminable split second. I would wake gasping and weeping from dreams, my concrete legs refusing the bidding of my panicked brain, horrified eyes turned to marble.

I tried a self-portrait. Another loser.

At the farm, the honeyed September light and the lazy, limpid river offered, as always, the cure, the balm for my bunged-up soul. At the farm, there is no reason for photography-as-inoculation, no fear and no danger. Just the land and the river and the sheltering cliffs, the comfort of the colossal trees.

Still, and not surprisingly, I concentrated on Emmett.

In each of these three pictures I saw something I liked: in the first, the solitary figure of the boy, in the next, the rush of water, made satiny by the slow shutter speed, and in the third, the V of the sky and the river.

Terrier that I am, at least in the pursuit of an elusive picture, I set out to marry all those features in one image, hauling the 8 × 10 camera and heavy tripod out into the river, slipping on the rocks, buffeted by the current, to set up in the riffling water at the lower rapids. I somehow managed to cut out the sky part of the picture in the next try, but still saw the potential for a good image.

Maybe lose the snorkel, I decided.

Now that I was on the scent, I was obsessed with getting this damn picture right. Day after day that balmy September I carried the camera and one film holder to the middle of the river across the mossy rocks. The water was waist-deep where I set up for the picture, with treacherous drop-offs into dark, fishy holes. After shooting the two sheets of film in each holder, I would swim, the holder high above my head, and get another, while dear, patient Emmett waited. I had six film holders, so we'd generally take twelve negatives each day—and most of them were failures.

They failed in many ways, sometimes because my wet fingers ruined the film, once when I dropped the film holder in the river, once because a flotilla of canoes came through, but usually because of dumb compositional mistakes on my part.

In this one he's too far out of the water,

then here there's too much light on the trees behind him, plus he's too far back, but I liked the satiny water.

Off-center here and don't like those clouds, or his hair.

Damn light-meter strap in the way here:

But now we're getting closer, got the hands right, still too far out of the water and the light is too bright behind him . . .

Okay, the hands are almost right here, but an awkward stance, still not a keeper.

Then, eureka.

Seven different days we had tried, maybe eight—but I knew we had it at last. No one was more relieved than Emmett, who had given up all those afternoons to the demands of the light—and of his mother. Children cannot be forced to make pictures like these: mine gave them to me. Every picture represents a gesture of such generosity and faith that I, in turn, felt obliged to repay them by making the best, most enduring images that I could. The children, picture after picture, had given of themselves when the dark slide was pulled, firing off a deadly accurate look into the lens; a glare, a squinty-eyed look, a sad expression, whatever I asked for, as professional as any actor. And in many cases, they did this while hot, hungry, tired, or, like Emmett, shaking with cold.

It was not unreasonable when he announced that it was the last damn time he would model in the freezing river (by then it was October), and for some reason I titled the picture "The Last Time Emmett Modeled

Nude," although I knew the nudity was completely beside the point. That certainly came back to bite me in the ass.

Not every picture required this Herculean kind of effort, but more than a few did. When I sensed that a good picture lurked just beyond my range of vision, I went after it with dogged intent. I'd get a whiff of a good one in an odd snapshotty picture, like this one of Virginia about to dive off the cliffs,

and after considerable effort and multiple tries, finally got it right:

That's the way many of these pictures evolved, their genesis in a failed image but one that had some rudiment of the eternal in it—like the hair plastered across the ribs, or the V of sky and river with Emmett.

But others came completely spontaneously; the camera was almost always set up off to the side and when something interesting happened, I would ask for everyone to hold still, maybe quickly tweak something, and then shoot.

I wrote about it in a letter back then:

You wait for your eye to sort of "turn on," for the elements to fall into place and that ineffable rush to occur, a feeling of exultation when you look through that ground glass, counting ever so slowly, clenching teeth and whispering to Jessie to *holdstillholdstillholdstill* and just knowing that it will be good, that it is true. Like the one true sentence that Hemingway writes about in *A Moveable Feast*, that incubating purity and grace that happens, sometimes, when all the parts come together.

And these pictures have come quickly, in a rush . . . like some urgent bodily demand. They have been obvious, they have been right there to be taken, almost like celestial gifts.

Gifts, indeed. Many pictures came to me in that lucky rush of exultation, the ones for which I had time to shoot only one, *one* sheet of film, those where I sank to my knees after shakily replacing the dark slide, eyes shut tight in thanksgiving and fear, fear that I'd screw it up in the developer, fear that the fraction of a second I saw was not the one on film, and in exhaustion, too, from the breath-bated moment, a tenth of a second with the expansive, vertiginous properties of Nabokovian timelessness, while before me the brilliant angel no longer radiant with the sun snatches up the towel and heads to the beach, the tomatoes are imperfectly carved up for supper, and my heart, my pounding heart, sends from my core the bright strength for me to rise.

8

Ubi Amor, Ibi Oculus Est

Remember that the file for the Mann murder-suicide was not deep in cold-case storage at the New Canaan police station? And that after thirty-five years it was sitting out on the desk in the records office when I asked for a copy? Wonder why? It's a strange story that speaks to the hazards of public exposure, which in turn illustrates what ultimately was for me the most chilling aspect of showing and publishing the family pictures.

In 2010 anonymous letters began arriving at a variety of places—mail-boxes of art critics, museum and gallery directors, college presidents, art professors, book publishers, collectors, newspaper offices, and, to the point of this particular narrative, the chief of the New Canaan Police Department, the head of the state police, and the attorney general of Connecticut.

The letters raved, in varying degrees of readability, that I had made my career by appropriating the work of an underappreciated and unnamed Virginia artist and that I was a fraud, a liar, a thief, and a *murderer*. Almost all were postmarked Richmond, Virginia, and typed on a computer, including the address labels. At first they were merely an annoyance to me and to those who received them, but as years went by and it grew clear they came from a committed and possibly deranged stalker, I became alarmed.

Various law enforcement authorities in Connecticut were also alarmed. Here is one of the letters they received, with redundant passages excised:

This letter is concerning the July 1977 case of Dr. Warren Mann and his wife Rose-Marie Mann in New Canaan, CT that was listed as a murder-suicide. I have come across some recent information that I believe is extremely important that could prove it was not a murder-suicide but indeed a double homicide. The culprits being Larry Mann the oldest son of Warren and Rose-Marie and Larry's wife the controversial photographer Sally (Munger) Mann.

Someone needs to check if Larry Mann was born having Arthur as his middle name. Arthur is what he uses as his middle name and it makes sense considering his father was Warren Arthur Mann. If so, we need to ask the question what the "TE" stands for in Laurence TE Mann, one of his aliases.

Logically with Larry Mann being a philosophy major in college and with what happened to Warren and Rose-Marie Mann Larry is taking the TE Mann as Teman, grandson of Esau from the bible, a.k.a. descendent of Esau. Larry Mann is relating himself as Esau and his brother as Jacob.

One of Larry Mann's other aliases Laurence A. Mannba a.k.a. Larry Mamba is a bold statement in itself. Esau was known to represent the hunter and bloodshed, he was the man known to have the love of violence and murder. Mamba—the deadly snake. Larry Mann, like his wife Sally, receives a natural buzz taunting the law to see how far he can go without being caught. The aliases would help him achieve this high.

If Sally's father Dr. Robert Munger or any Munger was used as alibis for Sally and Larry Mann's whereabouts at the time of Warren and Rose-Marie's death it would be a drastic mistake.

Dr. Munger is known as the devil in human skin and he would do anything to help his daughter continue the chain of destruction to destroy anyone and anything of goodness. He was known to make his extra money as the abortionist in the area when it was illegal.

Sally Mann hates Catholics and tries to set them up anytime she can. Someone needs to check if Rose-Marie Mann grew up Catholic since Sally and Larry chose to set up Rose-Marie during the crime scene. There is some crucial reason they chose Rose-Marie.

Rose-Marie and Warren Mann have been deceased now for over 34 years. Rose-Marie is innocent and she cannot speak in her defense about what really happened that July of 1977. Sally Mann has finally made the mistake to prove that she and her husband Larry Mann were responsible for a double murder.

It is time to clear Rose-Marie's name so she and her husband Warren can both rest in peace.

(The end of the letter noted that copies were sent to the FBI resident agency in Bridgeport, to the New Canaan police, to the Connecticut State Police, to various named public officials, and to a journalist at *The Hour* newspaper in Norwalk.)

Crazy as these letters seemed, the authorities who received them couldn't ignore what they were claiming. Late in 2011, unbeknownst to us, the New Canaan police reopened the case of the murder-suicide of Warren and Rose Marie Mann. At the same time, a capable detective for the Rockbridge County Sheriff's Department, Tim Hickman, began a local investigation into the origin of the letters, and proposed a long-shot request for help from the FBI at Quantico, Virginia.

The FBI has bigger fish to fry than a disgruntled would-be artist on a letter-writing campaign. It gets thousands of requests for help from local law enforcement nationwide and takes only a handful, so we were surprised when the Threat Assessment Unit agreed to meet Hickman at Quantico. They put several agents on the case and, together with Hickman, worked up a profile. It was a relief that they believed the immediate physical threat to me was minimal, but all the same the letters were getting crazier and more frequent. I worried when I appeared in public for speaking engagements or openings, and even found the seclusion of my life on the farm, which had always offered me protection and comfort, becoming a source of disquiet.

In the end, Hickman's open ears and old-fashioned gumshoe investigation cracked the case. The fruit bat letter writer was exactly the person the FBI profile suggested she'd be: older with an unsuccessful artist-daughter who lived at home, but (the Threat Assessment Unit got this one wrong) she also had a history of instability and physical violence. Once local law enforcement and the FBI confronted and strenuously warned her off in spring of 2012, the letters stopped.

Even now, writing this a year later, I still feel vulnerable and exposed, and I am even more mistrustful of our culture's cult of celebrity. Of the many unexpected repercussions surrounding the exhibition and publication of the family pictures, the widespread public attention and our seeming accessibility are still the most disturbing to me.

Looking back on that tumultuous decade, during which the skirmishes of the culture wars spilled into my territory, I have come to appreciate the dialog that took place, but at the time I occasionally felt that my soul had been exposed to critics who took pleasure in poking it with a stick. Many people expressed opinions, usually in earnest good faith but sometimes with rancor, about the pictures: my right to take them, especially my right as a mother, my state of emotional health, the implications for the children, and the pictures' effect on the viewer. I was blindsided by the controversy, protected, I thought, by my relative obscurity and geographic isolation, and was initially unprepared to respond to it in any cogent way.

For starters, I didn't realize the implications of allowing unfettered access to a journalist whose attentions I found flattering and whom I assumed to be a friend. Janet Malcolm wrote this wry assessment of the journalistic subject in her provocative book *The Journalist and the Murderer*:

> Like the young Aztec men and women selected for sacrifice, who lived in delightful ease and luxury until the appointed day when their hearts were to be carved from their chests, journalistic subjects know all too well what awaits them when the days of wine and roses—the days of the interviews—are over. And still they say yes when a journalist calls, and still they are astonished when they see the flash of the knife.

I said yes when the journalist Rick Woodward called and I was astonished at the flash of the knife. But unlike the Aztec youth, I wasn't expecting it; that's how naïve I was. In my arrogance and certitude that everyone surely must see the work as I did, I left myself wide-open to journalism's greatest hazard: quotes lacking context or the sense of irony or self-deprecating humor with which they had been delivered. During the two days of interviews, not exactly "wine and roses," that resulted in a cover story for the *New York Times Magazine*, I was a sitting duck preening on her nest with not the least bit of concealment. So I can hardly fault Woodward for taking his shots at me.

He wrote me afterward that he had "dined out for months" on the story, and I'm sure he did. It generated a large amount of mail to the magazine, all of which the editor was kind enough to send me, although reading it caused me the same furious pain that the article had, and that it was essentially self-inflicted made it the worse.

My intern and I read all the letters and divided them up into three crude piles: *For, Against,* and *What the Fuck?*

The *Against* pile (thirty-three) beat the others out, but not by much. Despite what I thought of as Woodward's unnecessarily heavy foot on the controversy throttle, nearly half were positive (twenty-eight), and not in the creepy way you might expect (an example of semi-creepy: "As an editor and publisher of a nudist related publication, I too am subject to public humiliation . . .").

Here's how the more negative, or in most cases, critical-but-trying-to-be-helpful, letters broke down:

Seven were from people who had either been abused as children or were themselves treating abused children. These were thoughtful, concerned, sometimes fraught letters. This opening sentence from a psychotherapist in Colorado is typical of the heightened feeling: "The cover article on Sally Mann stirred me greatly." Several recounted the writers' own painful life stories.

I went into therapy 14 months ago because of depression <u>never</u> thinking for one moment that there were incest issues in my past. After five months the horror of flash-backs and memories began. I was incested [*sic*] over and over and horribly tortured.

Much was made of the distinct personalities of my parents:

Her mother is described as having a sense of propriety; her father is described as being an aloof man and as having a sense of perversity. This contrasting parental style is regularly found in abusive families. . . .

She keeps a picture of her dead father in his bathrobe on her wall. Why a picture of him dead, why in his bathrobe, and why are the two combined?

All seven letters suggested that my father had abused me, and that I had repressed the memory and was unconsciously working out some kind of psychic pathology in my photographs. The then-popular theory that repressed childhood sexual abuse can remain susceptible to therapeutic recovery was, by 1992, beginning to wobble under scientific scrutiny (though you sure wouldn't know it from the confident assertions in the *Times* mailbag). I had stupidly planted this repressed-memory idea by telling Woodward that I had very few memories of what was, basically, an unmemorable childhood, and that my father had taken "terrible art pictures" of me in the nude.

A particularly agitated letter from Staten Island, with a postscript apology for the correspondent's "primitive method of handwriting," queried me from page one:

"Was it really art, Ms. Mann, or was it covert incest?"

It was neither. Not incest, not art, and, it turns out, not even nudity. I have now organized and scanned all my father's large-format negatives (as distinct from the casual snapshots he and my mother took) and am chagrined to report that they contain not a single nude photograph of me—an impressive feat of discretion on my father's part, given how much time I spent naked as a kid. I have no idea why I said that to Woodward, and I'm resigned to present-day readers making what they will of the apparent fact that I *falsely remembered* being photographed nude.

But so be it. Their concerns that my "inner child" is "harboring deep reservations" and that the pictures "speak more about the photographer's repressed memories of her own childhood than of her present relationship with her children" were misplaced. The facts are pedestrian and simple: what I had intended to convey to Woodward was that my pitifully few childhood memories were primarily based on photographs, and this was true.

And not just for me, either: I believe that photographs actually rob all of us of our memory. But having few childhood memories, and those being rooted in deckle-edged, curling snapshots, does not automatically qualify me for the repressed-memory club. If that were the case, nearly all the people my age would be spilling their guts on the couch about being "incested over and over again." We're not. We're just admitting that we're old, childhood was a long time ago, and we don't remember all that much because our human brains find only certain things, and sometimes odd ones, worthy of encoding as long-term memories.

After the repressed-memories camp, the next-best represented was the ketchup lobby, spearheaded by a clinical social worker. I was taken to task for the most self-mocking, flippant, two-glasses-of-red-wine-into-it comment *ever* about ketchup, or, rather, about the kids' use of it: "It's common and I will not have common children." Naturally, Woodward couldn't resist quoting that, but we'll skip the numerous letters of protest that begin earnestly with lines like "As a psychotherapist . . ." and continue to talk about, I swear, ketchup on fresh trout and my pretentiousness in setting the table with linen napkins in silver napkin rings.

The ones that stabbed me to the quick were the Bad Mother letters. If I was anything, I was a damned good mother, walking the razor-sharp line between being a "cool mom," as Woodward described me, and being the old-fashioned mom who insisted on thank-you letters, proper grammar, good conversational skills, considerate behavior, and clean plates, no matter what was on them.

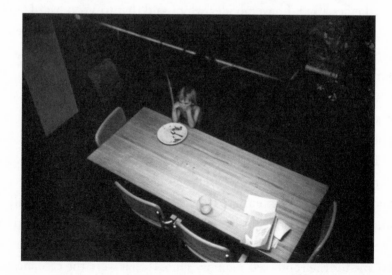

This is Jessie at 9:30 at night, still at the table after everyone else has gone to bed, sitting before a piece of flounder she refused to eat. I am not particularly proud of this moment, this clash of titanic stubbornnesses, but my children were the ones who would sit at our adult friends' tables anywhere in the world, eating whatever was on their plates and engaging dinner companions in evolved and entertaining conversation. And, yes, without being asked, write a thank-you note. Ask anyone: they were fantastic kids.

I can easily imagine the outraged letter about this picture from some concerned social worker, fretting about squelching a child's individual rights, or the power disparity between parent and child, or the abuse of trust or violation of bedtime hour or blah, blah, blah. I have the template for that complaint committed to memory from reading all the *New York Times* letters, many of which concluded as this one did:

Elizabeth [*sic*] Mann seems obsessed with situations which may prove disturbing to her children in a few years. . . . Time will tell whether and how much her children have been emotionally damaged by her photographs.

Even at the time, anguishing over these opinions and predictions, I knew that the crucial question for me as a mother was not whether the pictures were going to be respected in twenty years, but this all-important one: "I wonder how those poor, art-abused kids turned out."

Although the pressure and confusion gauges often buried their needles in the critical red zone, I continued to take the pictures, and I continued, with the help of the kids' patient, consistent, and loving father, to be the best mother I could be. The two roles were to a large extent kept separate. I walked the kids to school every morning and walked back to pick them up at three. I never forgot to sign the numberless permission slips and attended all their piano/flute/oboe/ballet recitals and soccer games. (Okay, so strictly speaking, that's not true, says Virginia. She just jokingly reminded me that I missed the All Regional band performance in Covington when she gave her oboe solo. And I bet there were some soccer games, too, but let's just say I did the best I could under the circumstances.)

With Larry holding the flashlight, I picked pinworms from itchy butts with the rounded ends of bobby pins, changed wet sheets in the middle of the night, combed out head-lice nits, and mopped up vomit. I baked bread, hand-ground peanuts into butter, raised and froze vegetables and every morning packed lunches so healthy they had no takers in the grand swap-fest of the lunchroom.

I also made many mistakes, as parents do, and I went through some powerful and painful self-examination. But, all the same, the Bad Mother accusation just couldn't stick, because taking those pictures was an act separate from mothering, and the kids knew the difference. When I stepped behind the camera, and they stepped in front of it, I was a photographer and they were actors and we were making a photograph together.

The Bad Mother letters usually raised the question of informed consent, but the kids were visually sophisticated, involved in setting the scene, and producing the desired effects for the images—and they were included in the editing of them. When the publication of *Immediate Family* was discussed, each child was given the possible pictures and asked to edit out any that he or she didn't want published. Emmett, who was thirteen at the time, asked to exclude this picture from the book.

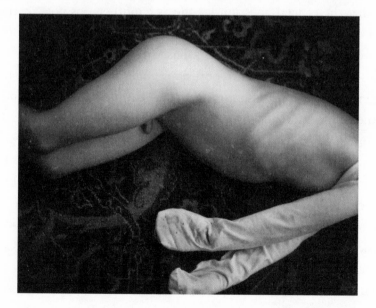

He, much younger, had been playing Bugs Bunny, and fell asleep still wearing the white legs of the rabbit. He was uncomfortable not because of the nudity, but because he said those socks made him look like a dork. It was a question of dignity.

That may have been the issue with Virginia's edits as well. Like Emmett and Jessie, nudity per se was of little concern to her. She removed this picture, "Pissing in the Wind," from the book possibilities, but, like Emmett, has given me permission to include it here.

Maintaining the dignity of my subjects has grown to be, over the years, an imperative in my work, both in the taking of the pictures and in the presentation of them. For example, as my father weakened with brain cancer, I tried to photograph him, in the manner of Richard Avedon or Jim Goldberg, whose work I admire.

But I put away my camera when I began to see that photographing his loss of dignity would cause him pain. (Once, after his death, I was asked what he had died of, and I replied, "Terminal pride.") I did not take a picture on the day that Larry picked up my father in his arms and carried him like a child to the bathroom, both their faces anguished. To do so would have been crossing a line.

It's hard to know just where to draw that stomach-roiling line, especially in those cases when the subject is willing to give so much. But how can they be so willing: is it fearlessness or naïveté? Those people who are unafraid to show themselves to the camera disarm me with the purity and innocence of their openness.

Larry, for example. Almost the first thing I did after I finally met Larry Mann in 1969 was to photograph him, and I haven't stopped in the years since. At our age, past the prime of life, we are given to sinew and sag, and Larry bears, with his trademark stoicism, the further affliction of a late-onset muscular dystrophy. In recent years, when many of his major muscles have withered, he has allowed me to take pictures of his body that make me squirm with embarrassment for him. I called this project Proud Flesh.

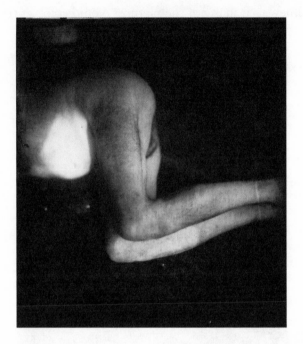

While working on these pictures, I joined the thinly populated group of women who have looked unflinchingly at men, and who frequently have been punished for doing so. Remember poor Psyche, exiled by the gods for daring to lift the lantern that illuminated her sleeping lover, Cupid.

I can think of numberless male artists, from Bonnard to Weston to Stieglitz, who have photographed their lovers and spouses, but I am having trouble finding parallel examples among my sister photographers. The act of looking appraisingly at a man, studying his body and asking to photograph him, is a brazen venture for a woman; for a male photographer, these acts are commonplace, even expected.

It is a testament to Larry's tremendous dignity and strength that he allowed me to take the pictures that I did. The gods might reasonably have slapped this particular lantern out of my raised hand, for before me lay a man as naked and vulnerable, and as beautiful, I assert, as Cupid. Rhetorically circumnavigate it any way you will, but the act of taking those pictures of him was ethically complex, freighted with issues of honesty, responsibility, power, and complicity. He knew that, because he is a sophisticated model, and he also knew that many of the pictures would come at the expense of his vanity.

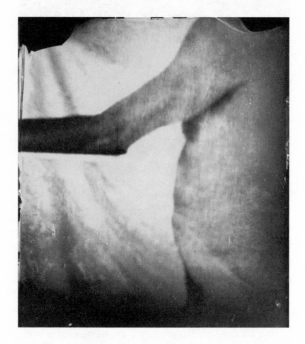

To be able to take my pictures I have to look, all the time, at the people and places I care about. And I must do so with both warm ardor and cool appraisal, with the passions of both eye and heart, but in that ardent heart there must also be a splinter of ice. And so it was with fire and ice, the studio woodstove insufficient to do him any good on the winter afternoons but with two fingers of bourbon to warm him, that Larry and I made these pictures: exploring what it means to grow older, to let the sunshine fall voluptuously on a still-beautiful form, to spend quiet afternoons together again. No phone, no kids, NPR tuned low, the smell of the chemicals, the two of us still in love, still at the work of making pictures that we hope will matter.

And it is because of the work, and the love, that these pictures I took don't disturb Larry. Like our kids, he believes in the work we do and in confronting the truth and challenging convention. We all agree that a little discomfort is a small price to pay for that.

⁓

Prophetically, one *New York Times* letter writer predicted an outcome for my children that did, in fact, come to pass: a "third eye," as this writer eloquently put it. By this she meant a shameful self-consciousness, a feeling of guilt and moral doubt about the pictures. And of the three, this most afflicted Virginia, my carefree, lissome river sprite.

That third eye was painfully drilled into Virginia's nervous system by Raymond Sokolov, a food writer who wrote a confounding op-ed piece in the *Wall Street Journal* in February 1991. He was knicker-twisted over government funding for art that the "non-art-going public" could find "degenerate" or in which a "line was crossed."

This 1990 *Aperture* cover set him off, an image called "Virginia at Four."

At a time when oceans of ink were being spilled on arts-funding controversies, Sokolov weighed in to observe, redundantly, that selective public funding is not the same thing as direct government censorship. As the government had neither funded nor censored my family work, its relevance to his argument was unclear. But Sokolov's piece, a tissue of banality and non sequitur that otherwise would have gone unnoticed, acquired an undeniably arresting force on the page, thanks to the accompanying illustration (for which no permission had been sought by the *Wall Street Journal*). The nation's largest-circulation newspaper cropped and mutilated my image as if it were Exhibit A in a child pornography prosecution.

THE WALL STREET JOURNAL WEDNESDAY, FEBRUARY 6, 1991 **A9**

LEISURE & ARTS

Critique: Censoring Virginia

By RAYMOND SOKOLOV

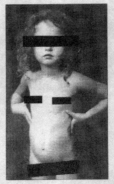

When we saw it, it indeed felt like a mutilation, not only of the image but also of Virginia herself and of her innocence. It made her feel, for the first time, that there was something wrong not only with the pictures but with her body. Heartbreakingly, she wore her shorts and shirt into the bathtub the night after she had seen the picture with the black bars.

Of course, this excited art-aware lawyers, because the Visual Artists Rights Act of 1990 still had some teeth, and they were prepared to use them to take a bite out of the *Journal*. I was glad to hear from them, pissed at the cavalier attitude about censoring my work, and spoiling for a fight. But, as it became clear that Virginia, just six, would be up against such a powerful opponent, a David to their Goliath, we backed off. The thought of the depositions she would face and the likely tone of the questioning by the opposing attorneys were important factors in our decision. Virginia's innocence was lost, and the third eye of shame was already in place. No need to blacken it.

We took her out to the pond up the road and tried to make a joke about it

but she was still upset and confused. Finally we suggested that she write Raymond Sokolov a letter, which she did:

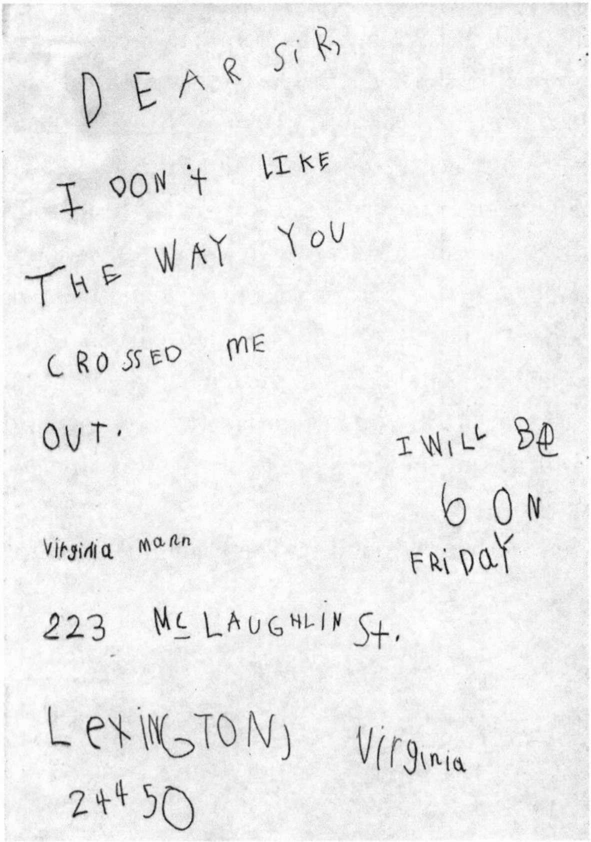

After some legal pressure on Sokolov and the editor at the *Journal*, they both wrote letters of apology to Virginia. But the last sentence of the letter from the *Journal* editor, Daniel Henninger, was particularly galling:

> The groups of people who often argue with each other about things like this would probably be better off if they gave each other something many people have forgotten called common courtesy.

How he thought this was an appropriate ending for a letter to a six-year-old, I cannot fathom.

The turmoil of that time was occasionally relieved by elements of humor, some of which were provided by the more oddball letters to the *Times*, in this case one that offered technical and compositional advice:

"Easter Dress" is at best a single, badly composed frame of an amateur home-movie which should have long ago been assigned to the attic.

"Fallen Child" is beneath contempt as it "uses" and manipulates and distorts this poor child for **no apparent artistic reason.**

Who would want to **own** this mistake? "The Ditch," too, removes two and a half heads as well as most of the upper body of the figure on the right. Cropping three inches off the right side could help (slightly) with the composition. But the arrogance of decapitation would still make this a "no sale."

While I appreciated their sincerity, I paid about as much attention to the writers of the compositional complaints as I did to the ones that insisted that

Susan [*sic*] Mann's pictures . . . are taking advantage of [the children] just as viciously as if she forced them to labor in a coal mine or a sweat-shop factory for long hours at low wages.

or the one, mincing no words, that called me "the most vulgar person of the year."

But I sat up and took notice of a few, for different reasons. For example, there was an inexcusably idiotic note from the writer Anne Bernays that brings up a familiar misapprehension about photography.

She writes in her assertive four-sentence letter that it's not the nudity of the children that people find troubling but what's on their faces: "They're mean," this total stranger to my children states with authority. "Mann has shown us children with ice in their veins; her kids give me the chills."

How can a sentient person of the modern age mistake photography for reality? All perception is selection, and all photographs—no matter how objectively journalistic the photographer's intent—exclude aspects of the moment's complexity. Photographs economize the truth; they are always moments more or less illusorily abducted from time's continuum.

The fact is that these are not my children; they are figures on silvery paper slivered out of time. They represent my children at a fraction of a second on one particular afternoon with infinite variables of light, expression, posture, muscle tension, mood, wind, and shade. These are not my children with ice in their veins, these are not my children at all; these are children *in a photograph*.

And if these kids give Ms. Bernays the chills in this picture,

then what about a different thirtieth of a second? This one, for example . . .

Now does she think they're so mean? Is she bundled up against the chill?

Even the children understood this distinction. Once Jessie was trying on dresses to wear to an opening of the family pictures in New York. It was spring and one dress was sleeveless, but when Jessie raised her arms she realized that her chest was visible through the oversized armholes. When she tossed that dress aside, a friend of mine, watching the process, asked with some perplexity, "Jessie, I don't get it. Why on earth would you care if someone can see your chest through the armholes when you are going to be in a room with a bunch of pictures that show that same bare chest?"

To which Jessie replied with equal perplexity at the friend's ignorance: "Yes, but that is not my chest. Those are photographs."

Exactly.

Let's carry this a bit further. Not only was the distinction between the real children and the images difficult for people, but so also was the distinction between the images and their creator, whom some found immoral. I'm going to go out on a limb here and say that I believe my morality should have no bearing on the discussion of the pictures I made. Suppose, for the sake of argument, that I actually *was*, as some *New York Times* letter writers suggested, "manipulative," "sick," "twisted," "vulgar."

Even if I were all of those things, it should make no difference in the way the work is viewed, tempting as it is to make that moral connection. Do we deny the power of *For Whom the Bell Tolls* because its author was unspeakably cruel to his wives? Should we vilify Ezra Pound's *Cantos* because of its author's nutty political views? Does Gauguin's abandoned family come to mind when you look at those Tahitian canvases? If we only revere works made by those with whom we'd happily have our granny share a train compartment, we will have a paucity of art.

Part of the artist's job is to make the commonplace singular, to project a different interpretation onto the conventional. With the family pictures, I may have done some of that. In particular I think they tapped into some below-the-surface cultural unease about what it is to be a child, bringing into the dialog questions of innocence and threat and fear and sensuality and calling attention to the limitations of widely held views on childhood (and motherhood).

So, it is fair to criticize that ambition, that project, to argue that I've done my job clumsily or tastelessly, to tell me that I'm a maker of "badly composed frame[s] of an amateur home-movie," as one letter writer did, or to wish to see restored the view of children as decorative cherubs with no inner lives of their own. But nowhere in that dialog about the work should my private character as the maker of the pictures be discussed. Nor, for that matter, should the personalities of the children, the actors and models, enter into the (metaphorical) picture.

By the same token, I was in no way personally obliged to answer my critics; to do so would have been beneath my dignity and that of the work. Happily, this stance was a luxury I could afford because the job of defending the pictures had been taken in hand by a number of impressive writers and thinkers, among them Anne Higonnet, Vince Aletti, Janet Malcolm, Katherine Dieckmann, and Luc Sante. Like Cy Twombly, I tried not to read what was written about my work, though occasionally a review or article would get floated past me, often with interpretations so rudderless, ill-rigged, and in every other way unseaworthy that I marveled they made it out of dry dock.

When Mary Gordon attacked my work in the summer of 1996 she went after my favorite image, "The Perfect Tomato" (see page 130), asserting,

> The application of the word "tomato"—sexual slang for a desireable [*sic*] woman—to her daughter insists that we at least consider the child as a potential sexual partner. Not in the future but as she is. The fact that the children are posed by their mother, made to stand still, to HOLD THE POSE, belies the idea that these are natural acts— whatever natural may be.

I felt this required a response and replied:

> It is a banal point that no artist can predict how each image will be received by each viewer, and that what is devoid of erotic meaning to

one person is the stuff of another's wildest fantasies. Mary Gordon seems to have these aplenty, but it is her retailing of lurid impressions of "The Perfect Tomato," a photograph of unassailable purity, that elicits this rebuttal.

To back up her denunciation, Gordon homes in on the offending title. I am now informed that "tomato" is slang for a desirable woman among the hard-boiled gumshoes of certain faded detective novels (a meaning which the *OED* does not recognize). I cannot imagine that this sense is ever used today except in ironical allusion to that genre. Certainly I had no thought of it when I gave "The Perfect Tomato" its whimsical title, a nod to the only element in the picture that's in focus. When I turned and saw my daughter dancing on the table that day I had no time to make adjustments, just ecstatically to swing my view camera around and get the exposure. There was no question of trying to retake the picture; it was, to pilfer a line from W. S. Merwin, "unrepeatable as a cloud."

"The Perfect Tomato" is one of those miracle pictures in this series which preserve spontaneous moments from the flux of our lives. For other images, we replayed situations that had arisen—pace Gordon—"naturally" or within the evolving circumstances of a photo session.

Oscar Wilde, when attacked in a similar ad hominem way, insisted that it is senseless to speak of morality when discussing art, asserting that the hypocritical, prudish, and philistine English public, when unable to find the art in a work of art, instead looked for the man in it. But as much as I argued this same point on my side of the pond, other voices still insisted that, as a mother, the rules were different. This is a typical paragraph from a *Times* letter in which the complainant asserts a mother should not:

... troll the naked images of her children through waters teeming with pedophiles, molesters and serial killers. Sally Mann's photos not only put her children at risk, but all the other children in Lexington, Virginia as well.

This got to me, too. All the other children of Lexington?

If ever there was a man who knows about "pedophiles, molesters and serial killers," it is Kenneth Lanning, formerly a member of the FBI's Behavioral Sciences Department. Fretting about this letter, I cold-called the department and lucked out by being referred to him. I asked if we could talk about these spectral, nightmarish figures and whether I should be concerned about them. I also hoped to get from him, in effect, a declaratory judgment as to whether my studio was going to be subject to the kind of ungentle attention that his agency paid to photographer Jock Sturges's when they entered it in 1990, confiscating much of his work and precipitating a long, costly legal battle.

Sturges's difficulties around the images made on a nude beach in France and the ongoing controversy around the work of Robert Mapplethorpe had made clear that we were in the throes of a full-scale moral freak-out over the photographic representation of nude children. Into this turbulent climate, I had put forth my family pictures. Although barely a quarter of them depicted a nude child, I was unfailingly described as the woman who made pictures of her naked children, an assertion that inflamed my critics, many of whom had never actually seen the work. I remarked then that I had trustingly sailed those images out like little boats onto rough seas and there was no fetching them back now to safe harbor.

Such was the innocence of the era that I had only the vaguest notion that child pornography existed and had certainly never seen any. The World Wide Web didn't cast itself over Rockbridge County until 1994, and even then most people didn't have access to the Internet until 1997. Imagine that—like talking about a world without fire. My only experience with perverts had been as a kid, seeing the wet lips and open zipper of a man in the back of the Lyric Theater who gestured to me while I felt my way to the restrooms. When I called Ken Lanning, I had a lot to learn.

We went to see him at Quantico in April 1993. The kids were with us and got a tour of the place before he sat down to look at what I had brought, the entire series of family pictures to date. When he was finished he slowly gathered up the pile of 8 × 10 inch contact prints in a sheaf, tapped it against the table to even the edges, and looked over at us. He spoke at some length, a sad, too-knowing smile playing occasionally across his face. He said what I already knew: that some people would be aroused by these pictures. Then the smile, and he said, "But they get aroused by door handles, too. I don't think there is anything you can take a picture of that doesn't arouse somebody."

He stressed that in his profession, context and perception were all-important, and I remarked, somewhat wryly, that they were all-important in mine as well. I certainly knew that the context of place was important in my family pictures, but I also knew that I was creating work in which critical and emotional perception can easily shift. All too often, nudity, even that of children, is mistaken for sexuality, and images are mistaken for actions. All contact is not necessarily sexual, all looking is not transgression, and of course appearances can deceive.

The image of the child is especially subject to that kind of perceptual dislocation; children are not just the innocents that we expect them to be. They are also wise, angry, jaded, skeptical, mean, manipulative, brooding, and devilishly deceitful. "Find me an uncomplicated child, Pyle," challenged the journalist Thomas Fowler in *The Quiet American*, adding, "When we are young we are a jungle of complications. We simplify as we get older." But in a culture so deeply invested in a cult of childhood innocence, we are understandably reluctant to acknowledge these discordant aspects, or, as I found out, even fictionalized depictions of them.

Another shape-shifter is desire—there is sexual desire but there is also maternal desire, marrow-deep and stronger than death. When the doctor handed Emmett to me, tallowy and streaked with blood, it was the first time I'd ever really held a baby, and here he was, the flesh of my flesh. I was gobsmacked by my babies: their smell, the doughy smoothness of their skin, the paper-thin pulse of fontanel. I loved the whole sensual package with a ferocious intensity. Yes, it was a physical desire, a parental carnality, even a kind of primal parental eroticism, but to confuse it with what we call sexuality, inter-adult sexual relations, is a category error.

In the pictures of my children I celebrated the maternal passion their bodies inspired in me—how could I not?—and never thought of them sexually or in a sexual context, remarking to Rick Woodward, "I think childhood sexuality is an oxymoron." I did not mean my children were not sexual; all living creatures are sexual on some level. But when I saw their bodies, and photographed them, I never thought of them as being sexual; I thought of them as being simply, miraculously, and sensuously beautiful.

Once the work was out in the world, I was puzzled why that sensuous beauty should be signposted as controversial while at the same time magazine pages were filled with prurient images of young girls, all aimed at selling commercial products. From the pile of complimentary *Times* letters, four spoke directly to this distinction:

> After closing the magazine to ponder the cover photograph, I then reopened it to page two, a Revlon Ad, and was confronted with photos more offensive than anything I read or saw in the Sally Mann article. Why should there be an uproar over a woman who portrays her children nude in an artistic medium, while no one bats an eye at the pages packed with semi-clad models prancing and pouting, exploiting their sexuality for commercial purposes?

Ken Lanning understood and noted the difference between the images of my children's bodies and those of the pornographers or of the profane consumer culture. That day in Quantico, he reassured me on some points but cautioned me on others: no, law enforcement wasn't coming after me, he said, but I was in for a rough time nevertheless.

He was right on both counts.

While Lanning seemed to think it unlikely that serial murderers and molesters were coming for the children of Lexington, or even just mine, it seemed to me that we were in some jeopardy. When we published *Immediate Family* in 1992, my expectation was that it would be received rather like *At Twelve* (1988)—with some modest attention, selling its small press run over the next decade mostly to the photography community. That's not what happened. Within three months the first printing of 10,000 sold out and we were reprinting, a sales pattern that continued.

Suddenly I was overwhelmed with mail, faxes, phone calls, and strangers knocking at my door. Not even living in little Chitlin' Switch protected us. During those first two years I received 347 pieces of fan mail, much of it addressed simply "Sally Mann, Lexington, VA." These fan letters came with photographs, of course, but also books, journal pages, handmade clothing, thirty-five preserved butterflies, jewelry, hand lotions, porcupine quills, Christmas tree lights, shark's teeth, recipes, paintings, a preserved bird, mummified cats, chocolate chip cookies, and a hand-painted statue of the Virgin Mary with a toothy demon on a leash.

Except for those that went straight into the weirdo file, I answered them all. Often I wrote on the back of failed or unwashed prints, a practice I regret now when I find them offered on eBay, and the more I answered, the more letters came. I was reminded of someone, Gen. Ulysses S. Grant, I think, who, when asked by a reporter if he got a lot of fan mail, responded with something like, "Not nearly as much as I did when I answered it."

There were some letters with troubling return addresses citing inmate numbers in correctional institutions and some that gave off an indefinably creepy vibe. But the creepiest stuff of all, and the cause of the fear and surveillance that I mentioned in the letter to Maria at the beginning of chapter seven, were the six years of fantasy, supplication, and menace issuing from the computer of one obsessive who lived in an adjoining state. This man was our worst fear come true, troubling our waking and sleeping hours for years; to this day, despite the fact that he has moved overseas (where he has a job teaching children), our daughter Virginia reports nightmares about him.

Using sometimes his real name, more often a transparent alias, and occasionally posing as an author researching a self-help manual for "recovering pedophiles," this guy, like the fruit bat letter writer at the beginning of this chapter, began his assault with an epistolary carpet-bombing of editors and journalists. But his were not letters of complaint; more worryingly, they asked questions about the kids.

Many recipients tossed these letters into the trash, but other people, alarmed, forwarded them to us. This creep was tireless: he wrote to journalists, curators, and editors asking for unpublished gossip, and to the kids' schools, asking (repeatedly) for assignments, yearbooks, grades, contest entries, and artwork. When he received no response from the schools, he got a local man to try his luck at getting the material.

A suspicious clerk was on duty at the medical records department in the local hospital when our stalker's official-sounding request for the children's birth certificates came in; fortunately, she called me about it. Subscribing to the local papers to scan them for our names, he would taunt us with his knowledge of ballet recitals, school honor rolls, and lunch menus. Once he sent registered-mail letters to the kids, and I had a friend sign for them, not wanting him to have even a signature.

Those who received his outpourings were regularly informed of his being "bedridden with love sickness for the Mann children," of his desire to receive "a blessing from the Mann family's holy presence," and of his resentment of us "for stealing my piece of the pie, so I hoped somehow to steal it back from them."

For years, I was sleepless with fears of Lindbergh baby–like abductions, and made sure that the windows were locked, that the house was always occupied, the children accompanied by an adult, and that the police made extra turns around the block. Of course I contacted Ken Lanning, who gave me advice but who was limited in what he could do, as were private protection agencies. A psychiatrist who read the letters suggested purchasing a box of rhino shells for the shotgun and a policeman concurred, reminding me to be sure to drag the body thus dispatched over the threshold and into the house.

The cumulative effect of this creepiness was, paradoxically, almost to make our stalker the family member he claimed he wanted to be. Though I didn't carry Larry's picture in my wallet, I started carrying this man's, and would watch for him with something close to the ardor of a lover, checking cars, peering down dimly lit library stacks, scanning the audiences at public appearances for an ordinary face that thousands of faces resemble. In a 1994 letter to the attorney, writer, and activist Andrew Vachss, I characterized the experience this way:

A curious phenomenon has occurred in this stalking process: We almost feel as though this guy is a member of the family. He is mentioned more frequently than many blood kin, and his presence is felt in every aspect of our cautious lives. We anticipate his next move with the fierce watchfulness of passion, albeit a warped one.

This strange familiarity, in a peculiar twist of the familiar adage, breeds not contempt but a kind of acceptance. We live routinely now with a hitherto unendurable amount of stress. Each time it ratchets upwards, we adapt to it. In accommodating it, we normalize it.

This is probably a familiar experience for anyone who has been stalked but I find our practical assimilation of him and his needs unsettling.

This is the first time I've publicly referred, in any detail, to the shadow this weirdo cast for so many years. I knew of course that it would only validate those critics who said I put my children at risk. And it will make their vengeful day when I admit now that they were in some measure correct. Unwittingly, ignorantly, I made pictures I thought I could control, pictures made within the prelapsarian protection of the farm, those cliffs, the impassable road, the embracing river.

That's the critical thing about the family pictures: they were only possible because of the farm, the *place*. America now hardly has such a thing as privacy, at least not of the kind we had at the cabin. For miles in all directions, there was not a breathing soul. When we were on the farm we were isolated, not just by geography but by the primitive living conditions: no electricity, no running water, and, of course, no computer, no phone.

How natural was it, in that situation, to allow our children to run naked? Or, put another way, how bizarre would it have been to insist on bathing suits for their river play, which began after breakfast and often continued long after dark, when all three would dive like sleek otters for glow sticks thrown in the pool under the still-warm cliffs?

They spent their summers in the embrace of those cliffs, protected by distance, time, and our belief that the world was a safe place. The pictures I made of them there flowed from that belief and that ignorance and, at the time, seemed as natural as the river itself. But they unquestionably changed our lives, and I am asked many times if I would make them again, knowing what I know now.

And, what do I know, exactly? Here's a memory refresher from the letters:

That some people feel the children could not have understood the implications of the work, could not have made a mature decision about their participation.

That some people find photographs of naked children inherently problematic.

That they arouse some pedophiles.

That some people who see them experience uncomfortable transport to a childhood both Edenic and shadowed by menace, a childhood they may or may not have experienced in their actual past.

That some people think the very act of taking the pictures was transgressive.

That the wide distribution of the pictures could make my children into minor celebrities or targets for predators.

That I was risking social censure and legal action.

That publishing the images would lead some people to try to tarnish the privacy and innocence that allowed the imagery to be made in the first place.

On that last one, they were right.

When the spotlight of celebrity, which seems to shine more brightly in America than anywhere else, directed its beam on our family, it brought all those issues, heretofore unexamined, into bright relief. Viewers who knew nothing about us interpreted our lives, and the images were scrutinized under the mantle of scholarship or god-haunted righteousness.

The candy cigarette here was just a candy cigarette, not a metaphor for a life on the streets. Jessie's vamping was just that, not a predictor of future pathology, Virginia's back turned to the camera did not mean anything except that it was easier to yell at Emmett that way, and the stilts in the background were just stilts, not phallic symbols. All these interpretations of this fictionalized fraction of a second have been posited, as have many more, sometimes to our amusement and sometimes to our distress.

The writer Lee Smith, who once had a New York copy editor query in the margin of her manuscript "Double-wide *what?*" tells a perfectly marvelous, spot-on story about Eudora Welty when she came to Hollins College, where Smith was a student. Welty read a short story in which one female character presents another with a marble cake. In the back of the audience Smith noted a group of leather-elbowed, goatee-sporting PhD candidates, all of whom were getting pretty excited. One started waving his hand as soon as she stopped reading and said, "Miz Welty, how did you come up with that powerful symbol of the marble cake, with the feminine and masculine, the yin and the yang, the Freudian and the Jungian all mixed together like that?"

Smith reported that Welty looked at him from the lectern without saying anything for a while. Finally she replied mildly, "Well, you see, it's a recipe that's been in my family for some time."

As critics, journalists, and the curious public bore down on our family, we began to understand that our family recipe was not from the cookbook of mainstream America. The ingredients in our work were exotic and the instructions complex.

But, in the end, as our own marble cake has emerged, swirled with dark confusion and light with angel food transcendence, the answer is *Yes. Yes,* and *yes*, resoundingly, absolutely, we would do it all over knowing what we know now.

As ephemeral as our footprints were in the sand along the river, so also were those moments of childhood caught in the photographs. And so will be our family itself, our marriage, the children who enriched it, and the love that has carried us through so much. All this will be gone. What we hope will remain are these pictures telling our brief story, but what will last, beyond all of it, is the place.

PART II

My Mother:
Memory of a Memory Past

9

A Sentimental Welshman

When I get asked what one piece of advice I have for young photographers, this is what I tell them: if you are working on a project, and you're thinking maybe it's time to put it out into the world, make sure you have already started your next body of work. Not just started, either: you should be well along on it. You will know that the first project is finished when you find yourself joylessly going through the motions to eke out a few more pictures while, like a forbidden lover, the new ones call seductively to you. This new lover should be irresistible, and when it calls, you will be in its urgent thrall, making the work of your heart.

Toward the end of the decade-long family pictures project, that call came. I responded to it by taking pictures so warm and ingratiatingly likable, so unwearied by alienation, so lacking in the chilly elegance that frosted over art at the time, that I was certain I'd be pilloried for them. How could such emotional pictures, fetched out from the back rooms of my heart's rag-and-bone shop and given sincere expression—no trace of irony or ambiguity—not excite the scorn and condescension of worldly viewers?

A curator friend remarked that the other work he was seeing in the art galleries in 1997 was like a palate cleanser for the sweetmeats served up in my Mother Land show of that year. These pictures, taken in Virginia and Georgia, were as creamy and rich as the food from the region they celebrated. And with the impudence of beauty, they were unapologetic about it.

Where did the impulse to make this work come from? After those knotty family pictures, out of what genetic tapestry did these threads emerge, weaving their unconscious sentimentality into the new design?

Surprisingly, they didn't come from my father's family of colorful southern eccentrics, even though their family seat, Arlington, a well-known tourist attraction in Birmingham, had provided the setting for bodice-ripper novels like this one:

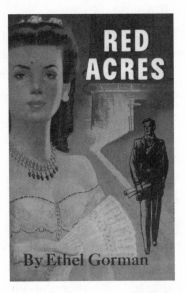

No, it wasn't from my father's side. Those strands of genetic sentiment came from my decidedly unsentimental Boston-born mother, whose ancestral past turned out to be hiding plenty of its own bodice-ripping. Until a few years ago, I knew almost nothing about her family background beyond the fact, revealed to me while studying seventh-grade history, that a paper in the safe-deposit box certified my mother as a *Mayflower* descendant.

That *Mayflower* ancestor was John Howland, a "lustie yonge man" who, according to Bradford's *Of Plymouth Plantation*, was swept overboard but managed to hang on to a dangling line long enough to be pulled to safety. Reading about him, I marvel at the contingency of my own existence, dependent here on the strength of a seventeenth-century piece of woven rope.

But no less marvelous is the strength of the genetic threads that, woven together, explain those romantic artistic tendencies otherwise unaccounted for by my personality or upbringing. These threads I have followed with all the diligence and groping optimism of a mythic hero, and with as many dramatic discoveries. I began this Knossian epic by cutting, one by one, the strings securing the boxes that I had hauled back from the nursing home after my mother died.

As if eager to spill their guts, they spewed before me letters, journals, account books, ships' manifests, stopped watches, menus, calendars, pressed flowers, scribbled love notes, telegrams, a ring from which the jewel had been crudely torn, dance cards, photographs, and newspaper clippings, all stashed away without system or order. For the hot half of the year, I bent into the angle of the attic eave and sifted through this wholly unsuspected, revelatory, and peculiar new past.

All my life I have had people tell me how wonderful my mother is—or, now that she is dead, was: how charming, witty, generous, beautiful, and smart. Smiling, I would agree with them, nodding my head, while the inside version of it shook side to side, silently rejoining, "Well, yeah, but that's because she isn't your mother."

But lately, disconcertingly, I have begun to think that maybe they were right. Certainly they were right about her being beautiful: that nobody disputes.

But I have come to think they were more right than I knew about the rest of it, too. This postmortem readjustment is one that many of us have had to make when our parents die. The parental door against which we have spent a lifetime pushing finally gives way, and we lurch forward, unprepared and disbelieving, into the rest of our lives.

Saul Bellow reports that for him it was like driving through a plate-glass window that he didn't know was there until it shattered. All that was left were the pieces, which he picked up painstakingly, right down to the last glassy splinter. But for me, the door analogy works better, the indifferent door that suddenly swings open, perfectly hinged, above the abyss.

In terms of beauty, I am a watered-down version of my mother. Where she had pure black hair, I had brown. And oh, if only I had gotten her dramatic widow's peak, never defiled with bangs. Below it, her eyes were a head-turning teal, on the order of those tinted contact lenses that were all the rage a few decades ago. Strangers would find themselves squinting at her eyes to find the telltale sickle of colored contact where it had slipped past the iris, but to no avail. The only one of our family who came close to her eye allure was my brother Chris, but mine are an ordinary greenish-gray. And she had height that I never achieved, plus some serious breasts that likewise checked themselves out of the genetic lottery when it came to my turn.

All the same, over the years, our physical similarities have been noted. A family friend once remarked, his gaze traveling between my mother and me, that he'd never really believed in the Immaculate Conception until then. And more startlingly, in the late 1960s on the streets of Boston, a passing stranger asked me if I was related to Elizabeth Evans. When I said yes, I was her daughter, he looked as startled as if he had just tumbled out of a time machine, which I guess he had, sort of. It turned out that my elderly inquisitor had not seen her in more than thirty years.

But that's where the similarities stop. There was a certain remove about my mother, hesitation and distrust suppressing her occasional, and quite charming, sauciness; hers was an absence rather than a presence. I know now that within her lay a grief too deep for tears.

Operating within her narrow emotional bandwidth, she was naturally suspicious of passion, of exultation, of fervor. The worst of her disdain for temperamental excess was reserved for her own father, Arthur Evans, whom she called "a sentimental Welshman." But I came in a close second.

In my early twenties, when a dear friend, MacCandless Charles, died in a plane wreck, I appeared at my mother's bookstore, weeping. She glanced up from running the cash register and by way of explanation to her concerned customer said dryly, "Oh, you know how it is, it's her first death."

When she had been that same age and, it turns out, had plenty of cause for her own weeping, she wrote this about her family:

> When I was sixteen, and I can remember the exact place on Cedar Street where this happened, I stepped back, almost physically, there on Cedar Street, and I never moved forward again. I stepped away from them and built up a shield. And I never went back.

And so she had, never stepping fully back into that family or any other, even ours, as far as I could tell.

In an immigrant society like this one, we are often divided from our fore-bears less by distance than by language, generations before us having thought, sung, made love, and argued in dialects unknown to us now. In Wales, for example, Welsh is spoken by barely 20 percent of the popu-lation, so we can only hope that the evocative Welsh word *hiraeth* will somehow be preserved. It means "distance pain," and I know all about it: a yearning for the lost places of our past, accompanied in extreme cases by tuneful lamentation (mine never got quite that bad). But, and this is important, it always refers to a near-umbilical attachment to a place, not just free-floating nostalgia or a droopy houndlike wistfulness or the long-ing we associate with romantic love. No, this is a word about the pain of loving *a place*.

Just like us southerners, the Welsh are often depicted as nostalgic and melancholic, their heads stuck in the past while pining for hopelessly lost causes. This attribution was conceived in the eighteenth century, and right from the beginning it was tied to a representation of landscapes: the blind bards of eighteenth-century fables are inseparable from the misty mountains in which they were imagined to strum their harps while giving voice to their *hiraeth*. Contemporary Welsh-speakers have continued that expression, linking memory and landscape most vividly in R. W. Parry's sonnet in which the longed-for landscape communicates to the human heart, "the echo of an echo . . . the memory of a memory past."

Distance pain is a real thing; *hiraeth* is not just a made-up neurasthenic disorder to which the Welsh and oversensitive, displaced southerners are susceptible. Looking through my long photographic and literary rela-tionship with my own native soil I can perceive a definite kinship with those fakelorish bards wailing away about their place-pain. And similarly, after months of research in my mother's archive, I am reasonably sure that some aspects of that sentimental Welshman, my mother's father, are woven through my psyche and have emerged in my own landscapes as "the memory of a memory past."

My grandfather Arthur Llewellen Evans was born in 1880 to Thomas and Ellen Evans, who by that time had already buried five sons in six years. Misfortune this severe is hard to contemplate, but that's the least of it for Thomas and Ellen. Their life together was a cliché-ridden smashup of the most overplayed themes of late Victorian fiction: social dislocation, debt, poverty, the fallen woman, and the caddish adventurer.

We can start with Arthur's English mother, Ellen, who before her third birthday had lost both her parents, her mother to a fatal illness and her father to the California gold rush. She was adopted by an aunt and uncle who owned a fashionable grocery store in Mayfair, and later in life she delighted in telling Arthur that she had regularly been "petted" by Charles Dickens, a patron of the establishment. Dickens called her "my little Nelly," and one wonders if she possessed something of the pure and untainted innocence of his famous heroine in *The Old Curiosity Shop*.

At the age of seven she was sent to a progressive boarding school, after which, at thirteen, she sailed to Paris to finish her education in music (piano and organ), art, literature, and French.

Certainly her education was as good as that of any girl in Britain at the time, so how it was that she fell in love with a stock boy at her uncle's store beggars the imagination. But she did, with my melodious-voiced, Welsh great-grandfather, Thomas Evans.

It's easy to imagine the furious objections of the aunt and uncle to the ensuing marriage and the subsequent decline in the couple's fortunes: money borrowed from relatives for a business, the failure of that and the next venture, the estrangement from family over the debts, a desperate emigration to Canada, and all the while pregnancies and deaths of babies. Shortly after the family moved across the border to New York, the second of the couple's surviving children, my grandfather, was born, and Thomas Evans, the onetime stock boy, landed a respectable job keeping the accounts of the wealthy Oneida Community.

So: why, after such a journey, would this man, with a loyal wife, an established income, three healthy sons, and another on the way, walk out on his family one morning and never return? No one knows, but it is suggested in my grandfather's writings that drinking was the culprit—apparently episodic and intense.

Ellen, having been abandoned first by her gold-hungry father and now her husband, was distraught and ashamed, too proud to tell her relatives back in England what had befallen her. She sold her family diamonds and rapidly went through assets that had included a modest inheritance from her uncle and aunt who ran the store in Mayfair. With great humility, she took in sewing, washing, and ironing but gradually sank into penury.

In careful handwriting, her son, my grandfather Arthur Evans, recorded the money he was able to bring into the family during that time, but it was not enough. His mother, Ellen, still unable to care for her four boys, was forced to farm them out to labor for local families in return for food. Arthur went to a man referred to only as Farmer Skaden. He was thirteen.

There is a decidedly Dickensian aspect to this servitude and separation from his family, but Arthur appeared to love his new home and take pride in his work for Skaden. He describes his work in his journals:

Rose at 4:30 AM, first chore getting the 16 cows up from the back pasture, milking half of them, a one-hour job, driving them back to the pasture. Feeding and currying the four horses and cleaning out the stables, then breakfast. Took the milk to Miller's cheese factory two miles down the road, bringing back whey for the pigs, then chores. Next out to the fields for the day's work . . .

(Reading this I think: "day's work"? Hasn't he just done a day's work?)

. . . plowing, dragging or harrowing, planting early in the spring, using, most awkwardly, a sidehill plow, hoeing corn, potatoes, beans . . . weeding onions, on knees all day long.

One year I hoed a ten-acre field of corn twice . . . forgot to mention rolling, the field always looked so nice after this operation. . . .

There was also water for the kitchen to be got, chopping and sawing kindling and stove wood, washing the buggy and two-seater, greasing and oiling the farm wagons and machinery, sharpening scythes, sickles and axes, feeding the hens and gathering the eggs, oiling the harnesses, salting the cattle, fixing fences, pulling mustard from the grain fields and Queen Anne's lace, everywhere; killing and dressing a fowl for Sunday dinner . . . and so on, indefinitely.

"And so on, indefinitely." Weary words from one so young.

There is no evidence of contact with his mother during his indenture, but for sure there wasn't a trace of his father, except for one curious and heartbreaking incident. About a decade after he disappeared, Arthur's father, Thomas Evans, made his way back to Oneida from Mobile, Alabama, where he had been slashing pine trees for turpentine. He came to the school that his four sons, the youngest of whom he had never seen, were attending. Standing at the fence as school was letting out, he asked a parent waiting beside him to point out the four Evans boys. After watching them walk past, he turned away.

Thomas Evans apparently made no effort to see his Ellen on that trip, although parents at the school reported the incident to her. Arthur wrote of his mother's frequent sobbing, their financial ruin, and her exhaustion from overwork. It was unnecessary to mention her heartbreak.

What I would give to see the letter that Arthur wrote his father, Thomas, when, at age seventeen, he finally tracked him down in Mobile (I can imagine what mine would have said). I don't have that letter, but what I do have is his father's response to it. He begins cordially enough: "Dear Arthur, I received your very kind letter of the 18th with profound surprise."

I bet. After thirteen years?

Thomas Evans goes on to say: "It makes me feel very glad to find that you have all been getting on so nicely notwithstanding a good many adverse circumstances."

Not the least of which was his desertion, of course.

He then has the effrontery to absolve Arthur's mother, Ellen, of any blame for those many adverse circumstances; such blame, he adds with late-nineteenth-century epistolary overflow, "is all mine and bitterly have I felt it, in fact my whole life since that unhappy day when I left Oneida has been one continual season of remorse and self reproach." A few lines down in the letter he offers this advice (hardly necessary in Arthur's case): "And please note as you read the biographies of Eminent Men that they have invariably been careful and kind to their mothers."

Surely Arthur must have already noted the kindness of Eminent Men toward their mothers, and, hoping to one day join their ranks, he wrote extravagantly of his own in a later journal entry:

> My mother was a woman of high intelligence and talent; generous, unselfish, uncomplaining with almost sublime, unflagging courage in the face of overwhelming and cruel misfortunes. Her devotion to her four fatherless boys, at the expense of her health, sight, strength and social position . . . was unparalleled.
>
> As passing years have made known all these things there came into my heart . . . pity for the pathos of it all.

On the other hand, what those Eminent Men had to teach him about how to treat a pathetically flawed father his writings do not reveal, but later in life when he wrote about Thomas Evans, he was charitable:

> I have no remembrance of my father. Many people at the Oneida Community spoke of him with affection and respect for his qualities of mind and heart. They said that he was a man of ability, talent and a capacity for leadership and friendship. He was also a fine singer and made a name for himself in that way. He was a great reader and well-informed, so they said.

Seven years later, Thomas Evans dropped dead on a street corner in Mobile. His burial expenses were paid for by my grandfather Arthur Llewellen Evans.

———

Arthur's arrangement with Farmer Skaden lasted through his teens, by which time his mother had married a German named William Hansen. Arthur was deeply pained by this second marriage and describes Hansen as "a cruel, evil, fearsome man, so brutal and terrible that I cannot bear to think of what my mother endured all those years."

Arthur entered Oneida High School in October 1894, graduating in June 1897. In that first year of high school, when he was fourteen, he met a girl his own age named Julie Keller, whom he described at the time as "the overpowering, all-in-all, fiercely passionate love of my life."

Carefully preserved in my attic archive is a crumbling, yellowed letter with Arthur's handwriting on the envelope noting, "First letter I ever received from Julie," and a postal service stamp that requests one penny more. This letter to Arthur begins "Dearest" and proposes a rendezvous for later in the week. But the postscript ominously reads, "If you have been at Brobly Dance you needn't trouble to come down. This is not irony."

There's no trace of irony in the eye of the young girl in the picture. She is straight-up lovely, and it was poverty, I am guessing, that prevented Arthur from proposing marriage to her upon his graduation from high school. His notes report that he worked at the Oneida newspaper, mowed lawns, tended furnaces, and continued to work back at the Skaden farm just to put himself through high school.

College was another matter. To pay college tuition he had to work as a schoolteacher for three more years, becoming a high school principal at age nineteen. By 1900 he had saved a hundred dollars and, as he put it, "I made the plunge," enrolling in Syracuse University. His resolute jaw-set, intense gaze and front-row-first position give some indication of his determination, setting him rather obviously apart from his classmates.

Despite that apparent strong will, when he wrote about his college experience he described himself as inferior in many respects:

Penniless, without adequate social status or training, physical attrac-
tiveness . . . musical or other talents or training that would find place
in college life; with mental powers sufficient for college work; with
capacity and experience in sustained work, hard or otherwise—
that's all.

Still, he managed to graduate in four years with a bachelor of fine arts
degree, summing up his achievements with this doleful assessment, written in the third person as if owning up to himself in the first person would
be too difficult:

As to most of the fine young men and women of his class . . . he
instinctively knew they were neither his friends nor admirers. And he
knew they were right in their judgments of him.

Despite this evident self-doubt, after loving her for fifteen years, Arthur
was finally in a financial position to ask Julie Keller to marry him. In his
journals from the time he praised her as

the graceful, gracious, fair and lovely girl . . . destined to mark forever the heart and soul of this boy with an ineffable something so
all-pervasive that no words of his can ever describe or express.

The modest wedding ceremony, which, according to the newspaper
accounts, "surprised their many friends," was held on June 12, 1909, at
Saranac Lake, New York.

Five months later Julie Keller Evans died of tuberculosis in his arms.

Their honeymoon and married life together, it turns out, had been spent at a sanatorium. She died on her twenty-ninth birthday. On that page of her daily calendar, carefully saved by my grieving grandfather, she noted in her unwavering handwriting, "I don't have any more birthdays."

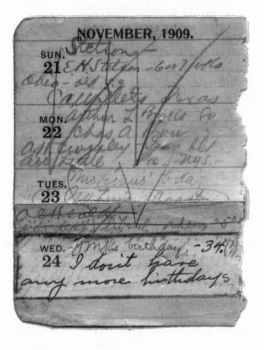

And then, incredibly, Arthur's life got worse. He met my grandmother, Jessie Adams, of Braintree, Massachusetts.

10

Uncle Skip and the Little Dears

My mother always suspected it was Jessie's wealth that attracted Arthur Evans, and who could blame the poor man for that? But she was good-looking, too. So tall and slender that she was nicknamed "Slats" as a kid, Jessie had inherited her mother Emma's distinctive auburn hair, pale skin, green eyes, chilly imperiousness and, important to this story, her sexual allure and appetite.

But more than that and more than her wealth, I suspect what Arthur, the immigrant tormented by his *soi-disant* lack of "social status or training," most desired about Jessie Adams was her illustrious ancestry. Early on when he wrote of her, he repeatedly noted her distinguished lineage, citing breathlessly that Jessie was

> a descendant of the original Mayflower passenger John Howland of the Plymouth Colony, and of the Adams line of the Massachusetts Bay Colony and eligible to join the Mayflower Descendants, and also eligible for the Colonial Dames and the Daughters of the American Revolution.

What Arthur doesn't speak about here is the miserable marriage between Jessie's mother, Emma Coles (the *Mayflower* descendant), and the man, Charles Jesse Adams, who gave her that esteemed surname, or how Emma's behavior presaged the calculating willfulness of Jessie herself. Nor did he note how that behavior stood in marked contrast to that of his esteemed mother, Ellen, or to his own stalwart and upright path through life.

There is far less information in the attic about Jessie's parents, my great-grandparents Emma and Charles Adams, than about Arthur's parents,

but there is enough to draw some conclusions about genetic tendencies—
and what we find isn't all that comforting for those of us likely to have
inherited them.

Emma Coles, my great-grandmother and the mother of Jessie, was born
in Braintree, Massachusetts, in 1867.

A twenty-seven-year-old physician named Samuel Holmes Durgin performed her delivery. Dr. Durgin, a graduate of Harvard Medical School,
had recently returned from military duty in a surgical tent with the U.S.
Army near Appomattox. He later, in a somewhat less dramatic résumé
addition, invented the wooden tongue depressor.

Other than these facts, I know nothing about young Emma; there is
hardly a scrap about her in the attic except that at age seventeen she married Mr. Adams, said in family lore to be a direct descendant of an Adams
my mother referred to as "the drunk son of the first President Adams."

(Between Presidents John and John Quincy, there are several sons who fit that description, and a cursory look on the Internet raises some doubts about this lineage.) The newlyweds decamped for Kentucky almost immediately so Charles could indulge his passion for raising racehorses.

There's an old joke question, "How do you make a million dollars raising horses?" I've heard this enough times that the reply is quick to my lips: "Start with three million," and that's just how it was with Charles Adams in Kentucky. Within a year of their arrival, my grandmother Jessie was born and the money, of course, was disappearing. Disgusted, Emma left Charles and with young Jessie returned to Braintree, where Charles eventually joined her, destitute.

But later, after the arrival of Emma and Charles's second child, known to me from my mother's accounts as "bad Uncle Carlton," Emma began a passionate and unconcealed affair with a married man down the street. In an unprecedented legal action that made headlines in all the Boston papers, she filed for divorce from Charles Adams for no other reason than having fallen in love with another man. And who was the other man? None other than Dr. Samuel Durgin, the attending physician at her birth, twenty-seven years her senior.

As you might expect, divorcing an Adams in Adams Central, Braintree, Massachusetts, made for an ugly scandal, and it went on for some time. My grandmother Jessie was even called to testify at the trial, but eventually Emma got her divorce and married the doctor, whose wife had conveniently died in the meantime.

What lessons Jessie took from this we can only guess, but by the time she was twenty-nine

and her path crossed with that of the luckless Arthur Evans, I'm guessing that the characteristics of "inner turbulence masked by outward austerity" with which my mother described her were well in place. That outward austerity not only hid her roiling passions, evidenced by a wrathful temper that my mother often described, but it also managed to make more than a decade of extremely profitable marital infidelity appear normal, even routine.

Yep, that's right. After all he had been through, poor Arthur had married a woman who openly cheated on him.

⌐———¬

By 1923, six years and two daughters (my mother, Elizabeth, and her sister, Molly) into the marriage of Jessie and Arthur, finances were tight. In my mother's journals is a suggestion that Arthur had run through a good deal of Jessie's money, but no indication of how he had done so.

Given what appears to be Arthur's natural frugality, I find it unlikely that he frivolously spent them into poverty, so most likely it was bad investing. Arthur had a low-paying job as an editor for a trade magazine, Jessie had a taste for finer things, and neither of them knew anything about managing money. I can easily imagine the young couple getting into financial straits.

I often wonder: was it money or love, or some combination of the two, that sent thirty-six-year-old Jessie into the arms of Harold Minot Gage?

Perhaps proximity played a part. The Gages lived two and a half blocks from the Evanses, their impressive estate taking up a goodly stretch of Cedar Street. Its five acres were beautifully planted with formal rose gardens, arbors, and vineyards. Evergreens lined the road, protecting the tennis courts, greenhouses, and putting greens from view. It must have been most unusual in those times to have a three-car garage, but the imposing Gage house did, and within were two Packards and a Cadillac.

The source of their wealth is not clear to me. A descendant of the Gages said that "Uncle Skip," as he was known to my mother, was a brilliant money man, although the money with which he was so brilliant appears to have come from his wife, whom my mother called "Aunt Ethel." Otherwise Uncle Skip had no job, traveling into Boston once or twice a week to look after monetary affairs but in general passing the time with his lover, Jessie—and in the company, surprisingly, of Aunt Ethel and Arthur.

Despite this flagrant affair the foursome was inseparable. Two nights a week they ate together and then played bridge late into the night. The two couples bought land and built a house on Lake Sunapee in New Hampshire, although it was the Gages' money that paid for it, and they spent every summer there together for more than a decade.

My mother described tranquil days spent lying on the pier, her feet dangling in the water, reading. She listed the now-classic books in her journal: *The Wind in the Willows, Winnie-the-Pooh, Alice in Wonderland, The Three Musketeers, Anne of Green Gables, Tom Sawyer, Little Women, Pride and Prejudice, The Moonstone, Emma, Persuasion*, and *The Prisoner of Zenda*. She gave credit to Uncle Skip for igniting a love of reading that she carried with her all her life.

She described him as:

Nearly ugly, with sparse reddish hair and a great beak of a nose, but at the same time most attractive, dapper, wonderfully charismatic and vital. He was witty and intelligent, incredibly well read and he dominated whatever group he was in with his brilliant mind and great humor. . . . He had an interest in everyone he met. He made people and books vivid and exciting.

At the house on Lake Sunapee Uncle Skip would build a fire in the fireplace, gather Molly and my mother, whom he called "the two little dears," and read out loud to them: Thackeray, the Bulldog Drummond novels, Trollope, and Dumas. He taught the girls to play bridge and tennis and to always wear red on the dance floor. My mother remembered it as the happiest time of her life.

But the affair between Uncle Skip and Jessie also caused some disturbing moments at Sunapee. Once, when Molly and my mother were still very young, a violent argument erupted between the two lovers by a smoldering trash pile a short distance from the house. As Molly and my mother watched from behind the screen door, Jessie and Uncle Skip, both red in the face, screamed and threatened each other as mephitic wisps of smoke curled around them.

When the two girls began to cry in fright and confusion, Aunt Ethel gathered them up and moved them away. By my mother's account, this caring woman took the weeping daughters of her husband's mistress into her arms and comforted them, murmuring that some things in this world can't be understood.

My mother and Molly, who up until the advent of Uncle Skip's beneficence had a distressingly frugal clothes allowance, now were dressed in the highest fashion. Their medical and dental bills were covered, as were dance and tennis lessons, plus camp in the summers. The Evans house was refurnished, the mortgage retired, and Jessie, for the first time, sported jewelry. Even the cheating grandmother Emma and Dr. Durgin came in for Uncle Skip's largesse: they received a beautiful antique dresser and a velvet sofa. Several times the two couples, with the Evans daughters (the Gages' sons were already grown), traveled to Europe, always first class, touring the Continent in flamboyant luxury.

And all this very obvious prosperity continued after the Evans household lost its only source of regular, if modest, income: Arthur was now jobless. But although there was no income (save what my mother would later refer to as "that which Jessie earned on her back"), when the girls were in lower grammar school they were sent to the private Thayerlands School, then on to Thayer Academy for middle school, and finally, when it came time for boarding school, Uncle Skip decided that they should be sent off to the radical and expensive Stamford, Connecticut, school Edgewood.

By this time, Arthur, pictured here with jauntily cocked hat behind Jessie, with Aunt Ethel to his right, was of course no longer sharing a bed with his wife and had been banished to a small bedroom in the attic of the house, which he mordantly referred to years later in a letter to my mother as his "sky parlour."

Down the steep attic steps he would tiptoe early each morning, softly unlatching the stairwell door by my mother's bedroom and passing through to the tiny second-story bathroom. There my mother described hearing the click of the chamber pot against the enamel toilet bowl as he emptied its contents before tiptoeing back upstairs so my mother and Molly could prepare for school.

It was from his attic bedroom that Arthur dispatched a thirty-four-page letter to Jessie, two floors down, passionately citing fifty-three reasons why their daughters should not be sent off to Edgewood School, several hours away. He handed his wife the letter on the back stairs.

But it didn't matter what his feelings were: Uncle Skip was paying, and off they went.

Among her admonitions to her growing daughters, my mother reported that Jessie often repeated this one: "Marry and divorce as often as you think you have to, but don't be any man's mistress."

This counsel must have been foremost in Molly's mind in the summer of 1927 when Uncle Skip, Aunt Ethel, Jessie, and the "little dears" set sail for Europe on the *Empress of France*. Their first-class stateroom suite, with its gilt Empire furniture and plush carpets, had a connecting door between the Gages' cabin and Jessie's bedroom.

Somewhere halfway across the ocean, Molly witnessed a sexual act between Jessie and Uncle Skip, the nature of which is suggested by the fact that she immediately developed a painfully sore throat. She insisted she was hemorrhaging, as she had the summer before when her tonsils were removed, although there was no evidence of inflammation.

After landing at Cherbourg, Uncle Skip engaged a doctor whom my mother remembered as a Napoleonically short Frenchman to examine the hysterical child. Speaking only French, he calmed Molly enough to look down her throat but found nothing wrong. But he could not convince Molly that she was not bleeding to death, so within three weeks of their arrival Uncle Skip booked Jessie and the girls return passage on the *Olympic*, sister ship to the *Titanic*.

By the time they disembarked in New York, Molly was restored to perfect health. Arthur, who had not been part of this grand European tour, met them at the harbor. Making sure his daughter was all right, physically if not mentally, he took the night train alone back to Boston.

It was not until four years after Molly's throat episode that Jessie was apparently struck by the inherent contradiction between her affair with Uncle Skip and her stated position on being a kept woman. She sat the teenaged sisters down, telling them with candor about the nature of her relationship with Uncle Skip. My mother, apparently ignorant of what Molly had seen between Jessie and Uncle Skip on the ship to Europe, naïvely inquired, "But, Mama, did you go the limit?" To my mother's abiding amazement, Jessie dreamily replied, "Yes, and it was wonderful!"

So after fifteen years of a profitable and sexually satisfying liaison, Jessie abruptly severed the relationship with Uncle Skip. In my mother's words, "Mama sent him off on a 'round the world cruise to find someone else."

He went on this cruise with Aunt Ethel, of course, and they were successful, returning to Braintree with a Mrs. Butler, whom he and Aunt Ethel immediately brought to dinner at the Evanses. My mother vividly remembered the event—it was a summer evening, and she and Molly had helped Jessie cook, serve, and clean up after the meal, which, however bizarre, was apparently quite congenial. After the Gages and Mrs. Butler left, my mother laughingly recalled "a delectable little touch," Jessie's indignant harrumph: "That woman dyes her hair."

The dyed hair must not have bothered Uncle Skip (or Aunt Ethel), for Mrs. Butler continued to live with them as Uncle Skip's lover until 1937, when he died in the Roosevelt Hotel of stomach cancer (incidentally, the same form of cancer that would kill Jessie a few decades later). At the funeral, on one side of the aisle was Aunt Ethel, the two sons, and their wives, and on the other side were Jessie, Molly, Mrs. Butler, and a hitherto unknown mistress who had preceded Jessie, a Mrs. Hamblin.

For all the years after Mrs. Butler was installed, Uncle Skip's payments to Jessie never stopped. Money continued to arrive at the Evans home in envelopes Aunt Ethel addressed herself with postmarks from all over the world: Europe, the Far East, South America. Even after Uncle Skip died, Aunt Ethel continued to pay for my mother's and Molly's tuition and expenses, all the way through college (during which time Molly suffered a breakdown and attempted suicide). With the exception of one short-lived reconciliation with Jessie, characterized by fiery and violent nighttime arguments that sent my mother crying to her room, Arthur Evans continued to live in the attic.

⸻

What a story. Imagine my dismay, week after week up in my own attic surrounded by journals and piles of string-tied letters, piecing these facts together, cross-checking and confirming as the picture got bleaker. Every improbable account is documented: it's all true and in so many ways surpassingly sad.

It prompts the question: What part of these lives, of this dolorous DNA, has made me who I am? Looked at in a certain way, this is not such a promising inheritance: the calculating, cheating, explosive, manipulative women and the maudlin, sentimental, self-doubting, alcoholic, family-abandoning men—"ppp," as my father would occasionally note at the bottom of his medical records: "piss-poor protoplasm."

But in much the same way that I have begun, years after her death, to reevaluate my mother, I have also gradually come to realize how strangely modern my ancestors were: sexually adventurous and exigent, they confronted in their own ways personal dilemmas and proclivities for which society at the time offered no resources or guidance. So maybe I needn't worry overmuch about my flawed genetic makeup: out of all those possible ancestral traits, the one my mother was convinced I inherited so directly as to be intravenous was her father's Welsh sensitivity. All things considered, there's nothing terribly ppp-ish about that. I'll certainly take it over the unmeltable sliver of ice that those same ancestors stabbed into my mother's young heart.

It wasn't until I read the line about "stepping back" in her journals and pieced together the complexities of her family relationships that I began to understand what had so damaged my mother. She kept the sorrows of her past hidden, like the stolen fox secreted beneath the cape of the Spartan youth in the ancient Greek morality tale. The young man, rather than reveal the dishonorable truth when waylaid by his elders, answers their questions with unblinking equanimity, all the while squeezing the fox tightly to him. Finally the grown-ups are satisfied and allow him to pass, but by then the fox has torn the boy's abdomen to shreds. I believe my mother discovered, like that stoic Spartan youth with the gut-gnawing fox, that when we cloak the past, like the fox, it will injure us. Now, when I push her oral history cassettes into my old player, I can hear the pain in her voice that she attempts to disguise with a wry, detached amusement.

Unfortunately, I am one of those women, and I know a lot of us, who somehow can't seem to get over our anger and hurt where our mothers are concerned, and who are determined to do better with our own daughters. We don't, of course. We fall into exactly the same patterns, or new ones equally damaging, and watch ourselves do it as helplessly as bystanders at a curbside shooting. Now, when I speak to similarly angry women whose mothers are still alive, I press upon them this advice: try again, and this time, listen better.

I am ashamed to open up the bulging folder of Maternal Slights, many written in a hand shaking with fury on scraps of paper snatched up the minute the door closed behind my departing mother's back. Of course, they say as much about me as about my mother: the mean pettiness of my impulse to document her failings, my complete inability to see myself mirrored in her, and my indisputable tendency to hold a Balkan grudge. But the folder is also a how-to manual for not becoming her, and many of the stories within are hilarious.

There is hardly a Christmas that my own daughters and I don't at some point sing out in unison, "Oh, thank you, Grandma! Best Western! My favorite shampoo! And in such cute little bottles!"

She was a master of the backhanded gift

> ### GREETINGS OF
> ### THE SEASON
>
> *These were too tall
> for my shelves —
> Happy holidays — and
> much, much love*
>
> *B./*

and, still clearly remembering those pre–Uncle Skip years of poverty, was extremely frugal. On Larry's fortieth birthday, she subtracted the $17.38 cost of the freezer-burned leg of lamb she had given me to cook for his dinner party from his $40 birthday check.

For years I bore particular rancor at her perverse refusal to participate in the births (or the subsequent lives) of our children. After Emmett's delivery we shouldn't have been surprised at her birthing behavior with the next two, but each time we were. On the evening I went into labor with Emmett she came to the hospital with my father, the éminence grise of the OB floor, and watched my labor from the doorway. But just before eight, as I was being wheeled into the delivery room in that delicious ten-centimeter interregnum between pains and pushing, she disappeared. My father reported later, as he sat with me in the recovery room, that she hadn't wanted to miss *M*A*S*H*.

Two years later, when I went into labor six weeks prematurely with Jessie, we called my parents at 2:00 a.m., scared and in need of someone to stay with Emmett while we went to the hospital. Larry heard my mother roll over and say, "You go" to my father, who did.

No better with the third, Virginia, whose delivery happened at the you'd-never-believe-it-if-it-was-in-a-novel exact minute of my mother's departing flight for an Arizona vacation she had booked knowing it was within a week of my due date. The other two kids were at home with the flu, cared for by our dear friends K.B. and Hunter. Still, that's when you could really use a mother.

But I didn't have that mother, not then and not ever, really. I created a lot of heavy weather about it over the years, but now I'm not really sure why. I had Gee-Gee, who was the best mother a child could want, and at eighteen I had Larry. And besides, I was probably too obstinate and ungrateful to get any advantage from a mother anyway. Plus, by not being a regular 1950s bridge-playing, stay-at-home mother, she got a lot of important things done, many of which have gotten folded up in the selvage of the opening curtains of the new era in America: she stumped for the progressive Adlai Stevenson, chaired the Lexington Interracial Committee, and founded the local League of Women Voters chapter. But, best of all, with a political interest sharpened by having heard in person two of the twentieth century's greatest orators at the height of their rhetorical careers (FDR at his first inauguration and Hitler at the 1937 Nuremberg Rally), she took on the infamous Virginia poll tax.

This blatant attempt to disenfranchise black voters levied a then-onerous $1.50 tax to vote in any election—local, state, and national. Along with the so-called literacy test, the poll tax was a shameful hold-over from the earliest days of Jim Crow, still thriving in many parts of the South. It stuck in my mother's northern craw, and she decided to see who else opposed it among the people she encountered each day on her errands. She typed up a simple statement and under it stuck a few sheets of blank paper on a clipboard that she carried with her for twenty-eight days in October 1963. She did not go door-to-door; her stated intention was to demonstrate to Governor Albertis Harrison, the man responsible for the equally odious policy of Virginia's Massive Resistance, that "there were more people who oppose the poll tax than you believe."

Taped together, the petition reached twenty feet and had five hundred signatures, and after she sent it to the governor it earned my mother, described as "a Lexington housewife," a big picture and page-two story in the *Richmond Times-Dispatch*.

(Note the little Twombly sculpture off to the left sandwiched between St. Somebody and the decanter of crème de menthe.)

If one thing defined my mother from the time she sat listening to Uncle Skip read to her at Lake Sunapee, it was her love of books and reading.

In the early 1960s she single-handedly raised the funds from skeptical and often hostile local governments to establish a thriving regional library and bookmobile, which replaced the three shelves of ratty loaner books in the corner of McCrum's drugstore.

For sixteen years she ran the university bookstore at Washington and Lee, bringing in writers as diverse as Truman Capote, Howard Nemerov, Betty Friedan, Tom Wolfe, and James Dickey. The last she was proudly escorting around the bookstore when he paused and tapped the spine of his popular novel *Deliverance*, announcing, "best work of fiction since Faulkner's 'The Bear,'" to which my mother surprised herself by delivering her first and only expletive, to my knowledge: "Bullshit."

It was through books and her annual return to Lake Sunapee, for which she pined all her life, that my mother staved off the pain of a childhood populated by liars and depressives whose sexual messages were confusing, to say the least. Particularly poignant and symbolic is this tale of her last trip, late in her life, to Lake Sunapee, which she described as her own Golden Pond.

She arrived at sunset and stood looking out from the porch of the cottage that the Gages and the Evanses had shared. The Gage family still owned it, and since there seemed to be no one around she took the time to indulge in a moment of nostalgia and romantic reminiscence as she looked out at the shimmering lake.

Her eyes traveled along the pier that extended into the water, the pier where she had spent so many summers reading and playing during what she said was the only really happy time in her life. At the very end of the pier sat a figure in a lounge chair silhouetted against the late afternoon sky. It was a Gage grandson, now middle-aged, and my mother, overcome with emotion, headed down the stairs and along the pier bathed in the glow of homecoming at sunset.

As she approached the man she realized he was masturbating.

11

The Southern Landscape

Most of what I have discovered about my mother's family history, while unfamiliar in its details, felt strangely recognizable to me on an emotional level. The curious tapestry of fact, memory, and family legend that emerged from my attic seems to suggest antecedents for certain aspects of my character that have always been mysterious to me—the occasional but intense bouts of sadness, my romanticism and tetchy sensitivity, the plodding work ethic, and my tendency toward Talmudic hairsplitting, fractiousness, and unrest. These genetic threads bind me invisibly to the past, and especially to my stoic, passionate, and sentimental grandfather, Arthur Evans.

For example, I have always been susceptible to some form of opportunistic sorrow—of the deepest, most soul-wrenching, step-off-the-cliff variety. I once burst into tears while pouring out a pot of unused salted water intended for cooking summer corn that hadn't arrived. The terrible futility of it all, the clear beauty of the wasted liquid, enriched by salt, strange, essential, powerful, ancient salt, vortexing down the drain.

This must be the sorrow of those Welsh forebears. And now I suspect that's where I got my tolerance for peasantlike, toilsome labor as well. When reading the detailed passages in Arthur's journals describing his dawn-to-dusk chores that conclude "And so on, indefinitely . . ." I am put in mind of my own willingness to plug away in the darkroom, from dawn to way beyond dusk. Perplexing all my friends in the photography community and aggravating my family, I have always insisted on making every print myself, even the 40 × 50 inch landscapes.

For almost two decades I virtually lived in the darkroom, figuring out how my problematic negatives should be printed and struggling with my enlarger, a 1919 Eastman Projection Printer that possesses a level of technological sophistication that would cause a caveman to drum his fingers with impatience. Each day I would make as many prints as my washers could hold (twelve) or as I could stand to make. I would often reprint an image several days in a row, tossing out hundreds of sheets of (now precious) silver printing paper, noting each day's detailed printing instructions on the negative's envelope.

Often enough, some end-of-tether frustrations are penciled in exhausted scrawl ("Please spare me from ever having to print this again") or, on another envelope: "<u>THIRD</u> fucking printing: If I ever have to print this goddamn picture again, heaven forbid, watch contrast/darkness in lower half and . . ."

When all was going well, I would print a new picture each weekday, starting early on Monday after getting the children off to school, usually around 8:30. If I worked steadily, making test strips of each section of the print, I could finally stitch together all the tests and make the first full print after lunch. Once I studied it further, I usually spent a few more hours tweaking the tiny details, burning here, dodging there. Then, after walking the kids from school and getting them settled in with homework, the robotic, factory-like production of the final prints would begin, rarely ending until the late night hours.

The next three days were the same until Friday, when, with the help of a series of long-suffering assistants, all the prints from the week were flattened and obsessively inspected for imperfections in surface or variations in print quality.

The weekends were spent rewashing and reflattening any prints that had emulsion problems, updating the editions book, sleeving and then filing the completed week's work. Then on Monday, I would start over again, *"And so on, indefinitely . . ."*

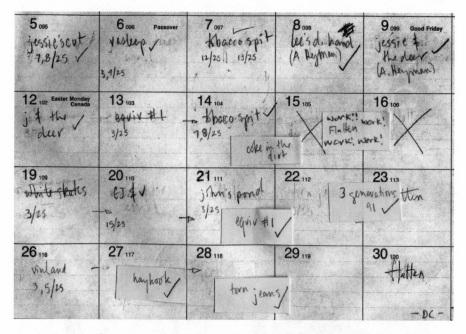

As I got to know my grandfather through his writings in the archive, I found kinship with him in the perseverance and attention to detail common to both our working lives, and in other ways as well. (Although I like to think I wouldn't have been so spineless as to end up living in the "sky parlour" while my spouse cheated on me downstairs. But who's to say?) He earned his living as a writer, albeit at rather pedestrian jobs, and went to great pains to set down the story of his life for his two daughters. But it is when he writes of his work in the landscape that I feel a particular affinity, despite the geographic disparity between Farmer Skaden's fields and my own. His occasionally overwrought prose accords especially well with my own *hiraeth*-rich writing from the 1970s, and it, in turn, aligns with the landscape photographs I made in the 1990s.

That inherent relationship between my writing and photography has never been clearer to me than it is now. The early poetic language and my later elegiac landscapes each served as primary, repeating threads running through my life, the warp and woof of memory and desire. Look, for example, at how this short essay I wrote in January 1969 ties in with a picture I made some twenty-three years later:

206

A Summer Passing

The air of late August lies heavily on our land with the thickness of water. Moving through it, I feel the fluidity of the heat suck at me, then swirl away at my passage. I drive slowly so as not to raise the dust. There are ripples of heat in the valleys, and when a faint breeze arises, the forms of torpid cattle appear in the dry motion of the high grasses.

This is the upper field, high above the river, which funnels the eye toward the looming mountain. Now, in the rising heat, its form can barely be seen, although it is just a few miles away. I look for it and barely see the outline in the sullen gray of mid-afternoon.

The trees appear exhausted with drought; the morning dew is quickly gone and the limp leaves droop. The only sound is the chirring of grasshoppers and cicadas. When they pause, seemingly at once, there is complete silence over the fields.

I begin my descent into a small dip in the field and the fringe of grasses at the edge ripples as I pass. I can see the moist spot where the summer catnip grows. I pull off the two dusty ruts and head toward the patch of green, catching the first wisps of mint and moisture. The air is fragrant and cooler. I pause in the stillness for a moment, then climb again toward the gate and back into the sun. A cow stirs but does not rise at my passing.

Remember how difficult it was for me up there at Putney? The penetrating nostalgia and longing I felt for the farm, the love paeans I wrote about it? "A Summer Passing" was one of them, written for an English assignment from Ray Goodlatte. It was meant to be a "rendering," which I gather from Ray's red notations throughout the first draft is a form of writing allowing only objective absolutes; no metaphor, no ambiguity, just the facts, ma'am. Not exactly my strong suit.

I couldn't be expected to render my passion for the farm in such spare language, especially this particular part, the upper fields. I wrote about those velvety undulations over and over again, even while on the beaches of Paros in 1972, when I should have been having the time of my life. It's hard to imagine, but there I was, looking out at the wine-dark and pining for them:

> *. . . Where all my life*
> *By the one river*
> *The upper field . . .*
> *The one place*
>
> *This has become*
> *All grief*
> *And all desire*
> *For me.*

And if I couldn't do justice with words and certainly not the "just the facts, ma'am" kind, I tried with my camera, composing silver poems of tone and undertow, the imagery saturated still with the words of authors I read in my teenage years—Faulkner, Whitman, Merwin, and Rilke. Many of my (poem-)photographs would sing those words, heady with beauty, ponderous with loss, right back to them.

That visual-verbal love song tuned up in earnest for me on a late morning in July 1992 when I took the first serious southern landscape, a day in which the heat was exactly as I described it in "A Summer Passing." We were living at the cabin and several other people had come for the weekend. The river was already dotted with bobbing children, their excited cries bouncing off the cliffs. I pulled on a thin shift and loaded my camera into the truck, not really knowing what I was going to photograph but feeling the need. Larry, feeling another need, offered to go with me, and we took off for the upper fields.

I had been undeviatingly photographing the kids since 1985, remarking once to a friend that my passion for those pictures was so intense and blinkered that I could drive right past the moonrise at Hernandez that so dazzled Ansel Adams if I was on the way to get a good picture of the kids. But on that July day, I was overcome with farm lust, wordless and undeniable. Driving with the camera from the cool river to the sweltering upper fields, we followed the animal pathways through the grass, stopping to make an occasional picture.

At the time, I didn't care whether the pictures I was taking were any good, or how I was going to inscribe my deep love of place, this time with photography, in a way that could begin to explain it. I hadn't made a picture in the landscape for at least a decade, although recently I had found myself swiveling the camera away from the kids just to watch the randomly edited tableaux pass across the milky rectangle of ground glass. Often a beautiful landscape would surprise me there, ambushing me with the allure of its self-sufficiency.

And I was, at that time, conspicuously vulnerable to ambush. The children were reaching the age I referred to as filial shear, and as the landscapes overtook my family pictures, their figures began to recede from my gaze. In this, one of the very last of my large-format photographs of the three of them together, the children are but tiny distant blurs, attenuated by the heat waves coming off a quenched bonfire.

This gradual move from the family pictures to the landscapes was a shift from what I thought of as our private, individual memories to the more public, emotional memories, those that the past discloses through traces inscribed on our surroundings. Working in the inexhaustible natural pageant before me, I came to wonder if the artist who commands the landscape might in fact hold the key to the secrets of the human heart: place, personal history, and metaphor. Since my place and its story were givens, it remained for me to find those metaphors; encoded, half-forgotten clues within the southern landscape.

There were plenty of those clues that July morning in the upper pastures, where the vine-oppressed trees looked like stooped giants shambling along what had once been a fence line, and a plangent humidity filled the fields, exactly the way it did when I wrote in March 1969:

> *A heavy scent of honeysuckle hung*
> *In thick, sweet layers over the land*
> *And the ripples of heat echoed the rhythm*
> *Of vines twined around the trunks of trees,*
> *Dangling from their branches.*

Larry and I drove slowly through the pastures to what we now call Dead Boy Hill, just to the left of the catnippy swale I had described in my "rendering" twenty-three years earlier. We set up the camera, facing east toward the Blue Ridge. In the primordial, mint-and-honeysuckle-smelling stew of midsummer, the platters of Queen Anne's lace balanced motionless on their spindly supports and the distant hills were muzzy with moisture.

The lens I was using was from the old rosewood 5 × 7 inch camera that my father had used when he was young man in Dallas. It was uncoated, susceptible to flare, and barely covered my 8 × 10 inch film. Because the shutter was sluggish and unpredictable, I always set a shorter time than my light meter suggested. I took a few pictures, bracketing to either side of the recommended exposure time to accommodate the vagaries of the system.

When I pushed the dark slide into the last film holder, I felt my impatient husband pushing against me and my dress rising up around my hips. And there we were again, just like the lovers of 1970 when I wrote of us in just such a moment, also here on the farm and in these same fields:

Our breath
Caught like a needle
On the skin of water

You said "Will it be here?"
"Here where the grass
is so tall?"

And I thought
Yes
Yes here

Certain moments in the creative process, moments when I am really seeing, are weirdly expansive, and I develop a hyperattuned visual awareness, like the aura-ringed optical field before a migraine. Radiance coalesces about the landscape, rich in possibility, supercharged with something electric, insistent. Time slows down, becomes ecstatic.

I once read an account by Hollis Frampton about a man named Breedlove, who broke the world land speed record on the Bonneville Salt Flats. Near the end of his second run, his car spun out of control at 620 miles per hour, severing telephone poles, flying through the air, and crashing into a salt pond.

Emerging unscathed, somehow, Breedlove was asked by a reporter to describe his feelings. Speaking on tape for an hour and thirty-five minutes, he described in a sequential and deliberate way what occurred in a period of 8.7 seconds. In this detailed 9,500-word monologue, Breedlove indicated that in the interests of brevity he was condensing his account, doing his polite best to summarize a much longer story. As Frampton points out, "his ecstatic utterance represents . . . a temporal expansion in the ratio of some 655 to 1."

It's a good thing that I usually photograph by myself, because I fear such a ratio could be applied to my own utterances when the good pictures are coming. Profligate physical beauty is easy to find in the South, but what gins up the ecstasy is the right light, the resonant, beating heart of that light, unique to the South. The landscape appears to soften before your eyes and becomes seductively vague, as if inadequately summoned up by some shiftless creator casually neglectful of the details.

Making a photograph in these conditions is a challenge, even for modern film, and the resulting image often appears to have been breathed onto the negative; a moist refulgence within deepening shadows, details dissipating like those in a painting by Turner. I loved that effect, and, with a hectic flush of near heatstroke, would load up my equipment as the humidity rose and the sun sank, heading to the hills in the eventide. To whatever extent it is possible to photograph air, I was going to try to do it, and to whatever extent photographs can reveal the dark mysteries of a haunted landscape, I set out to make them.

It was the same goal I had when I wrote, decades before:

> *Recovery of the small truths; the upper fields,*
> *the smells, sounds: The local.*
> *This much is not sentimental;*
> *. . . To recover and clarify the deposits,*
> *their grace so fragile, so various.*

When I was well into the pictures of the local Virginia landscape, I was asked by the High Museum in Atlanta to participate in a commissioned project with the self-explanatory title *Picturing the South*. Having seldom done commercial work or commissions, I was a bit unsure about working within a defined concept and under a deadline, but it seemed to dovetail nicely with my renewed interest in the southern landscape, so I accepted it.

However, I wanted the work for *Picturing the South* to be different from the images I was making in Virginia. Having never quite gotten over the aesthetic blow that the Michael Miley glass negatives dealt me twenty years previously, I looked back to them for inspiration. I got way more than I bargained for. His pictures completely changed the direction of my work for the next fifteen years.

This simple Miley landscape, for example:

Look at the subtle solarization of the lower half of the image and the crisp leaves in the upper, the soft light glowing through them. And those edges! Where, nowadays, do you see that white flare on the edges? It's not fogging, but some mysterious incursion of ghostly radiance creeping in all around. Try getting a picture like that with conventional film or, even more unlikely, with a digital camera or your phone.

And yet I did get a picture like that, forty years after my aesthetic consciousness absorbed that remodeling wallop from the Miley negatives.

And when I held this miraculous 8 × 10 inch negative up to the light, the fixer dripping down my forearms, and saw those radiant edges, I was transported back in time to another attic, the attic at the university where the 7,500 Miley glass negatives were stored.

I had run across them entirely by accident in the late summer of 1973 while searching for some arcane piece of darkroom equipment. Pushing up into the topmost level of the journalism building at Washington and Lee, my adjusting eyes dumbfounded me with the sight of a floor untraversable for the piles of glass negatives. They appeared to be many different sizes, from 2 × 3 inches to mammoth plates of 16 × 20 inches, and were stacked like badly shuffled cards or leaning against the walls, unsheathed, coated with dust, scratched, and sometimes broken, glass shards scattered about the rough-hewn flooring. Having worked with the 5 × 7 inch view camera for the last year while abroad, I wasn't intimidated by the size of the plates and began sorting through them, blowing off the dust and holding them up to the motey light coming in through a round window in the eave. Mostly they were portraits of students from the local schools, but occasionally I ran across an image unlike anything I'd ever seen.

Like this one:

Apparently Miley, in addition to photographing Robert E. Lee, enjoyed traveling around Rockbridge County taking pictures, in many cases damn near the same ones I was taking a century or so later.

Several of the pictures I recognized as my own farm, the exact river scenes I had known since childhood.

Although he didn't have quite the bizarre cast of characters that Mike Disfarmer of Arkansas or Charles Van Schaick of Wisconsin had, Michael Miley still took some eye-popping portraits:

What was this nameless, pain-haunted woman entrusting to the untender indifference of time? When I first printed this image in 1973, that question inspired a series of poems, *Early Pictures*, which became part of my master's thesis for my creative writing degree at Hollins College.

> *The print is pinned above the typewriter.*
> *Her molten eyes press for my attention*
> *. . . behind them*
> *the appalling plunge of promises . . .*
> *She dressed in the black lace of lost nights*
> *and her eyes*
> *lunged toward the lens.*

Many of Miley's pictures were memorable like this, and I realize now how often I have retrieved them from my deep pictorial reservoir to unconsciously reinterpret them.

If Michael Miley were peering over my shoulder as I make comparisons between his work and mine, I'm sure he'd be appalled by the shoddy technique of my pictures and the way I am inspired by what, for him, were probably his most embarrassing failures: the overexposed, weirdly stained, solarized, and fogged images that he, for whatever reason, didn't scrape from the glass. But, not to get all woo-woo about it, possibly I am looking at those failed Mileys with what E. P. Thompson called "the enormous condescension of posterity," and in fact Miley hadn't scraped those images from the glass because he hoped that one day someone would hold them to the light, gasping at their percipience just the way I did. Either way, he surely would have forgiven me if he had watched how, throughout the late 1970s, I cleaned, printed, and filed his life's work, saving it from ruin.

That time spent studying the wet-plate collodion aesthetic, though not rewarded monetarily, paid dividends when it came time to execute the High Museum commission. Not yet equipped for making actual collodion plates, I found I could mimic them using ortho film, a graphic arts film characterized by extremely high contrast. After a full decade of taking the family pictures, whose aesthetic success depended on technique so precise as to out-Ansel the most meticulous Adams, I decidedly welcomed the careless aesthetic of shooting with ortho.

I'd never been exactly conscientious about metering the light to the perfect Zone 5 middle gray, but with the unpredictable ortho film and a light-bouncing shutterless brass lens, I now hardly bothered to take readings at all, using my hand and the dark cloth to control the light.

When the time came to develop the negatives, if there was a tray of used-up print developer headed for the drain I'd just slop the ortho in it; no pre-soak, no painstaking temperature control, no replenishment, and, best of all, no darkness. Ortho could be processed under the safelight.

I was having fun again, just like those first months with my father's Leica. The process with the ortho was so much less freighted and required none of that meticulous capital T Technique, which can be, as the poet Charles Wright once observed, like a spider's web without the spider: it shimmers and snags but it doesn't necessarily kill. I was hoping to do all three: to shimmer, to snag, and to kill . . . and have a good time in the process.

And I did for a while, but after a year or so of working with ortho I found more shimmer than snag and kill, and decided to make the technical and aesthetic leap to wet-plate collodion. This required a complete retooling: an 8 × 10 inch camera set up especially for wet plate with custom-made film holders sized for glass, a traveling darkroom for the Suburban, and a collection of esoteric and explosive chemicals.

With the help of France and Mark Osterman, who had modernized the old formulas, I slowly learned all the arcana and found that I loved the whole process. Polishing the glass with a compound so ancient that the tin had a thirty-nine-cent price tag on it from a long-extinct hardware store, I welcomed the stupefaction produced by the humble buffing motions. Preparing to "flow the plate," I would reverently unscrew the collodion bottle and when it emitted its fragrant hiss of heavy ether take in a lungful. Then with the splay-fingered grace of a French waiter carrying a tray, I balanced the glass plate and poured the thick amber collodion onto it, watching for the chilly frisson as the ether evaporated.

The exotically tempting smell of ether—the drug of choice for Rimbaud, Rossetti, and Verlaine, poets of the age of decadence—produced in me a sense of genial well-being and didn't do a thing to diminish my natural romanticism. It also didn't appear to diminish my motor skills (though my liver might have taken a beating), or my tendencies toward ritualistic creative expression. When I was shooting with collodion, I wasn't just snapping a picture. I was fashioning, with fetishistic ceremony, an object whose ragged black edges gave it the appearance of having been torn from time itself. The whole operation had a contemplative, solemn, even memorial feel to it. There was gravitas to the act, as if it were a form of Holy Communion, a sacrament my upbringing had left me woefully unfamiliar with.

At the same time, despite the solemnity, I tried to remain flexible and open to the vagaries of chance; like Napoleon, I figured that luck, aesthetic luck included, is just the ability to exploit accidents. I grew to welcome the ripply flaws caused by a breeze or the tiny mote of dust, which ideally would settle right where I needed a comet-like streak, or the emulsion that peeled away from the plate in the corner where I hadn't liked that telephone line anyway. Unlike the young narrator in *Swann's Way* praying for the angel of certainty to visit him in his bedroom, I found myself praying for the angel of uncertainty. And many times she visited my plates, bestowing upon them essential peculiarities, persuasive consequence, intrigue, drama, and allegory.

Similar in ways to working with ortho film, I found the wet-plate collodion process could give both freedom of expression and the satisfaction of ceremonial process, as if someone had sewn Jackson Pollock's paint-slinging arm onto a body controlled by the brain of Seurat. It was the perfect technique, I now realize, for the granddaughter of that sentimental but methodical Welshman to use on her travels to the nostalgia-drenched Deep South.

And so in 1998, right after bluffing Virginia Farm Credit out of the loan for the farm, I set out on the first of my several trips down into Alabama, Mississippi, and Louisiana. The Suburban was packed to the headliner with coolers of film, smaller coolers with food and booze, nearly identical cylinders of sleeping, film-changing, and tent bags, the lunchbox-sized, primitive cell phone that Larry insisted I take, folders with heavily annotated maps, and in the far back, the darkroom with stacks of frame-quality glass, silver-blackened trays, and explosive, burping bottles of ether-based chemicals.

Because it was a chilly early spring day when I started out, I drove with the windows rolled up. By the time I'd been on the road for a few hours, I realized that I was drunker than if I'd been knocking back shots of moonshine. Quickly rolling down the windows, I was spared a traffic stop in which I would most certainly have been arrested for driving, shit-faced drunk, what was effectively a rolling bomb.

So explosive is ether, I was once told by an alarmed pharmaceutical rep, that even flicking on a faulty light switch could cause a canister to blast apart. I had called her to inquire casually about the twenty-liter tank of ether that UPS had dropped, I feared literally, at the house while I was out shopping. When I found it plunked down in the driveway, bare naked like some pudgy unexploded nuke, I had rolled it onto a handcart and hauled it into the shop where the wood furnace that heats our entire compound was burning away.

The pharma rep so terrified me about the volatility of the ether bomb next to the woodstove that I hung up, ran down to the shop, and rolled it back out to the driveway. Grasping it around the midsection, I placed it gently in the front seat of the car, buckled it in tighter than if it were Baby Jesus, and drove like a little old lady to VMI, whose chemistry department I had alerted to our arrival. Creeping along the parade ground, I was met by cadets dressed in what looked like Tyvek. Stopping traffic, they unloaded my own little Fat Boy and put it in their freezer room for me to draw down into smaller containers.

I took a number of those smaller bottles, swaddled in bubble-wrap, for the trip south, praying that my rolling darkroom *cum* bomb didn't get rear-ended by some meth-head who'd unknowingly met his chemical match. Once I got to the warmer temperatures, I kept the windows down and, sober, made Mississippi by nightfall. That's when the ecstatic time began, and it had nothing to do with ether.

In *Poetics of Music*, Igor Stravinsky distinguishes between the regular old, precisely quantifiable kind of time, and that giddy, bedlamite, psychological time we all know and crave (to varying degrees). For me, once those shotgun shacks began to appear along the road, I broke through into that transcendent dimension of revelation and elation that gleefully eludes Stravinsky's quantifiable time. The lazy shafts of late evening Mississippi sun heightened this time-unraveling sensation, illuminating vortices of cotton flies, like hundreds of bright, slow-motion tornadoes alighting upon the dark fields. I took lungfuls of the yeasty, essential smells that came in my open windows, the sweet stink of exuberant fecundity.

I stopped whenever I saw something that felt like a photograph or held some mystery or happened to catch the light in an alluring way: half a baby doll thrown in a ditch around which vultures circled, a cotton-ginning operation sending up spumes of light-struck dust, a burned-down clapboard church. Barely touching the accelerator, I stuck my head out the window, resting my chin on my wrist and watching the scenery crawl by with the calculating attitude of a cat measuring the distance from floor to countertop. Occasionally I'd glance into the rearview mirror to discover a string of cars, their drivers anxiously craning their necks to see what the holdup was. I would continue this until it was too dark to photograph (although one night I made a two-hour exposure, this one on Lake Pontchartrain)

and eventually find a campground where I could pull in under the mur-
murous pines and use the cinder block bathhouse illuminated all night by
bug-swarmed amber bulbs.

Early in the trip I met a friendly couple at a lecture in northern Mississippi. I told them what I was doing, and they asked where I was staying.
In the back of the Suburban, I told them, then, as a joke, asked them if
they wouldn't happen to have a furnished antebellum house in Louisiana
where I could live for a week. Oh, and ha-ha, I wanted this, too: not just
a free house, but a free house with killer pictures within a few feet of the
back door.

After sharing a glance, they turned to me with apologetic dismay and
said that their family had such a house, but it was in Mississippi, three
miles from the Louisiana border. Could it possibly suit anyway?

Of course I took them up on it, and this, I swear, was the killer picture
right outside the back door the very first morning:

Not only was the key under the mat as promised, but the sheets were clean and the refrigerator stocked. Occasionally I'd come in exhausted and hungry and there on the counter I'd find a still-warm casserole covered with tinfoil. As is the genteel southern custom, a serving-sized spoonful would be missing from it, with a note saying they just couldn't finish it, and hoped I "might get some use out of it."

This gesture, a slice out of the ham or a sliver from the pie, is to ensure that the recipient is not made uncomfortable by the generosity, but in my case, their generosity extended well beyond a casserole, and I was already uncomfortably far in their debt. On the morning I left, they brought me fresh biscuits and homemade sausage.

Total strangers. The kindness of total strangers: the sweet gestures of blind trust and welcome, the common and miraculous somehow made one. It makes me weep. I weep for the great heart of the South, the flawed human heart.

The road out of Greenwood, Mississippi, slices through loess hills soft as spoon bread, dropping down precipitously into the black ferment of the Delta. As I made my way down, oncoming drivers laboring up the steep lane opposite never failed to raise from the steering wheel a welcoming forefinger, the universal farmer's salute. And not just the congenial black faces behind the wheels of the low-slung Grands Prix and Catalinas, but also the good ol' boys in late-model, multi-antennaed white F-150 pickups, the NRA sticker on the back window just below the shotgun.

It was just such a truck that I heard coming slowly across the fields where I was photographing a burned-down ruin of a plantation house; I knew that distinctive Ford engine noise. Not that I could see it; I couldn't. I was stuck under the darkroom curtains at the back of the Suburban with a newly sensitized plate that I wasn't about to ruin by looking out.

The problem was, I was in deep trespassing shit. I had been driving way out in the country, miles from any paved road, when I had seen these siren-song columns, the home they once supported long burned to the ground, surrounded by live oaks trailing Spanish moss. Irresistible. The hitch was that they were behind a fence hung every several feet with No Trespassing signs, and they purported to mean business: "Trespassers will be Shot," "Violators will be shot, survivors will be shot again." That kind of thing.

Like Odysseus untied, tantalized by the vision of these columns, I pushed the Suburban through a gap I found in the barbed wire, sailed right in, and set to work. When I heard the pissed-off sound of that truck approaching I knew I had more problems than a run-over dog. Under the dark cloth I prepared my most ingratiating grin.

The engine cut off, and everything was silent save the ticking of cooling metal. After a few uneasy moments the door opened, and I heard footsteps approaching. In the pause that followed I imagined a gun barrel being raised by a Bull Connor–ish man to that part of the dark cloth where my back, given the evidence of the legs below, would be.

"Awful nice day for taking a picture," the gentlest of southern voices spoke to the dark cloth. Inside it, I couldn't believe my ears.

Or my eyes, when I emerged and saw him. He didn't look mean or angry at all; in fact, he had the benign, lazy look of somebody who'd gotten into a sizeable mess of nookie the night before. Hiking himself up on his tailgate while I shot this picture, his eyes now intent beneath the tufted beam of his brow, he tore out page after page from a spiral-bound notebook on which he had drawn maps of other easily trespassable places.

By the time I packed up my stuff, he had stacked a chaddy-edged pile of scribbled pages on my passenger seat, promised to call his friends to ensure their help, and invited me back to meet the missus. The proverbial hospitality of the South may be selectively extended but it is not a myth. The man was as gracious to this brazen trespasser as if I were Tocqueville back for a second visit.

The whole trip was like that: kind people, moldering ruins around every turn, and perfect weather, like some parallel state of grace. Everywhere I went, even the drabbest, most mongrelly backwash was enlightened by a glimmer of possibility.

One evening, after a day of driving, I stopped at the edge of a raw expanse of logged-over red clay. From the open window of a nearby newly built fake plantation home, naked of trees and propped up with Styrofoam columns, came the ravishingly beautiful, perfectly phrased chords of Beethoven's *Pathétique* sonata. Transfixed, I leaned against the Suburban as the familiar notes, infused with a professional passion and restraint, drifted across the wasteland. Unrestrained myself, I walked up the porch steps, cupping my hands against the flyspecked window screen to discover within the pianist Simone Dinnerstein sitting before a Chickering grand piano, attended on her right by a man who had suffered the ravages of leprosy. At once: the humdrum and the miraculous, the inelegant and the ineffable.

The South is made up of such contradictions and juxtapositions: the gracious splendor of its lost world founded on a monstrous crime and the often retrograde, repellent politics of its modern one elucidated in an accent and vernacular that are lyrical like no other. A culture in which a spritely little blue-hair, while ringing the foot bell under the dining room rug for minted sweet tea to be served, can say, twinkling with pleasure at the memory, "Oh how I miss Jasper. I got that nigger from the warden at Parchman and kept him 'til he died." And this in a honeyed and melodious accent that for a moment sugarcoats the hateful words.

The sound of the language: I once knew a woman who hired a man with a mellifluous southern accent to read to her young son each night so that he would always remember those pulpy vowels, the gentle mitigation of the consonants. The reader was from South Carolina and spoke with a wetlands calm, but to my ear the most beguiling accent of all belonged to the Mississippian Shelby Foote. Like most of America, I had fallen in love with his speaking voice in Ken Burns's Civil War documentary, but before that I had fixated on his earlier, written one, especially in the passage from his novel *Shiloh*, quoted at the outset of this book, about southerners being "in love with the past . . . in love with death."

On one of my trips, I passed through Memphis, where Foote had lived since 1952, and, finding him listed in the phone book, drove around his neighborhood with the deluded yearning of a groupie, hoping to find him walking his dog or pressing quarters into a parking meter outside a coffee shop.

I shouldn't have been surprised that I didn't find him; I had learned that my quarry was elusive the year before, when I tried to get permission from Foote to use those lines from *Shiloh* in an exhibition catalog. Each time I called he was out of town. Two nights before we were to go to press, I conferred with Edwynn Houk, whose gallery was publishing the catalog, and, having no permission, we reluctantly agreed we'd have to pull the quote. The next morning, Edwynn was riding the train into Manhattan and overheard a couple talking about the adventures they'd had downtown the night before . . . with Shelby Foote! Tapping the nearer traveler on the shoulder, Edwynn introduced himself, explained the problem, and was rewarded with Foote's location in the city, from which written permission was speedily dispatched.

But it seemed that was as close as I was going to come to hearing his voice in person, so I gave up the search in Memphis and stopped by instead to see my friend the photographer Bill Eggleston, in his magnolia-shaded brick home, stumbling into a midday birthday celebration. As we sat around the table, Leigh Haizlip, Bill's longtime girlfriend, came dreamily down the stairs dressed in a 1940s slip that I would swear was the very one worn by Maggie the Cat. Her hair was tangled, her face puffy with sleep, and her breasts swayed inside the nylon boob pockets. She was the sexiest, most ravishing creature I had ever seen, moving toward us like an underwater plant, stopping to pour a glass of bourbon.

If those had been my five birthday candles, I would be wishing to look at that sight forever, but who knows what Bill's wish was. He made it, and we ate the cake and took a stroll in the backyard, where there was a small, old-fashioned pool. Then I mentioned Shelby Foote. Bill brightened and said, Good Lord, of course he knew Shelby, so let's go right on over to his place and say hi. Delightedly I piled into Bill's car, which looked to have belonged to his grandmother, and off we went.

Fan that I was, I clung to every word of Bill's Shelby Foote stories until he said that the last time he'd gone over to visit Shelby unannounced like this in midafternoon, Shelby'd answered the door in his boxer shorts. Whoa, I said, no, no, no, we can't take that chance, and reluctantly we reversed course. I left Memphis richer for having seen the vision of Leigh but poorer in the Foote department. The next day, after one more lowlife night in a campground, I headed down toward civilization at Bill's first cousin Maude Clay's place in Sumner, Mississippi.

As always, I picked the least traveled, most remote roads, exiguous pale blue lines on the map, certain in my bones of the memories residing there. Driving through those vine-hung dirt roads, the slender grasses on the verge bent with dust, I was improbably enough listening to Joseph Conrad's *Heart of Darkness* on tape. Though a world apart from Africa, it was impossible for me not to think of the misery extracted at every turn in those roads, just as it had been impossible for Marlow to paddle up the Congo unaware of the "groves of death" lying within the shadows along the riverbank. For me, the Deep South was haunted by the souls of the millions of African Americans who built that part of the country with their hands and with the sweat and blood of their backs. I was moving among shades, aware, always, of their presence.

Flannery O'Connor once said that the South is Christ-haunted, but I say it's death-haunted, pain-haunted, cruelty-haunted—just haunted, period. I knew my pictures were haunted, too, but in a different way from the ones I had made closer to home. I had come south looking not so much for the scars of the Civil War, but for something even more fundamental and, paradoxically, more elusive.

The pictures I wanted to take were about the rivers of blood, of tears, and of sweat that Africans poured into the dark soil of their thankless new home. I was looking for images of the dead as they are revealed in the land and in its adamant, essential renewal. One death in particular had haunted me since childhood, that of Emmett Till, which took place in Maude Clay's home territory. On my way there, I traced the route his murderers had taken in his last hours, beginning with the fateful (and possibly apocryphal) wolf whistle in Money, Mississippi, passing along the Tallahatchie River,

and winding up on a balmy, serenely yellowish afternoon at the very boat lock from which fourteen-year-old Emmett was heaved into the river, naked, blinded, beaten, a cotton gin fan lashed with barbed wire to his neck.

When I visited, Emmett Till's murder was conspicuously unremarked upon in Sumner (although recently Maude sent me this picture of a sign that was erected on the newly cleared riverbank and immediately shot up)

River
Site
This is the site where Till's body was removed from the river. It was then taken to Greenwood, MS. Then the body was sent back to Money, MS for burial. Via a phone call from Till's mother, "not to bury her son", the body was then taken back to Greenwood. The body was then sent to Tutwiler, MS for final preparation to be sent to Chicago, IL.

so I was lucky to have Maude, the granddaughter of the former owner of the land, to show me the exact site. It was a trek, well off the road and iso-lated from any signs of life. She helped me carry my camera, bushwhack-ing a path alongside the cotton fields to the water's edge, and I was glad for her company, feeling unusually vulnerable and alone.

Having pushed our way through the thick brush and scraggly trees to get to the riverbank, I was disappointed by the humdrum, backwashy scene before me. How could a place so weighted with historical pain appear to be so *ordinary*? Was there a photograph anywhere in this unalluring scrub?

I put on my photo-eyes and squinted into the hazy afternoon sun. With my hands I formed a rough 8 × 10-inch dimension, cropping out the old wringer washing machine caught in the vines upriver, imagining the sun breaking all the Kodak rules by milkily pouring into my wide-open lens aperture. I set up the camera with increasing excitement. There was, in fact, something mysterious about the spot; I could see it and feel it, and when I released the shutter I asked for forgiveness from Emmett Till.

Fighting our way back out of the brush, we were startled to come face-to-face with a water-stained piece of lined notebook paper tacked to a spindly trash tree, admonishing us to confess our sins. So many sins, indeed: the voice of Emmett Till, the voices of myriad others like him, an irrepressible chorus of pain, humiliation, and deferred hopes.

Maude drove with me the next afternoon on the dirt access roads alongside the cotton fields, mile after mile. We chatted as we drove, but even distracted as I was I still slammed on the brakes when I saw the roughly human-shaped concrete mound off to the side of the fields.

"Oh," said Maude airily, "it's how they bury people out here in the summer," and, sure enough, at the bulbous end of the mound were the remnants of one of those plastic funeral wreaths designed to be stuck into ground more yielding than this.

I wondered who lay beneath that concrete. Could my deadbeat, drunk great-grandfather Thomas Evans have been uneasily buried on just such a piece of marginal southern land? How does one come to be entombed with a gusher-load of concrete? Did this person die working in the cotton fields and then someone pragmatically called for a cement truck to pour a sarcophagus atop the body?

Out in the middle of nowhere, I contemplated this paradoxical scene so emblematic of the plucky, undiminished South, a no-frills monument to the intractability of the overworked soil and the practical, impoverished, generous people who have long tried to wring a living from it.

Ever since those lonely, purplish Putney nights, reading and writing about the South, I have tried to nail down just what it is that makes it at once so alluring and so repellent, like fruit on the verge of decay. Ultimate beauty requires that edge of sweet decay, just as our casually possessed lives are made more precious by a whiff of the abyss. We southerners, like Proust, have come to believe that the only true perfection is a lost perfection, buying into our own myth of loss by creating a flimflam romance out of resounding historical defeat. In that nexus between myth and reality we live uncomfortably, our cultural sorrows, our kindheartedness, and our snoot-cocking, renegade defiance playing out against a backdrop of profligate physical beauty.

Every time for me, it's the beauty of the southern landscape that fires up that irresistible melancholy of golden nostalgia and inflames my genetically ordained *hiraeth*, spiraling down the DNA chains, southern-style. On these trips down South I succumbed to it without a fight.

I am reminded of the character in *The Prince of Tides* who said to his sister's shrink, "Southerners don't look at sentimentality as a flaw of character,

Lowenstein." Southern artists, and especially writers, have long been known for their susceptibility to myth and their obsession with place, family, death, and the past. Many of us appear inescapably preoccupied with our historical predicament and uniqueness, which, as the southern novelist Andrew Lytle once remarked, we can no more escape than a Renaissance painter could avoid painting the Virgin Mary.

My friend Niall MacKenzie, with his Canadian perspective, notes that we southern artists also display a conspicuous willingness to use doses of romance that would be fatal to anyone else. He likens us to the religious traditionalists of the Appalachians who handle venomous snakes without fear. What snake venom is to them, romance is to the southern artist: a terrible risk, but also a ticket to transcendence.

Occasionally on my travels, I drew that ticket, moving in the slow motion of ecstatic time, like Leigh dreamily descending the stairs. In my revisionist memories, I hardly recall those hundreds of miles offering no chance of a good photograph this side of the Second Coming. I have forgotten the many suppers of saltine crackers washed down with iceless gin, or the ballads I sang to keep myself awake on the highway, which even Emmylou could not have made remotely non-milk-curdling, or the nights sleeping in the backseat of the Suburban while the windows of the neighboring camper pulsed with blue TV light.

No, instead all that I remember is the rare, heart-pounding, brake-squealing lurch to the verge after glimpsing a potential image. My memories are of those euphoric moments of visual revelation, still fluorescing for me like threads in a tapestry in which most other colors have faded, leaving a few brightly, and sometimes wrongly, predominant. Tightly woven in the tapestry are the images I made, themselves informed by the inextricable past and its companions: loss, time, and love. In these pictures, and in the writing of them, the dropped stitch between the sentimental Welshman and his descendant is repurled. And the story depicted in the irregular weave is of a place extravagant in its beauty, reckless in its fecundity, terrible in its indifference, and dark with memories.

PART III

Gee-Gee: The Matter of Race

12

The Many Questions

Down here, you can't throw a dead cat without hitting an older, well-off white person raised by a black woman, and every damn one of them will earnestly insist that a reciprocal and equal form of love was exchanged between them. This reflects one side of the fundamental paradox of the South: that a white elite, determined to segregate the two races in public, based their stunningly intimate domestic arrangements on an erasure of that segregation in private. Could the feelings exchanged between two individuals so hypocritically divided ever have been honest, untainted by guilt or resentment?

I think so. Cat-whacked and earnest, I am one of those who insist that such a relationship existed for me. I loved Gee-Gee the way other people love their parents, and no matter how many historical demons stalked that relationship, I know that Gee-Gee loved me back.

My late friend the writer Reynolds Price repeatedly emphasized the importance to white children of this intimate care, especially to the writers and artists of the South, and he was right to do so. For many of us, being high-strung, odd, and complicated, it was crucial. As a child, I didn't have to ask myself if I was loved, a not entirely unreasonable question in the sometimes indifferent atmosphere of our household. Gee-Gee's love was unconditional, a concept I might never have believed in had I not experienced it. When the dogs and I came in panting and filthy from our adventures, Gee-Gee sent the cringing hounds away and made sure I had what I needed: food, a story, or a bath. And when I was teased to tears by my brothers and father, or scared, or hurt, I never wondered if I would be protected or comforted. I always was—by Gee-Gee.

Most mornings when I was very young, Gee-Gee would set me up on a yellow stepstool by the sink so that I could plunge my arms into the warm, sudsy water and mess around with the tin cups and mixing bowls she'd put in there. This activity would keep me occupied long enough so that Gee-Gee could get the clothes sprinkled and rolled up in preparation for the afternoon's weighty application of the iron. But one day, she had forgotten that there was a glass in the sink, and when it broke, it deeply sliced my little finger. I began squalling, and Gee-Gee rushed to me, pulling me from the stool and into her arms. I hollered more loudly when I saw the raw terror on her usually imperturbable face. Wrapping my bleeding finger in a dishtowel, she frantically tried to dial my father's office while I plunged and wailed in her arms.

My mother emerged from the cool of the bedroom wing and took over the phone, speaking levelly to Edna, my father's secretary. Hanging up, she assured us he was on his way. Gee-Gee carried me, still howling, to a chair in the dining room, where, at a certain angle, the road was visible. She rocked and comforted me, but it became clear at some point that it was she who needed the comforting. Gee-Gee was crying as she watched for the yellow streak of my father's car coming around the bend at the top of the hill.

No one ever doubted who really ran the household, and my mother used to joke about her own dispensability. Gee-Gee had long ago mastered what William Carlos Williams called "the customs of necessity," and to her devolved almost all the intimate aspects of our family life, the cooking, laundry, and sheet changing. After my brothers went away to school, I think she was mostly tasked with raising a lonely child in a household that cared very little for children. In 1958, three days before my seventh birthday, my parents went to France for six weeks to visit friends, including Pierre Daura, Cy Twombly's early art teacher (Daura's own early teacher had been Picasso's father, José Ruiz y Blasco).

In the late 1920s, Daura, a Spanish artist of some renown, and his friend the French artist Jean Hélion, had fallen for a pair of Richmond, Virginia, sisters studying in Paris. These well-brought-up girls summered about four miles from our farm, in Rockbridge Baths, so called because of mineral springs that bubbled up into a crude, algae-lined pool near their house. In exactly the same way as so many before and after them, these two European artists fell in love with Rockbridge County and spent their summers here, hanging out with their new American friends, my parents. I spent many summer afternoons of my childhood in that slimy pool, every inch of my body bubble-wrapped (a packaging concept as yet undreamed-of) with teeny-tiny sulfurous beads. Maybe one of those afternoons it was Cy I saw slipping into Daura's home for a lesson, its walls hung, salon-style, with two small Cézannes, paintings of the French landscape, portraits of Daura's wife and daughter, all topped off with a gorgeous School of Caravaggio over the stairs.

In any case, for those six weeks, while my parents were visiting the Dauras in Saint-Cirq-Lapopie and traveling around Europe, I was living at Boxerwood with Gee-Gee and the dogs. It was my first year at school and since Gee-Gee didn't drive, Clayton Campbell, the local taxi operator from whom Larry and I bought our plot of scrubland decades later, would arrive every morning at 7:30. I would climb into the backseat, where my feet didn't touch the floorboards, and Mr. Campbell would drive me to the whites-only public school, a tall-windowed, white-columned dump of a place with what Cy used to call "proper proportions."

I have no idea how Mrs. Huffman, my first-grade teacher, could have thought that an appropriate test of her students' readiness to transition to second grade was for each of them to choose and perform, unaccompanied, a song before the entire class. But she did, so Gee-Gee and I got out the *Fireside Book of Folksongs* and went through the index. Although Gee-Gee's hand repeatedly flipped the index pages toward Part Four, the Old Hymns and Spirituals, I went for "Clementine," in the Ballads and Old Favorites section.

Painstakingly I learned all six stanzas of the song, including the peculiar conclusion.

On the morning of our final exam, the class singing performance, Gee-Gee dressed me in the too-big homemade dress with tatting on the collar that she favored, and the taxi came to pick me up a little early.

Despite having sung "Clementine" all the way through for Gee-Gee that morning, I was terrified and could barely convince my party shoes to climb the stairs to the school entrance. Like many public buildings of the time, the main hallways of the school were spread with sawdust to absorb the puke and piss that were unavoidable in those primary grades. As soon as I walked through the door I could smell that it had already been put to the test. Apparently I wasn't the only one who was terrified.

One by one, my classmates were called to the front of the class to sing, all of them visibly shaking, some simply unable to perform. Memories of my performance of "Clementine" are mercifully unavailable to me, but I am not so lucky with this other: when Gee-Gee came to the classroom to pick me up and collect my final report card, I remember being afraid that my classmates would think she was my mother. I can hardly bear to even write these words.

R. S. Munger
FOURTH REPORT

Virginia Carter. In absence of Dr. R. S. Munger
FIFTH REPORT

Promoted to Grade _2_

On Sundays while my parents were abroad, Gee-Gee would dress us both up and take me with her to church.

FIRST BAPTIST CHURCH
Lexington - Virginia
1894 - 1960

It mattered a great deal to Gee-Gee how I looked when I went out with her. My lace-edged white socks had to be folded just right over my ankles, the frothy crinoline adjusted with the straps at the shoulders to exactly the level of my hem, and we both wore hats and gloves. Gee-Gee would not let us roll down the windows of Mr. Campbell's taxi for fear of mussing my hair, and by the time we reached the church, it was sweltering.

The dark sanctuary was sweltering, too. At the door, church elders handed out cardboard fans with a white-faced Jesus on them. With the rest of the white-gloved female congregants, we worked the fans metronomically, to little effect. Knowing nothing about church, I stood and knelt when Gee-Gee did, and we shared a hymnal. She had a beautiful voice and sang with the quavering, deep anguish and fervor of Odetta, whose music, with that of Joan Baez, was soon to pour nonstop from the family Victrola. When the entire congregation was in full throat, I felt as if a great wave had picked me up and was rolling me over. I went with it, tumbling like a pale piece of ocean glass, washing up outside the heavy doors at the end of the service. Blinking in the sudden sunshine of Main Street, I reached for Gee-Gee's hand.

Gee-Gee worked for my family until her early nineties. At age one hundred, with her hands curled into gentle claws, she died on Christmas Day, 1994. She was with us for almost fifty years, but to calculate by any form of numeric reckoning the moment-by-moment care and fidelity she tendered our family would be impossible. Yes, I know that she was paid to care for us, and that the notion of equality and reciprocity in an employer-servant relationship is inherently compromised. And I may get my ass kicked by those who think I am perpetuating the trope of the loyal housekeeper Uncle-Tomming her way to the unmarked grave. But Gee-Gee was not a caricature or a type; she was a very real and emotionally complicated person, who devoted a large amount of her time to raising an ungrateful and impertinent scalawag, the same one who now pauses to examine this relationship. I am reasonably sure Gee-Gee was as enriched, and occasionally appalled, by the experience of participating in our family as the rest of us were. And while our home may have been in some ways a replacement for her own, which was rent by racism and death, we did not take her for granted and we knew, even then, that her love was the real stuff that held our family together.

In some kind of cosmic irony, by the time Gee-Gee died her skin was paler than mine, and her long hair was as straight, fine, and white as any North Carolina mill child's.

Because of her broad cheekbones, her countenance remained generous and open, only sagging a bit when she took out her teeth to soak in a glass of water by the bed. Her wrinkled skin drooped below the now-visible arm bones that appeared to be no longer up to the task of lifting the heavy hands. She had been a powerful woman, not fat, just strong, built with the ageless sculptural proportions of the workingwoman. Diego Rivera would paint her, not Lucian Freud.

I seldom saw Gee-Gee in an everyday dress like this, but some mornings she wouldn't be in her uniform when my father honked the horn at her house at 7:30. When that happened, she would change in the furnace room by the kitchen. For everyday work Gee-Gee wore a white uniform, but on special occasions, when she was serving a dinner party or Christmas, she would wear gray with a tiny white apron.

I remember some rickrack around the edges somewhere, on the apron or the cuffs or both, but otherwise the effect was all business. That effect was reinforced by about a gallon of starch ironed so deeply into the fabric that I can still remember the distinctive tearing sound as Gee-Gee stuck her arms through the sleeves.

I knew exactly how Gee-Gee had gotten to be so good at washing and ironing because I had read about it in my well-worn *The Child's Story of the Negro* (1938), by Jane Dabney Shackelford.

Negro Washerwoman

Ms. Shackelford (an unfortunate name for an African American if I ever heard one) explained:

Even after the slaves were set free the Negro washerwoman had a great task to perform. Often her husband could not find work to do; but every community needed a laundress, so there was always work for her. When her husband was thrifty and worked regularly, his small earnings were often not enough to care for the family . . . If the children were sent away to school, their expenses were paid by a mother who was laboring over the washtub. Some of the most noted men and women of our race often tell of their noble mothers and the many sacrifices they made in order to give them an education.

This report was congruent with the life story of my own beloved washerwoman (except that she was widowed and had no "thrifty" husband), and, at the time, the sanguine cheeriness of Ms. Shackelford's description didn't perplex or confound me in the least.

On the worksheet at the end of the washerwoman chapter, I checked off the things that I did (and didn't do) for Gee-Gee—the *did*s are fibs, mostly, and the *didn't*s underreported by a mile.

SOMETHING TO WRITE

Below is a list of things that some children do for their mothers to make them happy. Write all the sentences that tell what you do for your mother.

1. I wash the dishes every evening.
2. I mop the kitchen floor.
3. I go to the store.
4. I mend my own clothes.
5. I give my mother a gift every Mother's day.
6. I darn my own stockings.
7. I try to keep my clothes clean.
8. I do all my work cheerfully.
9. I take care of the baby when mother is busy.
10. I cut the grass and rake the lawn.
11. I obey my mother.
12. I try to do my best in school.
13. I bring in the coal.
14. I sweep the sidewalks.
15. I take care of my mother when she is ill.
16. I take care of my school books and materials to save money for my mother.
17. I empty the waste baskets.
18. I put my toys away after I have finished playing with them.
19. I dust the furniture.
20. I make up my bed every morning before I go to school.

Gee-Gee had a problem with her feet, with finding shoes that didn't hurt.

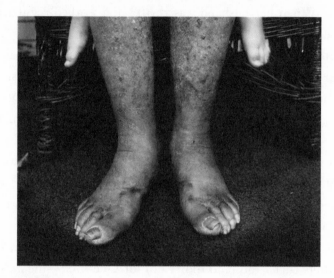

I remember standing in the women's shoe section of Leggett's department store and watching the tiny, hunchbacked saleswoman gaping up at my mother's gestured descriptions of Gee-Gee's feet. I'm guessing that my mother was doing this because she thought Gee-Gee might not feel comfortable shopping at Leggett's, where Colored and White signs on the stairway pointed to bathrooms in opposite directions. I have imprinted in my knavish memory an image of the hunchback kneeling over the barbaric-looking foot measurer clamped to Gee-Gee's metatarsal expanse, but this wasn't likely to have actually happened for the reason just mentioned, and also because there was no point in Gee-Gee's shopping, with her size-thirteen feet, in a ladies' shoe department.

So, where did she get her shoes, ill-fitting though they were? Only now am I wondering about these things. What about those uniforms? Who bought them? My mother? Gee-Gee? And from where? Was washing and ironing the uniforms part of her noble washerwomanly chores? When? At night, or on Sunday? And how did she get something as simple as her groceries? She had no car; she worked for us six days a week from eight in the morning until eight at night and her house was on top of grocery-less Diamond Hill.

I remember an ancient wooden building on the way down Diamond Hill that had a few shelves of extortionately priced canned goods, but no real grocery store until the upper part of Main Street, almost a mile away. This small store, unironically named the White Front, had excellent meat, gave out S&H Green Stamps, and it also allowed its customers, even black people, to charge food and be billed at the end of the month. I know that Gee-Gee had an account and must have shopped there, but then what? Did she haul all her week's groceries to the top of that hill in one of those woven metal carts the way I saw so many black women doing? But, wait; were stores even open on Sundays back then?

All these questions. The simplest, most elemental things.

What if her kids were sick? Or what if she was sick? (But of course she never was.) What if she had cystitis or diarrhea or menstrual cramps . . . surely she had those. Then, when she did, what did she do with those menstrual pads during her workdays at our house? And I guess she used the kids' bathroom; of course she did, but . . . when? If I ransack my memory, I think I can recall the crackle of her uniform leaving that bathroom, where she, like me, must have stared up at the etching of Napoleon on his deathbed from the toilet she cleaned.

During the day, she wore my father's discarded shoes, razor-sliced to accommodate the corns on her toes. But she arrived at work with her feet painfully crammed into whatever golden lily shoes she had found, wherever on earth she found them. She yanked them off as soon as things quieted down in the mornings and it was just the two of us. After wiggling her toes to restore the feeling, she would sit down on the stepstool and gratefully sink her feet into my father's laceless shoes, her stockinged toes protruding from the side slits.

Women wore stockings all the time then, even in the middle of the summer, and Gee-Gee would try to beat the heat by wearing hers rolled down to just above her knees instead of hooked to the dangling ends of a garter belt like my mother's. She often wore my mother's old silk stockings, whose gossamer runs enlarged into ladder-rungs as the day went on, the seams wobbling crazily. Stocking seams were a particular misery back then, but more for my mother than for Gee-Gee.

It was important for my mother's seams to run straight up her legs, two apparently converging lines that had the unintended effect of guiding the eye to their dark vanishing point. When my mother was going to town, she would close the bedroom door and twist her head around to examine her seams in the mirror. Then, a ritual familiar to almost any well-off southern white child of the 1950s would play out: powdered, lavender-scented, as cool and white as Lot's wife, my mother would emerge from her bedroom, grab up her purse and white gloves, and try to make her getaway.

Apparently both parties knew their roles in this drama, but to my observing eyes it seemed new each time it played out on the asphalt bib next to the black sedan beetled under the pine boughs.

"Mrs. Munger! Mrs. Munger!!" urgently issued from the slid-open kitchen windows.

My mother would stop, her expectant face belying the startled look she would try to put on it.

A beat.

"Mrs. Munger, you cannot go to town with your slip showing like that! And those seams! What would they think of me?"

For Gee-Gee, this was not a rhetorical question. She had reason for concern. Working for a Yankee, albeit one with a Dallas-born husband, was a problem for Gee-Gee, and my parents' oddball, liberal, atheist, country-club-shunning ways further complicated the picture. Curiously, that my mother insisted on exceeding the normal pay scale for her help, five dollars a week in the forties when they first arrived in Lexington, was no comfort for Gee-Gee. The anonymous, threatening letters my mother received as a consequence of this profligacy and the talk around town brought Gee-Gee to the attention of the community, which was not a good thing. Any black person could tell you: the less noticeable you were, the better.

Gee-Gee learned the rules of living in white society early on, though she revealed little to us about her childhood. What we knew was this: she was born to the very young daughter of a former slave in a part of the county where freed slaves had settled, known to this day as Buck Hill. Although Gee-Gee's mother was black, the man who raped her (or so it is logically presumed by her family) was white. It is likely that her mother died in childbirth because as an infant, Gee-Gee, born Virginia Cornelia Franklin, was brought to Lexington and raised by her mother's sister, Mary Franklin.

In her late teens, Gee-Gee married Wesley Carter and bore him six children, the youngest of whom was twelve when my mother, new in town and eight months pregnant with her first child, saw her coming down the post office steps. Struck by the image of this powerful, proud, and composed woman, my mother described her to my father in detail at dinner that night. By a twist of fate that to the end of her life still delighted and amazed my mother, the next day she answered a knock at the door to find the unforgettable stranger again. Virginia Carter stood tall and confident on the threshold, wearing a tweed Peck and Peck suit with a velvet collar so worn it appeared to be suede. Her broad cheekbones bespoke some Indian blood, her light eyes and almost straight hair something unspeakable. She asked if my mother needed help and was hired on the spot.

Gee-Gee's husband, Wesley McDowell Carter,

worked as a presser in the laundry room of the nearby Virginia Military Institute. He had problems with alcohol, and more than once Gee-Gee came to work troubled, her face blotchy. One night in the back room of the store on Diamond Street he rose from the card table, headed down the basement stairs, and fell, breaking his neck. Apparently, no one noticed right away, and it was more than a day before Gee-Gee was taken to his body.

Left with six children and a public education system for which she paid taxes but which forbade classes for black children beyond the seventh grade, Gee-Gee managed somehow to send each of them to out-of-state boarding schools and, ultimately, to college.

How did a widowed black woman pay for the housing, the food, the travel, and the tuition to educate six children?

By working twelve hours a day and by taking in linens to iron at night, linens stuffed into white sacks crowding her front door when my father took her home after all day on her feet at our house. What did he think when he saw those bags?

What were any of us thinking? Why did we never ask the questions? That's the mystery of it—our blindness and our silence.

Once in my early twenties, at one of the Friday night W&L cocktail parties, I went into the kitchen where a heron-like black woman bent over a sink washing glasses, her frilly uniform cap perched like a cockscomb above her glistening scalp. I struck up a conversation with her, and at first it was the usual pleasantries. When she learned who my father was, she straightened, turned from the sink, and, with her beaky eye on mine, said, "You can't know what it's like being colored. But I want you to know something about Dr. Munger. He always treated us like we were no different from white people. He didn't ever see color."

She turned back to her work, and when she was done with the dishes, I walked with her out the back door and watched her untie and fold up her apron, which she placed in the cardboard box I was holding for her. She leaned over and with flat palms to either side of her calves rolled her stockings down over her knees and off her long toes, putting them in the box, too. Then she stuck her bare feet back into her white service shoes and set off for home.

At the time, Larry and I lived close to the post office, where twenty-four-hour access to the mail slot invited the too-hasty deposit of a letter I drunkenly wrote to my father as soon as I got back from the party. I told him about the conversation with the birdwoman and expressed my admiration and love for him, a practice strongly disapproved of in our family. Our parents had installed in each of us an emotional thermostat with the dial turned down far enough to discourage even routine expressions of affection.

It was after midnight that Friday when I posted the envelope, addressed formally to Dr. Robert S. Munger. I envisioned it to the left of his placemat at lunch on Monday, the ivory-handled letter opener at the ready.

The instant my fingers released the letter into the brass slot, which read "Local Mail," I regretted it. The letter was over the top in every respect—for Chrissake, it was a love letter to my father. Suddenly sober and aghast, I fluttered my fingers into the slot, pushing my narrow wrist bones through the opening and working my arm up to the elbow. I waggled my fingers but touched nothing. Pressing further, my elbow bones now crammed into the opening, I twisted my arm to the side. Nothing. For a brief, horrible minute I thought I might not be able to retract my arm, but with some maneuvering I fetched it back. Cradling it against my stomach, I walked home.

Saturday morning I felt like crap, but kept my long-standing luncheon appointment at my parents' house. These lunches were important to Gee-Gee, and she went all-out on the menu. I found my father seated alone at the table, a small glass of sherry and his allotment of peanuts centered on the placemat before him, the mail stacked neatly to his left. He was staring out at his gardens with his usual mien of abstracted contemplation.

We spoke briefly, and I went over to the sherry bottle to pour out a medicinal hair of the dog. Snagging a *Harper's* magazine from the mail, I sat at my place and began to read. When we were done with the sherry, Gee-Gee poured iced tea into the unusually tall glasses that the Esso station gave out with gasoline purchases, then set the warmed plates on the mats. While he was waiting for the food, Daddy picked up the letter opener and began slitting the tops of the envelopes, one by one.

Bills, advertisements, and then, to my stomach-heaving horror, there in his hands was my letter. How had it gotten here in less than twelve hours? What about the Monday delivery? He slit it open, extracted the page of over-wrought prose, and read it through, pausing to take a cooling sip of iced tea.

He turned to me a bit quizzically, closed his eyes, and lowered his head in a bow, refolded the letter, and reached for the next envelope. Gee-Gee arrived with the fried apples and we began to eat. No further mention of the letter, ever, although after his death I found it in a file with a heading something like "Worth Saving."

The hands that were serving the lunch that day were bigger than my father's, with thick, heavily ridged nails glowing like pale beacons at the tips of the fingers. With unlikely balletic grace, Gee-Gee lowered the silver serving dishes to our left, two passes at each meal, a third if biscuits were involved.

Likely there were biscuits that Saturday lunch, as she always made them when we had fried apples and bacon. The apples came from an old orchard above the house and were small, green ones, Pippin or Northern Spy, and difficult to peel. Difficult for me, that is, but not for Gee-Gee. She would sit on the stepstool, the large bowl of apples beside her on the chest freezer, and, with a paring knife, unfurl a spiral of continuous peel, the whitening apple rotating in her pink palm.

When she was done, catching up the loopy tangle of peels in her apron, she would dump them in the compost bucket and carry the apples to the counter by the stove. Sinking a wooden spoon into the bacon grease stored in a sawed-off tin can, she would put the skillet on the burner and start the biscuits. Assuming the warm top step of the stool she had vacated, I would watch her from behind as she rolled out the dough and twisted the rim of a jelly glass into it, trapping the circle of dough in it long enough for her to shake it out onto the cookie sheet.

As far as I could tell, Gee-Gee herself never ate anything, save occasionally when she checked the seasoning from a pot on the stove. Otherwise, the only thing I ever saw pass her lips was ice water from a tin measuring cup that sweated on the counter. Maybe it was a good thing that she never needed to eat, because when we traveled together, as we did for vacations on the Eastern Shore, she could not enter the restaurants. When we stopped to eat at the Howard Johnson's, gratefully throwing open the doors of the hot car, Gee-Gee stayed behind.

Looking out from the big windows of the air-conditioned dining room, we could see her cooling herself with a First Baptist Church fan, Jesus's white face serenely waving in the backseat. Emerging from the restaurant with a tin-foil-wrapped cheese sandwich for Gee-Gee, which she would demurely place in her lap, and a Dixie Cup of water, which she would drink, we would resume our trip as if this were perfectly normal.

It's that obliviousness, the unexamined assumption, that so pains me now: nothing about it seemed strange, nothing seemed wrong. I never wondered where she peed on the trips to visit my brothers at school in Vermont. Could she hold it until we crossed the Pennsylvania border and the restrooms were integrated? Did any of us, besides her, wonder about that, about what would happen if she just had to go? How could I not have thought it strange that Gee-Gee not only never ate anything but also never had to *go*, never even got out of the car? How could I not have wondered, not have asked?

———

Like my two brothers, at Putney School I studied under a rotund, pipe-smoking, green-eyed black man named Jeff Campbell. It was Jeff who assigned, with the infinite despair of the defiler, the novels of William Faulkner.

Through the cold Vermont nights, the windows of my dorm room steamed up with southern gothic as I huddled under the bright Hudson's Bay blankets, grimly annotating the books Jeff had assigned: *Light in August*, *Absalom, Absalom*, *The Sound and the Fury*. My homesick romanticism thrummed to the melodrama: the violence, the undertones of sexual threat, the sense of moldering decadence, the cursed inheritance, and, of course, the inevitable haunted home place. That haunted home place, a metaphor for the South itself, was a house divided by the institution of slavery.

I am sure Jeff Campbell knew, as his long-nailed fingers, the forefinger yellowed from pipe-tamping, placed *Absalom, Absalom* like a sacerdotal biscuit in my palm, that this would be my moment of awakening, the one described by Graham Greene as the door to the future, after which the world is never again seen in quite the same way. Faulkner threw wide the door of my ignorant childhood, and the future, the heartbroken future filled with the hitherto unasked questions, strolled easefully in. It wounded me, then and there, with the great sadness and tragedy of our American life, with the truth of all that I had not seen, had not known, and had not asked.

———

The graduation ceremonies for the Putney School class of 1969 were held on a weekend in early June. My parents and Gee-Gee arrived Friday, and I could tell that Gee-Gee was not pleased with what she was seeing. The children of the wealthy were dressed like field hands, with dreadlocked hair and dirt between their toes. Gee-Gee glared at a black kid from my algebra class, and when he flashed the peace sign at her, his arm around a bell-bottom-wearing blond girl, she turned from him with a snort of disgust.

Oh, Gee-Gee, I thought despairingly: This is the future. Up here, we're all one.

Gee-Gee was having none of it.

On graduation morning I was late getting to the dining hall for breakfast, and all the tables were gone. Benches for the graduates and chairs for the visitors had been arranged at the eastern end of the room, with a processional aisle in the middle. The hall appeared to be empty, but squinting against the sun I saw a lone figure substantially anchoring the first row of the audience seating. Staring straight ahead, white-gloved hands folded in her lap and her back not even touching the back of the chair, sat Gee-Gee.

She must have brought with her that dreadnought of an ancient iron with which she had sent all six of her children through school, because she was wearing a perfectly pressed linen dress. It was a pale yellow, and centered above her bun was a pillbox hat made of the same fabric. A necklace of white plastic orbs, resembling the South Sea pearls that you now see oppressing the thin collarbones of ladies who lunch, complemented Gee-Gee's powerfully muscled neck. The skin swelled out above her too-small white pumps and her stockings had compression puckers where the toes were mashed in. No one had stocking seams anymore, but in every other respect she was as elegant and imposing as a dowager queen. (This picture of her at my brother Bob's college graduation a few years before my Putney graduation will give you some idea as to that serene elegance—especially in relation to her obnoxious charge.)

Before it occurred to me that a Styrofoam cup was absolutely out of the question, I walked over to her and offered her coffee in one. The concept of paper plates, cups, napkins, or plastic anything was anathema to Gee-Gee. It was she who kept the silver polished, the Wedgwood plates inter-leaved with circles cut from grocery bags, and the glasses wiped with old diapers washed so many times they were airy as cheesecloth. But to my surprise she accepted the coffee, and we sat for a while in the soft June sun.

A few hours later as the room began to fill for the ceremony, she was still in the same chair. When my parents arrived, my father stood to the side while my mother, in a prim little hat, slipped into the seat next to Gee-Gee. Directly behind them sat Ethel Kennedy, wearing white patent-leather boots, her brood sprawling around her, their shirts unpressed and hanging out of their khakis.

My mother and father leaned toward each other occasionally to exchange some whispered observation, but Gee-Gee remained straight-backed, staring ahead. I knew the warning signs. Her distress, even her occasional anger, was always accompanied by an ineffable and profound sadness: always the pursed lips, the closing of the eyes, perhaps onto visions of injustice and outrage, and the slow, tired shaking of her head, usually accompanied by an "umnh, umnh," which conveyed wordlessly the extremity of her disgust and sorrow.

Then it started, the eyes closing, the head slowly, almost imperceptibly moving from side to side. As if she could bear it no more, she reached out her immaculate white-gloved hand and with her forefinger tapped my mother on the arm.

The pillboxes came together and Gee-Gee put her lips to my mother's ear, whispering indignantly: *"Mrs. Kennedy is chewing GUM!"*

13

Hamoo

I had to learn many things about the South on my own. My parents tended not to speak in generalities about classes of people: they never disparaged poor mountain people as "white trash" or saw fit to mention the religious persuasions of local merchants. Early on, they became aware that seating the domestic help in the back of the car was a dated concept and, with much discomfort on all sides, convinced Gee-Gee to move up front. Over the decades they changed appropriately the terms they used to describe people of color: first "colored," then "Negro," and finally "Afro-American." Neither lived long enough to ever feel comfortable with the relatively new nomenclature of "black."

So I suppose it should not strike me as odd that a black woman taught me that contact with a black man could be dangerous, although I was so self-centered that I thought her concern was mostly for me. Before that lesson, one August afternoon in 1966, I hadn't really thought much about any of it. I had always seen, but not seen, black men on the fringes of white life, mowing, tending bar, or waiting for work in the shade of the big trees at the courthouse. There were a few black men who stood out as local characters: I remember silently cheering an insouciant Berkeley Hamilton as he drove a team of four horses along White Street. He was hauling a mountain of loose hay, whistling as he slapped the leathers and ignoring the increasing numbers of cars forced to drive through the droppings and dust he left in his wake. Even then, I think I sensed how dangerous his attitude was.

I had regular contact with only one black man back then. We called him Hamoo, a sweet man with few teeth who was soft-spoken and a heavy drinker. He came to the house to help Gee-Gee with the more onerous household chores, although Gee-Gee made no secret of her disdain for his "trifling" ways. I had no idea what his real name was (I recently found out it was Sam Hamilton) and didn't think it was strange that we called him by an appellation that might suit a cartoon character. Knowing black people only by their first names or nicknames back then was unremarkable. And conversely, the title "Miss" was always affixed to my first name when it crossed black lips, and, worse, "Master" often preceded my brothers' names, irrespective of their ages.

It was socially unacceptable to show deference to a black person. This lesson was taught to my Bostonian mother on her very first day in the South. In October 1939, my parents, married four days before in Braintree, Massachusetts, took the train to New Orleans, where my father had a job as a professor at Tulane Medical School. When they arrived, Daddy's imposing Dallas socialite mother, Irma Dumas Munger, was standing on the station platform.

Irma had grave misgivings when her much-beloved younger son announced he was marrying a Yankee she had never seen, evidenced by the telegram sent in reply to the news: "Slightly shocked . . . will arrive Sunday." This announcement in the Dallas paper says it all:

If Irma could have had her druthers, it would have been for a bride more on the order of the frilly one on the left, not the austerely modest one her son had chosen.

Dressed to the Neiman Marcus nines and smoking a cigarette in an elaborately carved ivory holder, Irma dispensed with the preliminaries as the newlyweds disembarked. Brandishing the *Times-Picayune*'s real estate pages, she announced that in all of New Orleans there was only one apartment suitable for them, so she'd signed the lease and had a few important pieces moved in. Located on Jackson Square in one of the Pontalba Buildings, the apartment came with a full-time maid, Ophelia Payne, plus a laundress and cook, all black. Irma had them lined up like a military unit when my mother and father reached the landing on the second floor.

Shaking each tentative hand, my mother greeted them using the proper honorific, "Good afternoon Mrs. Trask, Mrs. Payne, Miss Toutant." She had hardly stepped past the reviewing line before Irma pulled her aside and said urgently, "Betty, you must use the *first* names!"

Like most of the racial inequities she discovered in the South, my mother learned that this was just the way it was, stunningly unexamined.

Gee-Gee came to work every day except Sunday, but my memory of Hamoo is that his days were unscheduled, or, rather, scheduled by his level of sobriety. His job was to wax the parquet floors and wash the great expanse of windows in our Frank Lloyd Wright knockoff house, hauling back the itchy fiberglass curtains while wobbling on the stepstool. With a little help from our liquor cabinet, where the level of each bottle was marked for reference by my father with black grease pencil, he always left a little drunker than he came, his smile broader than when we picked him up in what was then known as Mudtown.

Lexington is a hilly town with a crease running lengthwise, north to south, all that remains of a once vigorous stream, now gone underground. In the absence of a railroad track, that geological anomaly offered the perfect racial divide. Mudtown began in the bottomland surrounding this shallow ravine, then rose eastward on the flanks of Diamond Hill, which gives this neighborhood the name that's used today.

On foggy mornings the coal smoke from the forge in Manly Brown's blacksmith shop would mingle with the wood smoke of the cook stoves in Mudtown, then nestle impenetrably among the wooden houses. When my white-knuckled mother pointed the black Chevy down the hill to pick up Hamoo, all we could see were the brick chimneys above the fog and smoke. As we poked down into the murk, the cobwebs running between the hood ornament and the antennae became dotted with moisture that resembled tiny lights. Our car moved as soundlessly as a lit-up party boat seen through the fog on the Mississippi, and we looked out at dark faces in the doorways, hearing the muffled cracks of knee-broken kindling.

Hamoo's house appeared to have been built on stilts, its rear door opening out into a deep void. It was unpainted clapboard and had windows covered with brown paper in which dry goods had been wrapped. Devil's shoestring sprawled in the yard, the gracefully arching branches brilliant with purple berries, and honeysuckle wound up the stilts. Approaching Hamoo's house, I caught sight of a male figure standing in a rear doorway sending an impressive arc of steaming urine into the yard. Sunstruck, perfectly parabolic, he sent it forth with a slight upward tilt to his hips, not guiding or even watching where it went but instead dangling his hands to his side and raising his face to the faint sun.

I knelt on the gray serge seat, my mother anxiously pumping the brakes, her left foot pressing the clutch to the floor while yanking on the column shifter. As we pulled to the front of Hamoo's house, she rolled down the window, peered out, and honked the horn. The horn stuck, as car horns often did in those days, its insistent bray bouncing off the ceiling of mist and against the hills on both sides of us. Mudtown resounded with it.

Children spilled from the doorways of homes so tiny that they appeared to be miniatures nestled in a crèchelike setting of cotton. They pushed through the screen doors, dragging bits of blanket behind them. Helpless and ashamed, I looked at them, and they stared back at me with eyes strangely serene as though informed by knowledge that precluded amazement.

My mother was beating on the tilted black circle of the horn, shaking the knurled Bakelite wheel, then kicking up at the steering column, dislodging her stocking seam into a rucked-up zigzag at the back of her calf. When the noise began, she had stalled the car in third gear, which was not low enough to hold us completely, and every so often the car would hitch itself forward toward the ditch with a reluctant, hiccupping motion. She appeared not to notice this, so preoccupied was she by the mutinous horn.

From the fog between two houses a giant emerged. He was wearing an overcoat and pants held up by a belt whose excess hung down from a buckle off to the side. He pushed through the gawking children and, as he easily cleared a picket fence, revealed a foot which resembled nothing so much as a crudely swaddled newborn. When he reached the window he spoke soothingly to my mother, who appeared to be trying to yank the steering wheel from the floor.

Reaching into the car, his hand enfolded the horn and gave it a twist. The braying stopped. In that sudden quiet the air seemed to collapse around us, like a gum bubble that pops across a freckled nose. My mother sat back on the seat with relief.

That wasn't the last time I was to see our white asses saved from automotive embarrassment, both times by a black man who accomplished his miraculous rescue in a similar way and with something resembling embarrassment.

But . . . embarrassment for whom? For us?

Yes, for us.

14

Smothers

Winters of the 1960s were stormier than those we have now, and deep snows were not uncommon. We lived at the top of a long hill on a country road that, once it passed our driveway, led on past the small whitewashed home of the Smotherses, a black mother and grown son. A little farther along was a cluster of shacks where white people lived, the grown-ups drunk and the children, as often as not, albino. This road was not at the top of anyone's plowing list, and sensible people out where we lived had chains ready to be spread out and fastened to tires at the first snowflake.

But not my daddy. Although he was one of only four physicians in the county and the only night he would not have to rise from bed and drive, sometimes for an hour or more, to a patient's house was every third Wednesday, he was still loath to put chains on his beautiful, zabaglione-yellow Studebaker. This modern, aerodynamic model looked the same both front and back—a slightly reptilian snout, backswept loins, and a tapering flank. It looked fast, and was, too.

But not with chains on.

One afternoon, Daddy picked me up early from Brownie Scouts because of the snow rapidly accumulating, and we headed toward home. With the long hill looming whitely ahead, Daddy instructed me to hold tight to the strap that looped from the headliner at the window. I grabbed it with both hands, and he gunned the Studebaker. Swinging into the oncoming lane, he cut the sharp corner at the base of the hill. The telephone pole whizzed by so close I jerked my hands free and ducked.

Wildly spinning the wheel, he corrected the drift, downshifted with a deft heel/toe, and then floored it up the hill. The nose of the Studebaker shoveled up plumes of snow, which blocked our vision as we roared into oblivion. But despite, or perhaps because of, the accelerator being jammed to the metal floorboards, the rear end began a series of gracefully diminishing fishtails, and we subsided into stasis. The snow gentled around us, restoring our sightline: two-thirds of the hill rose pristinely before us.

Then, slowly, the Studebaker began to slide backwards and sideways, my father futilely pumping the brake until both side wheels settled languidly but emphatically in the ditch. With a sigh, Daddy reached into the backseat, mated up the two worn handles on his black leather medical bag, and swung it onto the tilted front seat, where it slid down against my hip. I collected my book bag and scooted uphill toward his side of the car.

He pushed open his door, propping it with his foot, while I ducked under the wheel clutching my brown beanie to my head. Once I was out, I held the heavy door for Daddy, then let it slam, the weight of it seeming to sink the car more deeply into the ditch. But before we could start to trudge up the hill, the sound of clanking chains drifted up to us, and, with it, the distinctive, rancid smell of rotting trash. No mistaking that stench. We smelled it every Saturday when Smothers came to collect whatever trash we hadn't burned in our stone incinerator the week before.

I am sure Smothers had a first name; I knew his mother's was Betty, because she was the maid at the house of a friend of mine. But Smothers was always just Smothers. He and Betty kept pigs, so he gathered up the trash around town, sorted out the paper, glass, and metal, then fed the pigs everything remotely edible. His yard reeked, and his truck did, too.

We heard the gears shift down to first at the telephone pole, and the old truck began chugging its way up the hill, the smell getting stronger. As it drew alongside us, Smothers slowed, and the steady drip of liquid from under the tailgate now began to pour out, steaming and rank. The passenger-side window was jerkily rolled down, and the blue-black face of Smothers appeared.

"Mr. Smothers!" My father said cheerily, as though surprised to discover who it was.

"Doctor Munger," was all Smothers said, rolling up the window and pulling the truck past us and off to the side, where the snow began to melt in a line below the tailgate. Then Smothers loomed out of the snow. He was dressed in a dark coverall with knee-high black boots. Smothers smelled like rancid compost, too.

Daddy and I were fully snow-covered by this time, his bald head protected by a felt hat that he briefly tipped in welcome. Then, sensing Smothers' discomfort, he shook it to get the snow off, as though this was the intention all along, and replaced it. My galoshes rose above the thin Brownie socks with the dancing fairy on the cuff, but they were no match for the snow, which was drifting in around my ankles. I looked warily at the rivulets of brown liquid headed toward us, then at my freezing feet. Smothers had walked to the car and was dusting snow off the bumper.

"We'll just do the front," he matter-of-factly announced to my father, politely pluralizing the concept. And with that, he lifted the entire front of the Studebaker out of the ditch and back into the road. Returning to his truck, he fetched a chain, hooked the car to the truck, and told us to get back in. We resumed our seats, Daddy somewhat comically holding the wheel in the ten-two position. The steady clanking of chains and the slushing of our bare tires through the mixture of snow and compost runoff were the only sounds as we achieved the crest of the hill and our driveway just past it.

Twenty years later, on my way home after a weekend at the cabin, I stopped by a small grocery near my house, and in the parking lot was Smothers' truck, as noisome as ever. But Smothers himself, standing by the counter with a six-pack casually overtaken by his hand, was clean, smelling of Aqua Velva, and dressed up. His pants were a dark polyester check, he was wearing a yellow shirt, and his belt and shoes were a cracked white plastic material. Off to the side stood two white men, one a gelatinous pile of unintended self-mockery, the other stubby-fingered and wearing logger's boots. They did nothing to disguise their contempt for Smothers, snickering, glancing at the white shoes and the knee-bagging pants.

A bell on the door had sounded as I entered, and after it quieted I spoke to Smothers, whose eyes were fixed on the floor. Even after I spoke, he seemed reluctant to meet my gaze. Pressing the point, I stepped up to him, and for the briefest moment his expression brightened, then veiled over with an obvious attempt to spare me the embarrassment of knowing him. I took the cue and walked over to the coolers.

As Smothers dug into his pocket and uncrumpled his bills on the countertop, Stubby Finger stepped aggressively close to him, wedging the crenulated edges of his Dr Pepper bottle cap into the opener under the lip of the counter. As he pulled, the cap and a splash of sugary liquid dropped onto the white shoe below.

Smothers reached into his pocket, retrieved a folded handkerchief, and wiped his shoe. Then he stepped to the exit, turning to meet my eyes with a heartrending look of apology, and gently opened the tinkling door. I never saw him again. He died of a brain tumor several years later, his body wasted, in his aged mother's care. Even though I know it isn't likely under the circumstances, I see a pietà when I think of it.

15

The Kid on the Road

Driving back into Lexington from our neighboring town one August afternoon in 1966, I saw ahead of me on the side of U.S. Route 60 a dark, broken figure with a distinct hitch in his gitalong. Squinting against the afternoon sun, I tried to make sense of this jerky apparition that somehow reminded me of a sooty Tin Man. As I approached, it coalesced into a pointy-hatted black teenager with one crutch supporting the side of his body that had never grown and another dragging behind for balance.

I drove by him, then pulled to the side and hollered out a casual-sounding offer of a ride. His hat hid his face but everything about him bespoke indecision. I said, "C'mon, just hop in," instantly regretting the choice of verb, but relieved to see that he had begun lurching forward, shooting a backward glance. He came to the passenger side and got in the backseat. When he had settled the crutches, I pulled onto the road.

We drove in silence for a time, and then I asked where he was headed, which was Lexington, six miles east. Trying to sound as natural as possible, as though he were a boarding school kid like me out looking for posters for the new dorm room, I began asking questions about his family, where he grew up, and what he had been doing for the summer. When he said his family name, I knew it, or at least I had heard the name from Gee-Gee, and I was pretty sure I could find the street where he lived.

But on the outskirts of town he asked to be dropped off. I pulled over in a parking lot and got out to help, but he was well into it on his own and appeared to be in a hurry. He thanked me, turned away from my pleased face, and hitched away toward town. Since it was right there, I stopped by the Clover Creamery for a caramel milkshake before I drove home. As

I came down the drive, through the steamy kitchen windows I could see Gee-Gee preparing dinner.

Her specialty was fried chicken. Each week a freshly killed bird was delivered to us by a neighbor, who required a shot from the marked bourbon bottle in the sideboard to sustain him as he made his delivery rounds. Gee-Gee would singe the pinfeathers while the wrung neck and head of the chicken drooped out of her fist like a failed bouquet, and then cut it into the usual pieces. Maybe it was the fresh meat or maybe it was the depth of the hot oil or the seasonings in which she dipped it, but her fried chicken was so sublime that as we ate it we failed to notice the oil-splatter burns that peppered her arms or the sweat stain that spread across her uniform while the exhaust fan roared ineffectually above the stove.

She was about to cook chicken and biscuits when I got home that afternoon. I strolled into the narrow, hot kitchen, noisily sucking up the last of the milkshake and kicking off my Bass Weejuns.

"So," I announced, "I picked up this crippled kid on Route 60 today and gave him a ride to town . . . you know, Ernestine's nephew."

I went on, and Gee-Gee was listening, but then she was turning her body toward me with an ominous heaviness, as if a Henry Moore sculpture were being rotated 180 degrees. She had biscuit dough stuck to her hands, but above those hands was that wide face, shiny with sweat and . . . was it anger? Anger, at me?

No, perhaps it was fear but there was also anger, and it was taking over her features in a way I had never seen before.

With her hands in the air, the way a surgeon holds them to push the paddle faucets when he is prepped for action, she pressed me back against the wall with her floury forearms, and said in a voice I'd never heard, low and afraid, "Don't you ever pick up a colored boy again, no matter what, no matter who. You hear me?"

Despite having been so affected as a child by stories of Emmett Till's murder, it was many years before I realized that it was unclear just which of us Gee-Gee was most worried about.

16

Who Wants to Talk About Slavery?

The memories sketched in the preceding chapters provide a few of my personal points of reference for what the legal scholar Sanford Levinson calls "the brooding omnipresence of American history—race and, more precisely, slavery." No doubt about it, history is a big deal down here; but still, even among the competitive crowd of southern states, Virginia stands out in its obsession with the past. Somehow, though, we have neatly managed to elide out of our revisionist historical picture that latter clause, the "race and, more precisely, slavery" one, preferring not to acknowledge the abiding human spirit of slavery.

Physically, the reminders are everywhere. Prominent among them are some of Virginia's most iconic structures, from Jefferson's slave-built rotunda at the University of Virginia, where one of our daughters studied, to the slave-built colonnade of Washington and Lee University, which our other daughter attended. Of course, many Virginians choose not to be reminded of slavery and instead express their appreciation of the past in a Civil War–reenacting, R. E. Lee birthday–celebrating, Confederate flag–waving sort of way. Indeed, in 2010, Republican Governor Bob McDonnell contrived to announce the beginning of Confederate History Month with a formal declaration that omitted any reference whatsoever to slavery. This paradoxical refusal to own up to the horrors of slavery while glorifying the past of which it was a crucial element indelibly blots our ledger book and complicates the often dishonest narrative of our country's history.

The first slave ship to these shores unburdened her cargo in Virginia, and thereafter our majestic James River was compelled to carry the grievous burden of our country's slave traffic. No Southern state exceeded Virginia in slave ownership or slave trade: our soils were tilled, swamps drained, timber and minerals extracted, and our roads, cities, and universities built by the sweat of black backs.

The idea that Virginia stands in some kind of special historical and symbolic relation to American slavery has been discussed and debated ever since the 1975 publication of Edmund Morgan's *American Slavery, American Freedom*. For Morgan, Virginia history offered a microcosm of what he called "the central paradox of American history": the simultaneous rise and mutual reinforcement of American liberty and of slavery.

The success of slavery as an economic system in the United States depended upon the divisive effects of institutionalized racism, which other forms of slavery historically did not. Slaves were certainly mistreated throughout history, but however cruel the practice of slavery was in other societies, it did not rest on ideological racism to the extent its North American counterpart did. Morgan argued that our singular American racism was not a natural disposition carried across the Atlantic along with steel weapons and smallpox but rather a pragmatic attitude that had evolved as a way of preserving the stability of colonial society.

The greatest threat to that stability was thought to lie in the possible recognition of common interests between poor whites and slaves. To prevent such a nightmare alliance from taking shape, the law, the pulpit, and the press joined forces to deepen the perceived differences between the races by convincing white colonists that they were naturally superior; that they, whatever their social rank, were, as Morgan put it, "equal in not being slaves." As a cynically encouraged moral disease, racism has had regrettable staying power and, no matter how we deny it, is still employed as a subtle but potent political and psychological tool.

This racist legacy of slavery was said by Faulkner to be a curse on the entire South, white and black, the wounds of African Americans mirrored in our guilty white souls. Reading "The Bear" under my tented covers, way past Putney's "lights out" hour, I began to understand that he was right. "Don't you see?" he wrote. "Don't you see? This whole land, the whole South, is cursed, and all of us who derive from it, whom it ever suckled, white and black both, lie under the curse."

Now, some forty-five years later, the same Hudson's Bay blanket on the bed, here I am doing my best to visually articulate my sense of the unsettled accounts left to us by that brooding curse.

The first picture I took of a black man was easy.

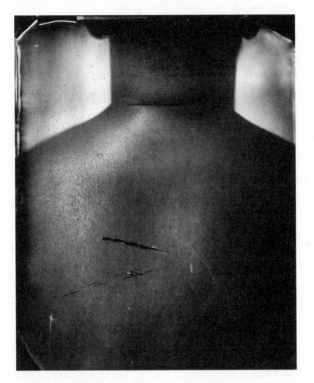

That's the way it sometimes goes for me: I start on a new series of pictures and right away, in some kind of perverse bait-and-switch, I get a good one. This freak of a good picture inevitably inspires a cocky confidence, making me think this new project will be a stroll in the park. But, then, after sometimes two or three more good ones, the next dozen are duds, and that cavalier stroll becomes an uphill slog. It isn't long before I have to take a breather, having reached the first significant plateau of doubt and lightweight despair. The voice of that despair suggests seducingly to me that I should give it up, that I'm a phony, that I've made all the good pictures I'm ever going to, and I have nothing more worth saying.

That voice is easy to believe, and, as photographer and essayist (and my early mentor) Ted Orland has noted, it leaves me with only two choices: I can resume the slog and take more pictures, thereby risking further failure and despair, or I can guarantee failure and despair by *not* making more pictures. It's essentially a decision between uncertainty and certainty and, curiously, uncertainty is the comforting choice.

So I soldier on, taking one dodo of a picture after another, enticed by just enough promising ones to keep going. Soon I encounter another obstacle: the new work, so precarious, unformed, and tender, is being subverted by my old work, which was itself once precarious, unformed, and tender but with the passage of time has now taken on a dignified air of inevitability. The new work has none of that apparent effortlessness, the after-the-fact infallibility that the old work so confidently glories in. No, the new work is always intractable, breech-presented, mulishly stubborn, and near impossible to man-haul into existence.

Eventually, the law of averages takes pity on me, as it is known to do for my fellow sufferer, the monkey at his typewriter, and doles out a miracle: a good new picture, at last. It brings me relief and reassurance, but no one else sees it for the milestone it is. Each time, friends and family dismiss my panic and despair, saying breezily, "Oh knock it off, you'll get another good picture, you always do. Relax!"

"Relax," I snort sarcastically to myself, shouldering the tripod to take another picture that is certain to be vapid, derivative, unhingingly bad. "Sure, you know all about it." How can they understand the paralyzing, dry-well fear I live with from one good picture to the impossible next? Who can know the agony of tamped-down hope between the shutter's release and the image in the developer? Or the reckless joy when I realize that, at last, I have a good one; eagerly, my ebbing confidence throws off the winding-sheet and resumes business at the old headquarters, a wondrous resurrection.

But, of course, it is also a fleeting one. It lasts about as long as the exquisite apex of a wave and, just as the wave takes the sand castle, it sucks my confidence out with it as it recedes. In its wake, it leaves the freshly exposed reminder that, however good that last image was, the next picture must be better. Each good new picture always holds despair within it, for it raises the ante for the ones that follow.

Every time it's the same. It's easy to prove to myself that good pictures are elusive, but I can never quite believe they're also inevitable. It would be a lot easier for me to believe they were if I also believed that they came as the result of my obvious talent, that I was extraordinary in some way. Artists go out of their way to reinforce the perception that good art is made by singular people, people with an exceptional gift. But I don't believe I am that exceptional, so what is this that I'm making?

Ordinary art is what I am making. I am a regular person doggedly making ordinary art. But as Ted Orland and David Bayles point out in their book *Art and Fear*, "ordinary art" is the art that most of us, those of us not Proust or Mozart, actually make. If Proust-like genius were the prerequisite for art, then statistically speaking very little of it would exist. Art is seldom the result of true genius; rather, it is the product of hard work and skills learned and tenaciously practiced by regular people. In my case, I practice my skills despite repeated failures and self-doubt so profound it can masquerade outwardly as conceit. It's not heroic in any way. To the contrary, it's plodding, obdurate effort. I make bad picture after bad picture week after week until the relief comes: the good new picture that offers benediction.

The early success I enjoyed in this new project gave me a false sense that not only would the good pictures come easily, but also that I understood my reasons for doing them in the first place. In general, I am past taking pictures for the sake of seeing how things look in a photograph, although sometimes, for fun, I still do that. These days I am more interested in photographing things either to understand what they mean in my life or to illustrate a concept. This work with black men, though inchoate and not yet even printed, seems to be a little bit of both.

The Platonic doctrine of recollection asserts that we do not learn but rather, with time and penetrating inquiry, release the comprehensive knowledge that came bundled with us at birth. In this concept, we each hold within ourselves "the other" by virtue of our shared humanity, with artists (in theory) being uniquely qualified to transcend their own identity and gain access to the unknown other through empathy and imagination.

Plato notwithstanding, it asks a lot of empathy and imagination both, not to mention photography itself, to help me understand my relationship with the black people in my life and to come to grips with the physicality of slavery. William Styron was accused of indulging in what Hegel called the "psychology of the valet" for his ambitious attempt as a white man to tell, in a detailed and personal way, a black man's story in *The Confessions of Nat Turner.* That criticism is specious: I think his Platonic pool of universal experience was all too happy to yield him the mysteries of history and human nature when he tapped into it. I hope that when I drill down to search my own soul's reserves, I might enjoy even a fraction of his access.

To compound the overall difficulty of tapping those reserves, I have established a rather stringent conceptual framework in making these pictures. Almost all my models are strangers, most know nothing about me as a photographer, and each session is limited to about an hour. When they walk into my funky-ass studio, miles from nowhere, they are guarded and suspicious; how could they not be? Who is this gray-haired old gumboil in her silverwear—clothes covered with silver nitrate stains—and what kind of pictures does she want? Not some quasi-sexual-stud bullshit, they hope, but they always couch it more diplomatically. The historically dishonest and slippery social ground upon which our brief friendships struggle for a foothold makes every emotion, every gesture, suspect.

In the more elastic medium of writing, even Faulkner couldn't, as Vincent Harding put it, enter "starkly white" into the mind of Dilsey, a purely fictional character in *The Sound and the Fury.* How then can I expect to introduce myself to a living stranger of another race, generation, and sex, then establish a relationship of trust, communicate my uncommunicable needs, reconcile four hundred years of racial conflict, and make a good picture all in one session?

⌐——⌐

In 2009, on the bicentennial of Abraham Lincoln's birth, the choreographer Bill T. Jones was commissioned to make a dance about him. Characteristically, Jones chose to relate Lincoln's legacy to the racial and social complexities that continue to haunt us today. In his dance/theater piece *Fondly Do We Hope . . . Fervently Do We Pray*, he addresses with movement and words our nation's history of slavery, but in a video about making it he acknowledged the doubts that haunted him:

> Who wants to talk about slavery, no matter how lyrical the terms, who really wants to talk about it? . . . What will the vocabulary be . . . how do I use the abstraction of arms and legs?

And sometime later, speaking with Bill Moyers, he said:

> To go back to slavery seems beside the point. But I think there was something . . . in what you said about it being about the body . . . the body is the thing that . . . connects us, the body is bought and sold, and the body is definitely the thing that will divide us. And slavery is the most horrible example of it. And it's simply abstraction . . . it is nothing more than an abstract gesture, heated up in the crucible of our association. It's useful for people to do that exercise. See something horrible through a formal lens.

The formal lens through which Jones chose to focus his examination was Walt Whitman's poem "I Sing the Body Electric." Among the many gifts of sensuality, unasked-for and risky, given to American letters by Whitman, this poem stands out for the intimately carnal language with which he describes the realities of a slave auction. Whitman and Jones, each through his own medium, sought the person inside the auction-block property, speaking about slaves as human beings, about their humanity, about, to get right down to it, their physical bodies. It's the body that's being offered for sale, bought and sold. It's the body that divides us, the body that gives value to the "product." Using song, dance, and Whitman's words, Jones heated up the crucible of our association, and I borrowed the idea, using the poem as a template for my own exploration:

Head, neck, hair, ears, drop and tympan of the ears,

*Eyes, eye-fringes, iris of the eye, eyebrows, and the waking or sleeping of the
   lids,*
Mouth, tongue, lips, teeth, roof of the mouth, jaws, and the jaw-hinges,

Nose, nostrils of the nose, and the partition,
Cheeks, temples, forehead, chin, throat, back of the neck, neck-slue,

*Strong shoulders, manly beard, scapula, hind-shoulders, and the ample
    side-round of the chest,*
Upper-arm, armpit, elbow-socket, lower-arm, arm-sinews, arm-bones,
*Wrist and wrist-joints, hand, palm, knuckles, thumb, forefinger, finger-
    joints, finger-nails,*
Broad breast-front, curling hair of the breast, breast-bone, breast-side,
Ribs, belly, backbone, joints of the backbone,

*Hips, hip-sockets, hip-strength, inward and outward round, man-balls,
    man-root,*
Strong set of thighs, well carrying the trunk above,
Leg fibres, knee, knee-pan, upper-leg, under-leg,
Ankles, instep, foot-ball, toes, toe-joints, the heel;

All attitudes, all the shapeliness, all the belongings of my or your body or of
    any one's body . . .
O I say these are not the parts and poems of the body only, but of the soul,
O I say now these are the soul!

These pictures are not a voyeuristic inventory of my models' physical properties. When asked what I am doing these days, I hesitate before responding, "I am photographing black men," because all too often the response has been, "Oh, like Mapplethorpe!"

No, not like Mapplethorpe. Not at all like Mapplethorpe.

What I want to do is find out who those black men were that I encountered in my childhood, men that I never really saw, never really knew, except through Gee-Gee's eyes or the perspective of a racist society. It's an odd endeavor, and the remarkable thing is that my models are willing to let me try. They are helping me find the human being within the stylized, memory-inflected, racially edged, and often-inaccurate historical burden I carry. The heartrending irony is that some of that burden was given me, out of fear and concern, by Gee-Gee.

Edification and understanding can be a felicitous outcome in the making of these pictures, possibly as much a part of the art as the end product, the image and print. Because of the clear, self-imposed parameters, this work could be seen as a form of performance art: an intense period during which the relationship that obtains between sitter and photographer both informs and becomes the art. Our different ages and gender deepen the transaction, but the social constructs of race, culture, age, background, and life experience contribute to the Gordian nature of the knotty moment. It is an intense time, probably for both of us, certainly for me.

I remember author Dorothy Allison saying once that if you don't break out in a sweat of fear when you write, you have not gone far enough. I'm going that far. It is not fear that's bringing on the sweats, exactly, but something else that has to do with the nature of photographic portraiture and why, since the 1980s, I have hardly made a portrait of anyone outside of my immediate family.

I once read an interview with Richard Avedon in which he asserted that a photographic portrait is a picture of someone who knows he's being photographed, and that what he does with that knowledge is as much a part of the picture as what he chose to wear that day. Avedon felt that his models had control over the results, that they were performing for the camera and implicated in what was taking place. Of course, he acknowledged that most of his models were professionals or public figures who knew exactly what the camera could do for them and to them. When pressed, he allowed that there were also those he called "the innocents, who have no idea what my agenda is, how or why or for what purpose I am photographing them and who are simply curious and at the same time generous with themselves."

Because I do not photograph the famous, my models are often "the innocents," and easy exploitation of their naïveté all too often results in good pictures. I think this is commonplace in photography throughout history. If you were to take a look, for example, at the contact sheet of the well-known Diane Arbus image of the boy holding a toy hand grenade in Central Park, you'd understand what I mean. But unfortunately, you can't because the Arbus estate will only permit reproduction in art books devoted to Diane Arbus's work (although, at the time of this writing, you can see the Arbus contact sheet reproduced many dozens of times by entering "Child with Toy Hand Grenade in Central Park" into Google). If it were reproduced here, this is what you'd see: eleven pictures on the twelve-image roll of a perfectly normal (if oddly dressed), knobby-kneed little boy standing arms akimbo and occasionally mugging for the camera. But your eye would go straight for the one in which for the briefest split second the exasperated child is shown spasmodically clenching his hands, one holding the grenade, and grimacing maniacally. This anomalous and life-altering split second in the life of the little boy is the one she chose, the one where he looks like a freak.

Of course she did. I would have, too.

The girl in this picture from my 1988 book *At Twelve* could not have known that her breast was visible from the vantage of my camera, but I did and took the picture anyway.

And I published it, because her face does not show, and because it is one of the best pictures in that collection.

How about this Edward Steichen image:

It depicts the robber baron J. Pierpont Morgan, who allowed Steichen a mere two minutes to make his portrait. How could Morgan have known that the arm on his chair was reflecting the light so that it appeared he was holding a dagger? Morgan was one of Avedon's "professionals," a public figure who had been photographed countless times. And yet the photographer held all the cards.

We always do. Exploitation lies at the root of every great portrait, and all of us know it. Even the simplest picture of another person is ethically complex, and the ambitious photographer, no matter how sincere, is compromised right from the git-go. There are nimble justifications for making potentially injurious imagery, some grounded in expediency and others cloaked with the familiar Faulknerian conceit: "If a writer has to rob his mother, he will not hesitate; the 'Ode on a Grecian Urn' is worth any number of old ladies."

But most of us are not Keatsian in our talents, so does our lesser work deserve what my friend the writer Jim Lewis calls "Faulkner's moral pass"? Lewis thinks not: "An asshole who makes great art is an asshole who makes great art; but an asshole who makes lousy art is just an asshole." And one wonders if being the subject of "great art" takes the sting out of painful representation. Maybe it does; perhaps the sting diminishes over time, particularly as the importance of the art grows. For example, does Dora Maar's discomfort over Picasso's representation of her really matter at this point? Still, the fact remains that many, I daresay even most, good pictures of people come to one degree or another at the expense of the subject.

When I work with these men, my goals are primarily to establish such a level of trust as to attenuate, if only for that short time, our racial past. But, secondarily, I hope to convince the total stranger before me that this work will be aesthetically resonant in some universal way and worth the risk he takes in making himself so vulnerable.

It's a tricky moment: taking the picture is an invasive act, a one-sided exercise of power, the implications of which, when considered in historical perspective, are unsettling. Photography is always invasive, but these experiences are consensual and, in the best hours, transcendent. I have had men, complete strangers, trust me enough to offer up physical character-istics about which they were sensitive—missing digits, scabby, eczema-ridden backs, surgical scars—with no prompting and no embarrassment in the quiet afternoon light of my studio deck.

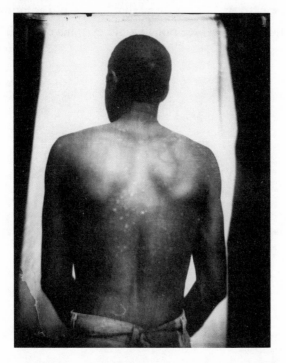

We don't speak much, but we both give, and take, something. At the most basic level, making these images is exploitive, reductive, and fraught. But at a higher level, which portraiture at its best can achieve, the results can also be transformative expressions of love, affirmation, and hope. If transgression is at the very heart of photographic portraiture, then the ideal outcome—beauty, communion, honesty, and empathy—mitigates the offense. Art can afford the kindest crucible of association, and within its ardent issue lies a grace that both transcends and tenders understanding.

But even if these image-making sessions can't bridge the seemingly untraversable chasm of race in the American South, and of course they can't, they still offer an oblique way for me to express my belated thanks to Hamoo, Smothers, and Ernestine's nephew. These men, and many others, suffered the ignorance and arrogance of my youth, and reached across that divide when they needn't have, gestures that required forbearance and courage that I was too blind to recognize at the time. Now, on my studio porch, I both reveal and invite vulnerability, gently, I hope, teasing open the doorway to trust, a doorway that leads from an immutable past to a future that neither Gee-Gee nor I would ever have imagined.

PART IV

My Father:
Against the Current of Desire

17

The Munger System

My father always said he'd kill himself before debility took him, and he did. After a ruinous year of unsuccessful treatments for a malignant brain tumor, we shouldn't have been surprised. Daddy had been waltzing with the cultural concepts of death since his youth, and I wonder if he hadn't long ago memorized the steps to his own danse macabre. I've also wondered if the numerical echo between his birth and death dates might have determined his decision to swallow thirty Seconals on the particular day he did, May 22:

Robert Sylvester Munger

Born 11-22-11

Died 5-22-88

Parenthetically, I can envision the even more satisfying inscription on my own tombstone, should I be so palindromically correct as to die on January 5, 2015:

Sally Mann

Born 5-1-51

Died 1-5-15

While my father was the kind of man who might have been tempted by the prospect of this kind of memorial congruity, he actually intended to die the weekend before he did—at least my mother said so. The whole family was converging on May 13, and if he could pull off his death the next day, the reunion and farewell could be tidily wrapped up together.

But he couldn't. Although it's an intriguing notion, I doubt that the eight-day delay had anything to do with the aesthetics of numbers on his tombstone. I suspect that as he contemplated it, a much deeper shadow than we can know fell between the idea and its execution. Although it's hard for me to imagine my father's resolve ever letting him down, I think on May 14 it did.

And anyway, how did he think he could pull it off in a house full of people? I guess he planned to do it after everyone was asleep, moving unsteadily through the house to his study, softly shutting the door. Then, he would have brought out, from wherever he had kept it all those decades, the brown glass bottle of Seconal, its label yellowed with age and flaking onto the table. Maybe he even went so far as to count out the pills and pour a glass of water. Not too much water, though, because he would have been worried about his bladder releasing; too humiliating, even if he were dead.

Earlier that year, he had grown afraid that he might wet the bed and had cut back on his water consumption. He grew less lucid and his thinking was screwball. Unaware of his fear of incontinence or of his dehydration, we thought he was dying. But a savvy hospice nurse, who knew him to be a man for whom adult diapers would be an unthinkable indignity, figured it out and made him drink. All the same, I bet that on May 14 it was a mere sherry glass of water he poured for those thirty pills, if he got that far.

Water or not, he didn't kill himself that day, choosing instead to spend one last weekend with his family, even if it meant inconveniencing them by a return trip in the near future when he could get up his resolve.

For the next week, my father, the papery skin of his bare head raw and inflamed from radiation treatments, resumed his solitary station at the windows facing the Blue Ridge Mountains. He watched helplessly as the disappointed crows he had trained to come to him circled raucously above the house. I assume he was plotting the next best death day.

May 22 was a Sunday, and a close friend of mine, Ronald Winston, was flying down from New York to visit Daddy. When Ron and my father met a few years earlier, each recognized something of himself in the other: a gentle courtliness, a double-breasted-suit-wearing kind of rectitude, and a wide-ranging, fusty erudition—qualities that for a generation had been uncommon.

I retrieved Ron, cuff-linked and immaculate as always, from the Roanoke airport and drove him to Boxerwood, where he and my father sat out on the terrace drinking iced tea and talking of their fondness for rare flowering trees, specifically *Cornus coreana* and *Franklinia alatamaha*.

Neither acknowledged that only death's looming specter, the long shadow of the great-winged black bird, would provoke a busy man to fly from New York to Virginia for less than two hours.

When I returned from taking Ron back to the Roanoke airport, my father was dying on the couch.

On July 5, 2011, as I wrote about that day in 1988, I received a call from a friend saying that Cy Twombly had died in Italy about an hour before. Immediately an image of Cy presented itself: the penetrating eye, his mannerly melancholy, his long fingers daintily picking at the tablecloth, and most especially the sense of stillness and gravity that seemed to accompany him, cohabiting somehow with his love of mischief and repartee.

My image is holographic; I can walk behind him as he sits at the kitchen table and see a scruffy patch of hair matted down from sleep—and it's in color, with sound, and in motion, too. I hear the little snort that often preceded a witticism and remember the way he demurely covered his lips before uttering something wicked. I can see him moving carefully across the studio in pale leather loafers, his wide-wale corduroy pants depending from suspenders.

When we parted a month earlier, I think we both knew that he was, as he laughingly remarked that day, "closing down the bodega for real." Instead of turning his big back and flapping his usual fey good-bye wave as he got in the car, Cy turned to face me and looked me directly in the eye. He said with discernible sadness and gravity: "You keep on working hard, sweetie."

His drawling voice, his wrinkled face, the gap between the front teeth—Cy is right here. Cy, who hated to be photographed, is still vivid in my memory. I hardly have any pictures of him, although he gave me this one that Robert Rauschenberg made of him at Black Mountain College, and showed me where he wanted it placed on my desk.

RR. EMC.

I am convinced that the reason I can remember him so clearly and in such detail is because I have so few pictures of him. That's unusual in itself, in this era of ubiquitous camera phones, but imagine a time a mere 170 years ago, when there was no mechanical way to preserve a face, an important experience, or the beauty of the natural world.

Before the invention of photography, significant moments in the flow of our lives would be like rocks placed in a stream: impediments that demonstrated but didn't diminish the volume of the flow and around which accrued the debris of memory, rich in sight, smell, taste, and sound. No snapshot can do what the attractive mnemonic impediment can: when we outsource that work to the camera, our ability to remember is diminished and what memories we have are impoverished.

Because of the many pictures I have of my father, he eludes me completely. In my outrageously disloyal memory he does not exist in three dimensions, or with associated smells or timbre of voice. He exists as a series of pictures. When I think of him, I see his keen, intelligent eyes cast askance at me, his thumb lightly resting on his cleanly shaved chin. And I see his thick forearms, the left impinged upon by the stretchy metal band of the watch I keep here still in my desk drawer, the sleeves of his white cotton shirt rolled to reveal his powerful biceps, his waist trim from an absurdly careful egg-whites-only kind of diet, girded round by the same cracked leather belt he wore for forty years.

But . . . here's the thing: It's a picture, a photograph I am thinking of.

I don't have a memory of the man; I have a memory of a photograph. I rush upstairs to the scrapbooks and there he is. I've lost any clear idea of what my father really looked like, how he moved, sounded; the him-ness of him. I only have this.

It isn't death that stole my father from me; it's the photographs.

So that's where I go to find him, to the deckle-edged, yellowing pictures that keep my father, Robert Sylvester Munger II, alive for me. He's there in the attic next to all those boxes from my mother's New England side of the family. But the tightly bound Daddy boxes seem somehow aloof and reticent next to the seam-bursting boxes of my mother's father, unlucky Arthur Evans. Those, by contrast, seem like eager schoolchildren, waving their hands, ready with the answer.

No answers spill out of Daddy's boxes; within them are almost no personal confessions of insecurity, or of modest pride or passion, or even much emotion, all of which I found in the neighboring Evans boxes. Indeed, even the primary questions about my father, never mind the answers, have taken me weeks to form after sorting out the contents.

Who was this man? How on earth did he turn out the way he did, given his upbringing? Would he have been a happier, more expansive person if he'd followed his great love of art, literature, and high culture instead of medicine? Indeed, was he happy at all? Did he feel his life was fulfilled in the same way as that of his namesake, Robert S. Munger? And most of all: why the fascination with death, especially the iconography of death, and from his earliest years?

If the story of my mother's family, of Emma Adams, Jessie Adams, Arthur Evans, and Uncle Skip, is primarily about unrealized dreams, flawed character, damped-down obsession, unconventional sexual behavior, poverty, grief, and depression, the predominant story from my father's side of the family, that of the first Robert Sylvester Munger, is of ambition perfectly realized, marital and professional fulfillment, of wealth and generosity, racial tolerance, an expansive, gracious lifestyle, and of obsession indulged.

This busy man, Robert Munger I, whose business, family, and civic concerns should have occupied every spare moment, was possessed by a passion that completely transported him, and I mean literally: his passion was the automobile. And, similarly susceptible to possession and obsession was his grandson, my father, Robert Munger II, the outwardly calm, respectable medical doctor with the questing soul of an artist. His was an improbable obsession with death, capital-D Death, which he pursued almost his entire life, until it caught him under its eradicating black wing.

As soon as I cut the baling twine that held the Munger box together, the cardboard flaps gently released, revealing this picture of the prosperous Munger clan gathered in Birmingham, Alabama, for Christmas 1922. With even a cursory look,

my eye was drawn to my eleven-year-old father's intelligent, curious face in the lower left corner.

And, when my eyes traveled upward, I was easily able to find his grandfather, Robert Sylvester Munger, the namesake who was also the family member my father most resembled, physically and intellectually.

The senior Robert Munger is standing among his children (he had four boys and four girls), their spouses and offspring, and gently leans toward his pensive wife, Mary Collett, whose rather unyielding bulk he appears to be coaxing into compliance by demonstration.

What he appears to be demonstrating is sweet and satisfied repose. His eyes are serenely closed, as, in fact, they would be closed forever exactly four months later when he died of pneumonia at age sixty-nine.

⁂

I have always referred to my father as a genius of a certain sort, but in fact, the real genius in our family was this man, Robert S. Munger I. And not only a genius, but also a financially successful genius and, more importantly, a generous genius: at his death in April 1923, the *Birmingham News* praised Robert Munger as "one of the greatest philanthropists the South has ever produced." The millions of dollars he gave away hadn't been inherited; he earned them all.

He was born into a hardworking farm family in Rutersville, Texas, a wisp of a town a hundred miles west of Houston. It now barely merits a mention in Wikipedia, having enjoyed its peak population of 175 right about the time Robert Munger was doing his level best to get out of there.

His father, Henry Munger, who ran a sawmill and a cotton gin in Rutersville,

was ambitious, tough, and hewn from sturdy early-American stock; his forebears had come over to Connecticut from Surrey, England, in 1630, just a decade after my mother's celebrated ancestor, half-drowned John Howland, was pulled back aboard the *Mayflower* and into the history books.

Born in 1825 and raised in Texas, Henry Munger was at just the right age to get caught up in the California gold rush, which, you may remember, also excited my great-great-grandfather from the New England side of the family, Ellen's father. But, unlike that family-abandoning wastrel who never returned, Henry Munger, made miserable by shipwreck in the Pacific and privation in the camps, headed back home to Texas after only two years out West. He walked the entire 1,552 miles.

This one surviving portrait of Henry, which I first discovered in the archive of a ninety-three-year-old Birmingham relation, was put to hard use, even standing in for the encoffined man at his wake after what the newspaper called "a brief but intensely painful illness."

It wasn't until later that I realized the portrait was cropped from a larger picture, which tells its own story about Reconstruction-era social relations in west Texas.

Even taken out of its racially troubling context, the one surviving photograph of Henry Munger appears to show the face of a sour, squint-eyed man. Here we may be confronting another of photography's treacheries over and above the medium's power to displace real memories.

At its most accomplished, photographic portraiture approaches the eloquence of oil painting in portraying human character, but when we allow snapshots or mediocre photographic portraits to represent us, we find they not only corrupt memory, they also have a troubling power to distort character and mislead posterity. Catch a person in an awkward moment, in a pose or expression that none of his friends would recognize, and this one mendacious photograph may well outlive all corrective testimony; people will study it for clues to the subject's character long after the death of the last person who could have told them how untrue it is.

When only one photograph survives, its authority is unimpeachable, and we are in the position of jurors who have to decide a case based on one witness's unchallenged testimony. Within my own attic archives, I can think of a picture that, if it were the only surviving photograph of me, might provoke some descendant to write: "She was a pinched, humorless woman, evidently incapable of enjoying any worldly pleasures. It is tempting to think that the beauty celebrated in the photographs she took was a means of externalizing the rapture and wonder she obviously could not feel within herself."

The power of any one photograph to falsify a person's character is, of course, diminished by the evidence contained in every other surviving photograph of that person. It would be an interesting exercise to determine if there's some threshold number of photographs that would guarantee, when studied together so that signature expressions were revealed and uncharacteristic gestures isolated, a reasonably accurate sense of how a person appeared to those who knew him.

But since we have just this one picture of Henry Munger, we have no way of knowing if it's a distortion or true to life. Studying it, I resist the impulse to make assumptions based on a fraction of a second snatched from time, perhaps the same second that a slight gassy sensation troubled his lower bowel. So, despite his crabbed countenance and the sense of prerogative he displays as he rides behind that joyless rickshaw hauler, I must take into account evidence of his character derived from other sources. Henry Munger was lauded at his death for his "modest and unpretentious" generosity, and in an even more important endorsement, my great-grandfather, Robert Munger, appears to have loved and respected his father, working devotedly for him in the Rutersville mill.

Early on, Henry Munger gave Robert the job of driving the oxen that pulled the logs bound for the sawmill. The *Birmingham News* reported that at nine years of age he drove that oxen team nearly seven hundred miles by himself through the sparsely settled and dangerous Texas outback. Can this really be true? At nine? Seven hundred miles?

Apparently it was, because later in life, Robert Munger made frequent mention of that trip, and especially what must have been the scariest part: sleeping out in the chaparral alone, with only his father's overcoat for warmth while "blood-thirsty marauding bands, insanely cruel, murdering and robbing" passed near him.

With such a brave and capable son becoming more indispensable on the farm each year, it must have been difficult for Henry Munger to spare Robert after he was accepted at Trinity University in Tehuacana, Texas, 150 miles away. Indeed, after only two years of college, where his son proved to be an excellent student in Latin and law, Henry urgently called Robert back to the farm, rewarding him with the cotton gin to manage as his own. He was just twenty years old.

Robert Munger was not a tall or physically imposing man, but every image I have shows him as strong and lean, even ascetic in appearance, much like my father. Raised under what were clearly physically tough conditions, he was self-reliant, courageous, competent, and, most of all, a hard worker.

He expressed his belief in the importance of hard work as a character-building expedient in somewhat pettish terms much later in his life in a letter to his sons that I found among my father's papers. (My daughter Virginia says that when she read this letter she was further convinced of genetic determinism, so strongly did it remind her of my voice lodged in her head.)

When he wrote this letter, Robert Munger was sixty-five and one of the most successful entrepreneurs and inventors in the South (we'll get to that). It's handwritten in elegant script on hotel stationery from a resort in Ormond Beach, Florida, where he and his wife, Mary, were spending the winter of 1919. Interestingly, he addresses the letter to just three of his four sons, those three he clearly believed were ungrateful idlers. The excluded son, I am pleased to report, was my grandfather, his eldest son, Collett Henry.

He begins by pointedly noting that he has received letters from almost everyone else in the family except the three sons, and he especially commends the four virtuous daughters. Then my great-grandfather describes an encounter on the links:

> We played just behind Mr. John D. Rockefeller this morn. And at the end of 9 holes he stopped and came back and was very cordial and sociable, and chatted with us quite a bit about Birmingham, business, etc. . . . As I told him good bye, I asked him if he knew he was a tenant of mine; I told him he was about the Best paying tenant I had, but I did not tell him his representative worked to his interests so well that he not only got it all back but <u>some more beside.</u> I'll tell him that next time . . .

Apparently leisure time didn't agree with Munger. He comes across in the letter as fretful and remarks that it is hard not to think about the work he has left behind. That provides him with the perfect lead-in to the point of the letter: He lays into those three slacker boys, Robley, Lonnie, and Eugene:

> We, Mama and I, feel like we can and should get away from home now . . . to regain some of the youth and vigor that we have lost in thinking and worrying over our children's affairs . . . and we are hop-

ing and looking forward to the time soon when they will do <u>something for us</u>, instead of our working or worrying over them—

We can then direct our energies into channels more for the good of our Community, our Country and our Church and in fact the wide world—Even while away down here we see opportunities and think of the great good we could do if we could just turn ourselves loose for the rest of our lives—

The agitated letter writer continues, contrasting himself, his own boundless drive and creativity, with the trifling trio who apparently have none of his ambition. He reminds them of how lucky they are to be inheriting the successful business he has established by dint of inventive genius and <u>hard work</u> (emphasis his) and of their responsibility to maintain its upward trajectory.

Papa Munger is seriously worked up by this time, eight pages into it, and his handwriting, which was restrained at the start, sprawls across the page, expanding and tightening in sync with his feelings.

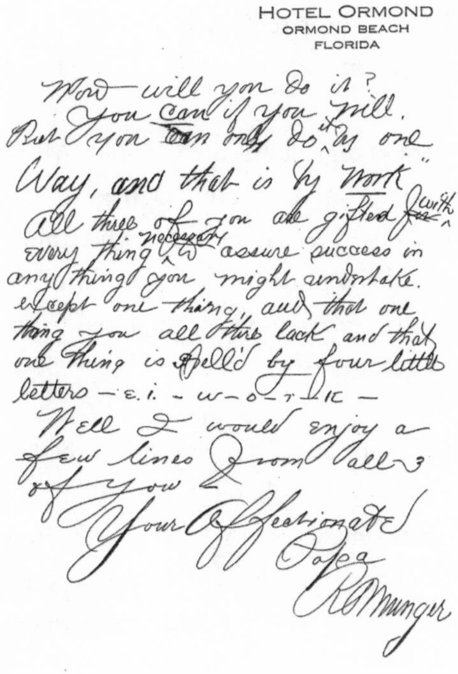

HOTEL ORMOND
ORMOND BEACH
FLORIDA

He continues with his exhortations:

> Now will you do it?
>
> You <u>can</u> if you will. But you can only do it by one way, and that is by **<u>Work</u>**.
>
> All three of you are gifted with everything necessary to assure success in anything you might undertake except one thing, and that one thing you all three lack and that one thing is spelled by four little letters—e.i.—**W-O-R-K**—
>
> Well I would enjoy a few lines from all of you—
>
> Your Affectionate Papa
R. Munger

His father, Henry, certainly never had to spell out those four particular letters—**W-O-R-K**—for "R. Munger." This good son, despite having been yanked out of the college he adored and recalled to the hinterland farm, proved to be a dedicated worker at his new cotton-ginning business. More significantly, the thwarted Latin scholar proved to be a brilliant business manager and, important for this narrative, unusually compassionate and empathetic.

Choosing to work alongside his men, Robert Munger learned the ginning process from the ground up. He began as an understudy to the lowliest among the workers, the "basket boys" who unloaded the cotton bags brought from the fields by mule-drawn carts. Straining under the weight of the bulging bags, these youngsters staggered to the feeder bins where they upended the bags and were rewarded by great mushrooming clouds of debris.

Once the dust settled, burly bin workers rushed in to press down the billowing mounds of cotton by hand, faces averted against the spumes of dust. The basket boys scuttled at their feet, gathering up lint cotton that had spilled on the floor, dumping it by the armload into the feeder boxes. Once the cotton was subdued, the feeder boxes were carried to the huge press box.

When the press box was packed full, the strong-thighed press men jumped in and began wadding and stomping down the buoyant cotton with their bare feet, sinking deep into the cumulate mound, often lost from view until, by dint of their furiously pumping legs, they gradually rose up through the suffocating mass into the turbid air that at last afforded their lungs some relief.

The mounting clouds of lint and dust that arose from the force of their effort coated everything in the pressroom and beyond, and over time coalesced into racemes gently swaying from the rafters and beams, drifting down to brush the passing faces with spidery tendrils—Miss Havisham's living room writ large. All the workers, despite wrapping their faces with moistened kerchiefs, coughed constantly and their eyes wept. The mortality rate was unavoidably troubling.

As it happened, despite being a pretty tough kid, Robert Munger himself had some pulmonary ailments, and when he began working in the gin, his health suffered along with that of his workers. Wheezing and coughing after work, he and his clever bride, Mary, whom he had married in 1878, began to speculate about a closed, mechanized ginning system that would minimize exposure to cotton dust. Although neither had any education in engineering or design, they bent to the task of realizing this concept, drawing by hand specifications for the complex mechanical operation they envisaged.

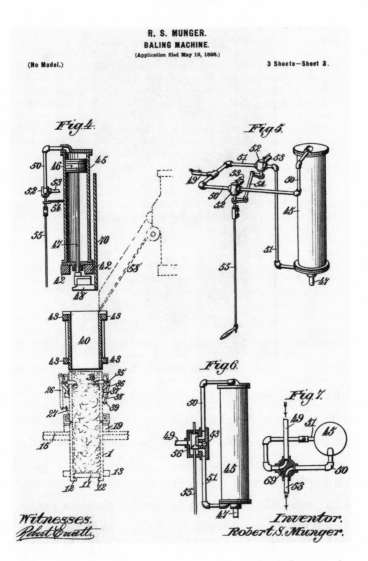

Reading accounts of this inventive charrette, which frequently required most of the night, I am struck by the parity and harmony in which they worked. Theirs was a remarkably modern and happy marriage, and Robert Munger's courtship letters from 1877 express an uncommon, almost instant, connection between them. Even more apparent in those courtship letters is his respect for Mary's impressive intelligence. She wasn't all that beautiful by the standards of the time, at least not in this view, which I found in the Birmingham archive.

But, take a look at this: see the photographer's address at the bottom of the picture? Staunton, Virginia. Thirty-five miles from where I live, Staunton is the nearest city to the north of our farm. How on earth did my great-grandmother, a teenage girl from Fairfield, Texas, get all the way to my backyard in 1875 to have her picture taken? And why?

Turns out, to attend a Staunton finishing school, the Augusta Female Seminary, and it seems to have worked: the next picture I found of her, taken back home in Texas at the time of her wedding to Robert Munger, shows a woman with considerably more polish. But there's still not a lot more in this picture of what were then considered the indicia of feminine beauty: pliancy, refined features, and a delicate, shy gaze. To the contrary, Mary has an almost masculine heft, her features are somewhat coarse, and there is a stubborn set to her jaw. She is a formidable woman.

In an interview years later, Robert Munger spoke of her as his indispensable helpmate and of her encouragement as essential to his success:

> She has always been my greatest inspiration. She has helped me and . . .
> been right with me through it all. She would stay up just as late as I
> did, and she always was up and fully dressed, no matter how early I
> had to leave in the morning to get to work. She would see that I had
> something to eat and [would give me] a hearty, cheerful send-off,
> and I didn't carry away with me any recollections of her in a kimono,
> either. She was as ready for the trials of the day as I was.

Apparently she was up to those trials, and together, in 1879, Robert and Mary Munger finished designing the improvements that were to revolutionize the process of ginning cotton and make them multimillionaires. He, or they, had designed a system by which the cotton, upon arrival at the gin, could be transported by pneumatic suction from the bins, sparing the half dozen or so workers from having to gather it up and carry it by hand. The cotton was filtered while being sucked up from the bin, cleaned of dust and trash, and delivered by a spiked belt to a battery of feeders. After passing through a more refined lint flue and primary compressor, it was then fed in a continuous batt along the moving belt to the mechanical press box for baling. No more basket boys. No more gasping, half-suffocated cotton stompers. No more Miss Havisham-y racemes.

In this clean and efficient process, the cotton passed from the wagon to the bale in one automated operation, requiring only a few men to run the machines rather than the eighteen needed earlier.

1900 Type Munger System Ginning Outfit with Vacuum Box and Belt Distributor Elevator

Obviously these refinements were gratifying from a humanitarian point of view, but, from a businessman's bottom-line perspective, they were momentous. Not only did they produce significantly cleaner cotton, but they also upped the plant's production by a peachy 25 percent. As the business grew, the expanding operation provided different, and safer, jobs for the workers displaced by the new technology. Robert Munger clearly was doing very well by doing good.

After working out the glitches in the new invention at his own little Rutersville gin,

Munger moved the whole burgeoning operation to Mexia, Texas. He patented his Munger Ginning System, and then spent four frustrating years peddling it to existing gin manufacturers. Inexplicably, none wanted to adopt and produce it, so, in 1884, at the age of thirty, he and Mary went back to the drawing board and designed the means of production for the equipment they had invented. Munger then borrowed money, found land in Dallas, built a large factory, and began manufacturing the Munger System himself.

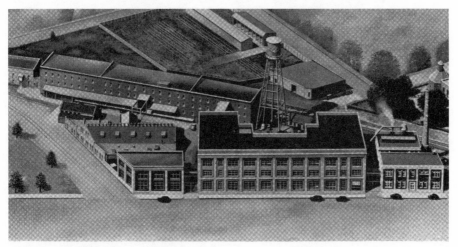

MUNGER IMPROVED COTTON MACHINE MANUFACTURING COMPANY FACTORY, DALLAS, TEXAS

By printing beautifully designed catalogs,

and going all-out on advertising,

The above is from a photograph of car which was loaded at Dallas, Texas, November 13, 1900, with Munger Compressed bales. Note that the car is *not entirely filled*, yet it contains 144 bales weighing 76,256 lbs. The distance left between the rows of bales on floor of car was 7 feet 7 inches, in which space 25 to 30 additional bales could easily have been loaded.

he was rewarded with rapid commercial success. Within a few years, his factory was so profitable that he sought a location for a second large plant in Birmingham, Alabama, strategically east of the Mississippi. Merging his company with several other regional ginning concerns, he formed the Continental Gin Company and moved the family from Dallas to Birmingham in 1892.

With the little Rutersville ginning shack still visible in his rearview mirror, Robert Munger's Continental Gin Company was soon operating six booming factories, with showrooms throughout the world and assets of well over $116 million (in today's dollars).

At the age of forty, just twenty years after taking over his father's gin, Robert Munger

was an extraordinarily successful and rich man. But it is satisfying to note that when I went looking for him in the pages of history, his abiding reputation is not as an inventor and wealthy businessman but rather as a humanitarian and philanthropist.

By all accounts, he genuinely cared for people, was unfailingly kind and courteous, and "his generosity knew no bounds." Much of my information about my great-grandfather comes from his obituaries, where, in an extensive front-page article in the *Birmingham News*, he was described as "a gentle, sweet soul whom neither applause nor riches puffed up. He never behaved himself unseemly." The same article stated:

Munger looked up to no man, and he looked down upon none. . . . He did not overlook the Negroes and he numbered his friends among the Negro race by the hundreds. There isn't a Negro church in Birmingham to which he has not contributed . . . and the Negro schools of the area have always found a ready response when appealing to Mr. Munger for funds. He also gave of his time and counsel.

In that era, how many prominent society figures could have had that written about them, or, more importantly, *would* have?

Apparently, those "friends among the Negro race" did not hesitate to express their reciprocal feelings for both Robert and Mary. When Mary died in 1924, within a year of Robert Munger's death, the following was received and published by the *Birmingham News:*

Tribute by a Colored Preacher

Please allow me the space in your paper to say a few words in regard of the beautiful life of Mrs. Robert S. Munger. . . . I feel that death has removed from Birmingham one of the greatest sympathizers with unfortunate humanity that ever lived in our city.

Very much like that of her late husband, she possessed a heart of sympathy for the poor, irrespective of color or creed. I feel safe in saying that there is not a church or institution of learning among the people of my race in Birmingham that these sainted hands have not aided and . . . thousands of colored people in Birmingham . . . are sorrowing with you in the loss of one who has done so much in the work of charity.

Rev. W. H. Hunt

In the same way that I was ignorant of the pathos and peculiarities in my mother's past, I knew almost nothing about my great-grandfather Robert S. Munger until I began digging around in those boxes in the attic. I had no concept, for example, of the magnitude of his wealth. Whatever had trickled down to my father had been soaked up in land, art, cars, education, exotic trees, and the trappings of a funky-charming southern existence by the time my parents died. I had known Munger was an innovator, something about cotton ginning, but had no idea of the originality and significance of his inventions. On the wall of my father's study hung pictures of him sitting proudly at the wheel of some old jalopy but, again, I had only the sketchiest notion of his involvement with the automobile. That a few buildings had been named for him I was perhaps aware, and I'd seen the gold and silver medals with his name engraved on them, but I knew nothing of the extent of his philanthropy.

Since I was deep in this search, I began to wonder what racial skeletons hung in the closets of that deeply southern side of the family, especially given the timing of Henry Munger's move to Texas. I had rested comfortably on the assumption that the Mungers, coming to America when they did, were Puritans hoping, as Garrison Keillor put it, to repress themselves here more than was legally possible at home. Often in New England families, Puritan origins foreshadowed a noble commitment later in the nineteenth century to abolitionism: that is the upside of the Puritan heritage.

But here the Mungers appear to have gone off-track. Henry Munger moved to Texas in the early 1850s, and it was not the repression of the self, but the enslavement of others that usually motivated such a migration of gringos to Texas in those years. The Texas Republic, whose constitution expressed an overheated enthusiasm for America's peculiar institution, had been created in 1836 in part as a way for slave-owners to keep their human property by effectively seceding from Mexico where slavery was illegal.

These are well-known facts, except possibly in Texas, and they only increased my trepidation as I headed south in the summer of 2011 to find out what I could about my southern ancestors. My mother's Boston side was pristine (in that respect, anyway), and, of course, it was also on the right side of Civil War history. But I feared the worst from Alabama and Texas.

I found it in a sad and provocative letter preserved in the storage chest of my ninety-three-year-old Birmingham relative. In this handwritten letter, J. H. Collett of Fairfield, Texas, the same seemingly open-minded man who had sent his daughter Mary 1,210 miles to be educated in Staunton, Virginia, describes to a cousin in Tennessee the purchase and resale of slaves:

An unusual case happened in the purchase of a family of six Negroes, a man and his wife and four children, age respectively from 12 to 21 years.

The owner came to town one afternoon and told me he wanted to sell the Negroes. I told him I did not have money to pay for them, and he told me that made no difference, and he asked me to go home with him and stay all night. I went.

The Negroes' cabin was some distance from the dwelling house and he suggested that we go by it and see the Negroes. When we got to the cabin the Negroes were eating their supper and he told them to all come out, that he had brought me there to buy them. The Negro woman said:

"Marse Jackson, that man is not able to buy one of us. I heard that a few years ago he came to Springfield with his pack on his back."

The owner called their names and their respective ages, and I made a memorandum in a little book that I had and put opposite each name my estimate of price. The owner saw my figures; it was a total of $5,000. Without hesitation he said, "that's alright."

When supper was over I wrote a bill of sale and he signed it. I then gave him my note for the $5,000 payable on demand. Next morning he had the Negroes loaded up in a wagon and they got to Fairfield before I did. And in a day or two I sold them to a man in our town for $6000.

I learned later why he sold them. His wife did not like the way he treated . . .

And at that cliff-hanging ellipsis the letter stops, leaving little doubt as to the sorry end of the almost certainly damning sentence. The remaining pages are lost to time—or to the editing instincts of a relative who thought they sullied the archive.

So, there it is: my great-great-grandfather, starting out with only the "pack on his back," bettered himself by buying and selling slaves. And it would be naïve to think those workers in Henry Munger's Texas gin were anything but slaves, hauling the bundles, stomping the cotton, and dying of the dust. Since he was eleven when the Civil War ended, Robert Munger himself never owned slaves, but I have often wondered whether his munificence to black churches and charities possibly sprang from guilt over his family's slave-owning past. As a child, having worked closely with his father's slaves, especially, one might assume, his contemporaries the basket boys, he surely saw them work until they dropped dead. This, it seems to me, might provide an impressive psychological explanation for Robert Munger's later generosity to African American causes.

However it came about, the compassion that provoked Munger's inventive successes continued well beyond his lung-saving cotton gin improvements. Early on, with an initial gift of more than $250,000, he established the Munger Benevolent Fund to be held in trust for the benefit of his factory employees in the case of sickness, injury, or death. In Gilded Age America, the era of the robber barons, this was an unusually progressive gesture. In other ways as well he was remarkably ahead of his time, especially in the respect he paid his wife. Munger's countless donations to charitable causes were always presented as gifts from both him and Mrs. Munger, extending into philanthropy the inclusive and respectful spirit that marked their marriage in so many ways.

This generous impulse came to the fore when, in 1921, Munger was awarded the *Birmingham News* Loving Cup, a very big deal back then, for distinguished and unselfish service in the South. The formal presentation was held at Birmingham's First Methodist Church, which was filled to capacity. In fact, the newspaper reported that as many as seven thousand people were turned away when the sanctuary was filled and the doors closed.

A reporter interviewed one woman as she stood weeping before the barred door. She told him between sobs that she had come all the way from Ensley (then a thriving industrial city outside Birmingham) to see Munger get the Loving Cup, and he quoted her entreaty in the paper: "He helped my son. He helped him when he needed help. I must get in: it means more to me than it does to you, or to the others."

Banging on the doors, the reporter interceded on her behalf, and the woman was admitted.

The newspaper printed several of the speeches lauding Robert Munger, and a description in one of them by a Mr. Stallings particularly caught my eye, for it might just as easily have been said about his grandson, my father:

> He is unobtrusive in his daily life, but a man of tremendous, quiet force, of broad sympathies and understanding, unassuming and genuinely anxious to benefit others. . . . In the carriage of his body there is a quiet pride, a feeling not of vanity but of instinctive power. He is a man of purity, warm affection, simplicity of manner and courtesy, singularly graceful and dignified.

At the conclusion of the speechifying, in front of the cheering (and weeping, it was reported) crowd, Munger accepted the trophy with "modest demeanor, halting speech and evident humility." He spoke briefly and then, to everyone's surprise, he stepped off the platform and over the chancel rail into the audience, stopping next to Mary. He spoke again to the hushed audience:

> There is one in this room . . . who has stood by me all these years, has been a true and devoted help, and inspiration, one who has never uttered a cross word to me, one who has aided and approved every impulse for good that I have entertained.

He handed her the impressive silver cup, kissed her, and sat down. The next day, he delivered the cup to a local jeweler with instructions for it to be inscribed with her name.

In my own marital experience, money has caused the most friction between Larry and me, but clearly this was not the case with Robert and Mary. Munger so trusted and respected Mary that, at his death in 1923, he left a fund in excess of $3 million for her to distribute to charities in her own name. He himself left much of his estate (estimated by the newspapers at the time to have been as great as $52 million, more than enough, it was said, to burn a wet mule) to be distributed to charity anonymously as well as in their joint names.

In fact, in going over his will and his meticulously handwritten accounts, it is obvious that far more money went to charity than to his children, though each child, as well as grandchildren (among them, my father) and step-grandchildren, got a generous plenty.

His will stipulated that, as with bequests made during his lifetime, his money should go to educational institutions, orphanages, homes for the blind, the fledgling YMCA, and various churches in the area, including, it was pointedly noted in the paper, "many Negro Churches."

In light of all of this, it seems odd that Robert Munger, a prosperous, fulfilled and enlightened man, devoted to his wife, and with every reason to enjoy the sleep of the virtuous, should be afflicted with debilitating insomnia. But apparently he was.

Mary blamed it on his excessively active brain, and there's no reason to doubt her. When his first Birmingham home, the Mirabeau Swanson house,

proved to be too close to the noisy traffic circle at Five Points Road for the delicate sleeper, he had the huge house placed on rollers and moved to a quieter location behind St. Mary's Episcopal Church.

But even there he found no rest, and in 1902 he retreated further into the countryside, purchasing a handsome Greek revival antebellum home known as Arlington. Thirty-seven years before, just twelve days before Robert E. Lee's surrender, the downstairs library of this home had been used by the Union Gen. James H. Wilson to draw up plans for the destruction of the nearby Oxmoor and Irondale furnaces.

This depiction by artist Max Heldman suggests that the house, then owned by Judge William Mudd, was commandeered by Wilson, and the caption below it asserts that Wilson's men "rolled the barrels of peach and apple brandy from among the cobwebs into the light of day," delightedly polishing them off.

However, a little research reveals a fact generally suppressed in accounts of Wilson's raid, which is that Arlington's owner, Judge Mudd, was a Union sympathizer. In fact, upon their arrival, Wilson and his men found the doors to Arlington thrown open to them and the hospitality gracious, but because Judge Mudd was a teetotaler I'm betting the brandy did not flow as described. Still, Mudd's Union complicity goes a long way toward explaining why Arlington was spared the grievous destruction Wilson's Raiders subsequently wrought on the surrounding communities.

It was not spared from ruin for long, however; almost immediately after the war Arlington fell on hard times. Having changed hands several times, its original 475 acres were whittled by subdivision down to 33. By the time my great-grandfather purchased it for the not insubstantial sum of $12,300 (more than $300,000 in today's dollars), it had been hard-used as a boardinghouse for fourteen years, then, sitting empty, had fallen into the poignant ruin of neglect.

With a solicitude verging on tenderness, Robert Munger dedicated himself to renovating this fallen beauty.

This took some doing, and letters from his foreman, Ed Norton, provide a depressingly predictable account of the rotted sills in the windows, failed column bases, the necessary steel beams for the listing portico, extensive lengths of copper guttering to replace the rusted drainage system, and the dire condition of the oak flooring damaged by heavy boots, including those of the Union soldiers.

In time, Norton got the basic structure stabilized and went to work on the details, tearing off the crumbling plaster from the lathing, running pipes for indoor plumbing, and replacing gaslights with electric fixtures. He reopened the fireplaces, and he and Munger figured out a way to send steam heat to the house through underground pipes from a boiler in an outbuilding. (This system is, in fact, close to the one we have here on the farm, although we, more primitively than the Mungers, use wood to fire the boiler.) Once the place was lit and heated, Mary jumped in, hanging curtains ceiling to floor, unpacking the Wedgwood china, polishing up the extensive silver services, and installing an enormous, multipaneled dining table for the family meals.

I'm not sure who is the most imposing of the three figures in this image of the finished living room.

The grounds required extensive improvements, and Munger hired the firm of Frederick Law Olmsted to design and plant a gracious pecan grove, the still-impressive remnants of which I walked through in 2011.

He leveled ground and built tennis courts . . .

and dammed a nearby creek, excavating a pond for swimming.

Then, dusting off the rollers he had used for the Mirabeau Swanson house, Munger moved two buildings to Arlington from across the road. The first he converted into a sun parlor and living quarters for the house servants. The second he made into a multicar garage.

Wait. A multicar garage in 1902?

Yes, a garage . . . because, in addition to his business, family, philanthropic, church, and community-related pursuits, Robert Munger's real passion was the wheel.

It started with bicycles.

Bicycling was, of course, a popular pastime at the turn of the century and central to a whole quasi-scientific cult of physical and moral health, but for Munger it was much more than that. He was big on sports in general: he and his family rode horses, played tennis, swam, hiked, and even boxed.

How he managed this I do not know, but, before they reached the age of two, Munger made sure every one of his children knew how to ride a bike. The child in the lower left of this picture, appearing to chat amiably with her older sibling as she pedals along,

is Margaret Munger, at *eighteen months old*.

So passionate was Munger about his family's two-wheeled adventures that all the children had special biking outfits

and bikes for the littlest children were custom-made, often in Europe.

I found no indication that his wife, Mary, who seems an even more unlikely bike rider than an eighteen-month-old, participated in this sport, but Robert Munger was often seen biking around Birmingham, dressed in a coat, tie, and hat, with his eight children, in order of size, pedaling behind him.

So it's easy to imagine the allure of the automobile for my two-wheeling great-grandfather when the first cars became commercially available at the turn of the century. Munger took his family with him from Birmingham to New York to buy their first car, a Winton, in 1902. The morning he took possession of it, he proudly took them all out for a little spin . . . *to Philadelphia.*

It took twelve hours.

Delighted, they motored back to New York and the next day headed out to Boston, twice as far. This trip, however, was not so much fun. They got a flat halfway there and discovered they had no jack. Ever the problem solver, Munger made a fulcrum of rocks and, grabbing up a rail from the side of the road, jammed one end under the car. He then placed his substantial wife at the far end while he and the boys repaired the tube. After this, he always carried a jack and a pick and shovel to smooth out the roads.

The inconvenience and the mess did not deter Munger, and the next year he bought three more cars: a 14-horsepower Packard, a 24-horsepower Packard, and a 1903 Winton. In short order, as motoring replaced bicycling as the primary family activity, the outfits became more extravagant and even the cars were decorated on occasion.

Not taking any chances on being incommoded if a chain broke or a tire was punctured,

Munger prudently insisted upon a horse-and-buggy backup that traveled a discreet distance behind the car parade.

Thus protected from breakdowns and loaded with picnic baskets, the family would head out of Birmingham in a caravan to a farm that Munger had purchased about nine miles out of town. Those nine miles took half a day to cover because, as his children reported many years later, each time they met a farmer on the road the whole line of cars had to stop. The chary horses were coaxed around the silent cars, and the curious children and adults were obliged a look at the cooling engines. Many Birminghamians reported that these encounters provided them their first automobile ride.

Apparently, four cars weren't enough, because the next summer, in July 1904, Munger and much of his family sailed to London, staying at the Midland Grand Hotel while the arrangements were finalized to purchase one more car, a French Panhard et Levassor. (Upon reflection, I realize that this may be the origin of my own family's long bedevilment by foreign cars—for example, after each unpatchable puncture the tires for this Panhard had to be imported from France. Because of its curious lack of a generator, the foreign-made battery would frequently run down, and Munger, in a risky maneuver, would insert platinum tubes into the combustion chambers and heat them with a blowtorch to fire the gas charge. *Wouldn't a Ford have been simpler?* This exasperated rhetorical question has echoed down the generations, right into my own.)

When the new car was delivered to the front of the hotel it caused such a commotion that police had to be called to control the crowds. Once the family got past the hullabaloo at the hotel steps, they began a 2,000-mile tour through England, Belgium, France, and Switzerland.

Apparently, everything went fine until, crossing the Alps into Switzerland, the brakes overheated and failed.

Without panicking, Munger put the car in the lowest gear and alternated between using the compression of the engine and the hot brakes to reduce the speed. But, wouldn't you know, in the nonconforming Panhard, the brake and clutch pedal had a peculiar relationship, and, unlike with most cars, using a lower gear ratio did not slow it. Consequently, as the Panhard gathered speed, Munger had no choice but to run the new car cattywompus into the side of the mountain.

All cars of that era were designed with a wooden door at the back of the car for entering the rear seating area, rather than doors on the side. The rear door had an interior seat hinged on it, and, once the door was closed, the seat was lowered for the unlucky occupant. Apparently on that particular day Mary had drawn the short straw and was sitting in the rear door seat when the Panhard hit the mountain and spun around, jamming the back door and trapping her in the car.

A rather large woman even in her youth, Mary in her later years had become even more ample, and it took most of the day to release her from the back of the car. The contemporaneous report from her son was that she was not at all amused.

So how cosmically coincident is it that later that week on the boat crossing back to London, Robert Munger happened to meet a buggy and car chassis designer? Naturally, he asked this Mr. Mullinax, a Frenchman, to help him remedy what was clearly bad automotive design. There on the bobbing boat, drawing on paper pressed down hard against the Channel winds, the two men designed a car chassis with side-entrance doors to the rear seat and a body made of steel rather than wood.

Once the designs were finalized, Munger bought a second Panhard and had the car shipped to London, where the original body was stripped off and the new, steel Munger/Mullinax-designed side-door body was attached to the chassis. When it was complete, the refitted Panhard was sent to New York City, where it was exhibited at the Waldorf so that American manufacturers could see and study the innovations.

Nothing in my research indicates that Munger patented this idea or realized any financial gain from it, but I suspect that the promise of a safer vehicle for his family, and the families of the future, was enough for the already abundantly wealthy man.

In an ironic twist, as he drove the new Panhard out of New York City after the Waldorf display, Robert Munger was given a speeding ticket by a New York City policeman on a bicycle.

⸻

Fifty-eight years later, it was a Florida policeman in a black Chevrolet who tried his damnedest to continue the tradition of ticketing car-crazy

Mungers. Only this time, in the 1960s, it was my lead-footed father the cop was pursuing. He and I had driven to Florida to a car race, where Daddy had thought it important for me to shake the hand of some dashing British driver, Stirling Moss or Graham Hill, I forget now.

It's true that taking a daughter to a car race was unusual, but one thing in our family was for sure: this Robert Munger's daughter wasn't going to be a milquetoast driver. Daddy had no patience, for example, with my mother's automotive timidity. She hadn't gotten her license until she was thirty-six and had never quite mastered the accelerator-clutch relationship. No, his daughter was going to know how to accelerate through corners, correct an incipient drift, downshift using toe and heel, and make an emergency stop, the one we practiced the most.

Driving lessons with Daddy were excruciating. We'd head out after dinner from our rural home, and without fail he would direct me toward Sellers Avenue, the street where the cool town kids hung out on the tree-shaded front yards. When we turned onto Sellers, he'd tell me to downshift and accelerate well past the speed limit. Then, as we roared toward the cluster of my school peers, he'd shout "EMERGENCY STOP!" and expect me to slam on the brakes with force appropriate to avoid hitting a caroming toddler.

I had no choice in this: if I didn't do it correctly, he wouldn't let me drive. I so passionately wanted to get my permit, which back then you could do at age fourteen, that I was willing to suffer the ridicule of the kids I most wanted to be my friends. Each time he yelled, I stomped the brake into the floorboards of the car, which screeched to a smoking halt while the hula hoops dropped to the ankles of my dumbfounded, yearned-for friends. Then while they watched, I would coax the gas back into the recalcitrant and famously tetchy carburetor of the time, and we would lurch up Sellers toward the Clover Creamery and his next demonic test.

The trip to Florida happened long before I even had my learner's permit, and we made it in his brand-new car, a creamy white Aston Martin DB-4. He had picked it up in England along with an orange marmalade appeasement for my irate mother and a blue Pringle cashmere sweater for me that was so soft it invited my grade school teachers to pet me like an animal.

The purchase of the Aston caused a significant disruption in my parents' marriage, which a friend once likened to a building in which a crucial foundation stone was really two powerful magnets with the wrong ends pressed together, the marital edifice held together by the pressure of the surrounding brickwork: the family, the land. My frugal mother objected to the expense, the ostentation, and the unilateral nature of the purchase, and my father's response to her upset was to ignore it. When my mother pressed home to him the financial consequences of buying such a car, his solution was to noisily replace the two measured ounces of good whiskey he drank every evening with tall glasses of weak iced tea. By his arithmetic if he did that for the rest of his statistically probable life, he would pay for his half of the car. My mother gave up.

The Florida races were hot and boring, and we stayed in a motor court that Humbert Humbert would have found too squalid. Each evening Daddy would rummage in his plaid suitcase and, from underneath the tin of tooth powder, bring out a flat, clear-glass bottle labeled conspicuously in his blockiest handwriting "HAIR TONIC." He would then pour himself a few brown ounces of the "tonic" in the motel's calcium-crusted glass and we'd sit out on the concrete slab breathing in the heavy scent of the citrus blooms and watching the lizards skitter around in the underbrush. Recently I found prints from the roll of film he shot while we were there and among them is not one image of anything but distant cars, blurry with heat and speed, racing around the track.

Nothing of me, of us, of the lizards, or the sleazy motel—not even one of me shaking the hand of whichever Brit it was on the rainbow-hued, oil-slick tarmac, all of which, in the patchy way of memory, I can remember. This offers further evidence that my theory about photographs stealing or, at the least, diminishing memories might be correct; those moments with their fragmentary but vivid details and smells and tastes are available to me because there are no photographic images of them. The only thing I can't particularly remember is the cars speeding by.

As we ourselves were speeding back from the races in the Aston Martin, my father noticed a Florida state trooper in the rearview mirror, the half-moon light on the roof of his car flashing crimson. Naturally, he floored it.

The power of the acceleration flattened me to the seat, but I didn't let on what a thrill this gave me. Staring impassively straight ahead, I could see out of the corner of my eye a drop of sweat hover at the tip of my father's intent, pointy nose as the needle went deep into the red part on the speedometer, pegging at 140, the limit. He went faster.

The minute he crossed the state line into Georgia, my father slowed, watching the mirror until the trooper hove into view, his panting Chevy shimmering in the heat coming off the pavement. Pulling to the side of the road, Daddy casually reached down with his left hand to pop open the bonnet, climbed out, and had a long, companionable visit with the trooper while they admired the six-inline cylinders under the hood. After a time, they shook hands; the trooper replaced his hat and returned to his jurisdiction. We continued home, hightailing it through the Georgia pine forests, my heart heavy with the secret of my father's impish illegality that I was instructed to keep from my mother.

Sometime later my car-challenged mother, mistaking reverse for first gear, gunned the Jeep into the rear of the Aston Martin and then doubly insulted it by insisting on having it repainted a Wedgwood blue that reminded her of their wedding china. On those days when he let me practice driving the Aston, the pleasure of the red leather seats, the throaty roar of the engine, the extraordinary handling through the corners, and the shiny wood veneer of the dash were diminished, heart-sinkingly, when I looked out across the now-blue bonnet.

—✦—

Here again, you can't tell me that genes don't matter. The elder Robert Munger sent his car passion sprinting along the DNA pathways, tossing the baton over the head of his relatively car-indifferent son (my grandfather Collett Henry) into my father's uplifted, eager hand and then into mine, similarly receptive.

It was not just the car thing: Daddy was such a perfect replica of his grandfather that he hardly needed that lackluster genetic vehicle, his father, Collett Henry. In every respect—appearance, intelligence, rectitude, compassion, imagination, and drive—Daddy was a veritable clone of his grandfather, another example of the Immaculate Re-Conception, however reproductively impossible.

There were two unique and formative things that he didn't get from his grandfather: his passion for art and his lifelong fascination with death.

Those were sui generis.

18

Leaving Dallas

Nothing about my father's privileged Dallas childhood would seem likely to have instilled in him this obsessive "death thing," as my perplexed mother used to call it. In fact, his was about as idyllic a childhood as any boy ever had.

Remember that page of sums that Robert Munger I wrote out, listing the inheritance for each child? You might have noticed that Collett Henry, his firstborn son, my father's father, appeared to get more cash than any of the others, $83,600 (a bit more than a million dollars today). Remember also the Ormond Beach letter in which Robert Munger stated that the other three sons didn't deserve to inherit much, being unfamiliar with the concept of **W-O-R-K**?

So it would seem that my grandpa Collett Henry was a go-getter, having decamped from Birmingham at a young age to set up a real estate business in Dallas, where the Munger name already had conjuring power. His uncle, Steven I. Munger, had stayed in Dallas to run that part of the gin business when the company headquarters moved to Birmingham and had become a prominent figure in Dallas society. When Collett joined him there, he found a spectacularly boisterous city on the make, full of gifted hicks like himself, newly minted as oil barons or captains of industry.

Naturally he was regarded as a most desirable catch among the Dallas debs, and so it must have thrilled the innkeeping Dumas family of Paris, Tennessee, and all of little Paris, when he married eighteen-year-old Irma Dumas in 1902. His wealth was ostentatiously noted in the *Paris Post-Intelligencer* account of the wedding, right after a description of the bride as exemplifying "the type of young womanhood that will grace and bless the home to which she goes."

Indeed, Irma (known as "Pan," short for pandemonium) soon graced and blessed the household with two healthy boys. The first was Collett Henry Jr., an affable good ol' boy who once, when I was on the way to Mexico during the July 1969 heat wave, invited me to his house in Dallas and cranked up the air-conditioning until the roaring fire he'd built in the fireplace became a necessity. The second was Robert Sylvester Munger, my father.

Daddy was cared for in his first two years by "Mammie" (yes, I swear)

and, when Mammie died, which by the looks of it was probably not so long after this picture was taken, by Hattie, until, at age fourteen, he left for the Choate School.

348

When he used to speak of Hattie, it was with clear emotion, a rare thing for my father. I am reasonably sure that he, many years ago, must have experienced the same harrowing heart-wrench that I recently did when I discovered that Hattie had left a hundred one-dollar bills folded into her will for the fair-haired child, my wealthy father, whom she had raised and clearly loved. Under the circumstances of the time, that number of dollars probably took her almost as many years to earn.

Hattie was not the only one who loved my father; his mother flat-out adored him.

It must have been reciprocal—take a look at that last picture; they almost could be lovers the way they are standing. Now, look at the picture full-frame:

On the right is easygoing, not too bright, destined to corpulence and heart attack, big Cadillac-driving, steak-eating, hard-drinking, country-club golfer Collett, my father's brother, with a girlfriend, careless and smiling. As if occupying a separate universe, in a time warp of Left Bank angst and ennui, separated by a few feet in actual space but a mile symbolically, stand my father and Pan.

You can see the same easy affection again here, Daddy with his arm around beaming Pan, affable Collett to his right, a cousin in front, on their way to Europe in 1928.

What kid would welcome his mother coming along to college with him? Worse even than that, installed there as his fraternity housemother? And, okay, even if you can feature that, where would you be standing when the photographer set up his tripod for the annual Sigma Chi fraternity picture, placing your housemother Mom front and center?

The very back row, right?

His hair slicked down and his feet properly mated up, there he sits, next to an elegant Pan, that same Left Bank beret rakishly tilted, her white leather-gloved hand, for once not holding a cigarette in its customary three-inch-long holder, relaxed against the fur coat.

By this time, 1931, Irma was a widow, her husband, Collett Henry, having dropped dead in Dallas of a heart attack one winter night in 1928 after returning from the theater. He was forty-eight. My sixteen-year-old father was far from home when he died, in his second year at Choate.

Daddy had lots of time to reflect on the capricious and devastatingly final nature of death on the long, bleak train ride home to Dallas that February. But there's plenty of evidence, photographic as well as anecdotal, that until the moment of his father's death, my father's life had been a carefree joyride full of the typical tomfoolery we now identify as quintessentially American.

As you might expect, guns figured prominently.

Never a hunter, and in his later years averse to killing of any kind (even household ants, to the despair of Gee-Gee and my mother), his imagination was nevertheless seized by guns early on, as this, one of his "High Art" photos, probably taken in his early teens, attests.

He often fished with his father in bass-and-bream-abundant Texas waterways

and, if the evidence of these teen pictures is to be believed, he somehow managed a loutish and peculiar marriage of guns and fishing . . .

I suspect a pistol figured into the demise of this five-foot rattler . . .

and I bet there were plenty of guns, along with the obvious alcohol, on his numerous underage trips across the border into Mexico.

Take a look at this picture for a second:

His bottle-chugging companion is wearing a tie, but, strangely, my sartorially fastidious father is not, a sign that he must really be snockered. (He had been nattily dressed by Pan since infancy, with no apparent resistance.) The cars in the background probably don't belong to Mexicans. If we could enlarge that license plate it would almost certainly read "Texas."

Sufficient evidence exists here of rich-boy hedonism to suggest that the elder Robert Munger's legacy of hard work and public-mindedness was in precarious shape. A lot of money had been passed on to a son (Collett Henry), who may have known the meaning of those four letters, **W-O-R-K**, but who exhibited none of the rectitude, brilliance, self-restraint, or abstemiousness of the father—and who died before fifty, effectively of excess. Now the namesake grandson, inheriting the automotive imperative,

and mixing it dangerously with alcohol, guns, and an indulgent, unaware, pampered, lavish lifestyle, seemed to be headed down the same path as his father.

But . . . he didn't go down that path.

Instead he became an erudite polymath, a lean, physically fit, quiet, compassionate, unpretentious, disciplined, courtly, multifaceted, some would say Renaissance man who put in thirty-eight years as a hardworking country doctor, who could instantly recognize a sub-par Cézanne or a perfectly executed Donatello, who knew enough to buy those Twomblys and Kandinskys, who was a culinary sophisticate, a lip-smacking connoisseur of coffee, a fervent horticulturist who single-handedly planted more than fifteen thousand exotic trees and shrubs that turned Boxerwood into the nationally known garden it remains, a speed demon who rode powerful motorcycles, flew his own plane and raced cars, and, though he would be astonished to read this, a father who terrified the living bejesus out of his children by his intelligence, his remoteness, and his magnetic righteousness.

So, what changed him? Why did he reverse course on the easy, well-worn path of wealthy Texas mediocrity? What sent him running—fleeing— from that Dallas lifestyle and turned him into a veritable reincarnation, in so many respects, of his august forebear, Robert S. Munger?

You already know the answer.

It's here, in this eerily prophetic and haunting picture on one of his earliest rolls of film:

At the death of his father, the black wing of death—the wing of the final crow—brushed my father's life. While it forever darkened the path of unfortunate Collett Henry, it paradoxically proved to be a source of light for his son.

19

Mr. Death and His Blue-Eyed Boy

Goddamn dogs. Heartbreak, every time.

A few years ago we took in a handsome pit bull whose former owner underestimated the difficulty of caring for a large and energetic dog. We folded him into our established pack of four females, the largest of them, Patui, immediately dominating the much larger Max with nimble footwork and a convincing display of ferocity. Max, a sweet-tempered dog, never challenged her and generally aligned himself with the two smaller dogs,

except when Patui needed him to step in as the closer in a varmint kill.

Most of the time Patui, a powerfully built, black SPCA mutt, can dispatch prey of just about any size, but in Max's second summer with us she had met her match with an exceptionally large raccoon. She called for help from Max while she circled the cornered coon, barking and feinting. He ran straight in, grabbed the endearingly cartoonish coon head, and gave a shake so powerful that spit and feces flew from opposing ends.

Then, with a kind of dusting-off-his-paws dignity, Max turned away and walked up to his perch on the high ground above the stable, leaving the raccoon for Patui. She picked it up and began her ritualistic triumphant parade around the yard, the body of the coon dragged in the dust like Hector's outside the gates of Troy. Max watched with satisfaction . . . and something else: a little touch of bloodlust.

After that first Max-kill, there were more and for each we manufactured a benign explanation: perhaps the fawn whose leg he proudly carried home had been killed by coyotes, and Max just happened by. And the entire deer, broken neck pressed hard against the fence, haunches gnawed and guarded over by Max—perhaps she had misjudged the jump. But when Max came home grinning from ear to bloody ear, a trail of pink saliva dripping from his massive jaws, I suspected the worst. It was much worse than the worst: retracing his path, I came upon our neighbor despairingly palpating the torn body of his daughter's pet donkey who stood weakly in her pen.

When she collapsed panting and quivering, he showed me the severity of her wounds, her enormous belly torn nearly open, her haunches shredded.

Wordlessly, our neighbor walked over to his truck and got his pistol and Bowie knife. A compassionate and capable man, he knows exactly where to shoot an animal for instant death, and it surprised us that minutes after his head-shot the donkey was still alive, with bubbling foam pulsing in and out of her mouth. Time was short to save the life of the baby, so he sliced a clean cut on the underside of her bloody stomach, peeled back the skin, and made another cut to enter her uterus. Within the pale caul lay a too-tiny hairless donkey, her hooves sharp, eyes squeezed shut as if against the rain starting to fall.

Fetching Larry and his tractor, we found a place not likely to be disturbed by bear and coyotes and dug a large hole, then hoisted the donkey into the lowered bucket of the tractor, the umbilical cord trailing limply as Larry drove her to it. I rode with our neighbor back to the house where I got out, crying and queasy, and he picked up Max, who was delighted at the prospect of an adventure. Driving him to the muddy pit, he cajoled the suspicious Max into it. This time the kill shot worked.

Once again my heart was broken over a dog, each heartbreak different from the next: lymphoma, heart disease, tumors, injury, kidney failure, old age, cancer, Lyme, seizures . . . and now this.

I had seen that heartbreak in my father, too, with dog after dog. Those moments were about the only times I remember ever seeing him cry, but my older brother Chris said he once saw him cry on a different occasion.

He said it was when Daddy was reading out loud to our mother, a charming holdover from their early marriage when they read Faulkner's "The Bear" to each other on hot New Orleans nights. What Chris heard him reading was a passage in C. P. Snow's book *The Two Cultures*, in which Snow discusses how modern culture enforces a split between the practices of science and art and the difficulty of reconciling those two impulses if they reside within one conflicted person. I believe my father was such a person, and as he read he wept for the loss of his own rich world of ideas and art to that of medicine.

This defining existential struggle within my father is illuminated in the symbolic bookplate he designed while in medical school at Tulane. Having seen the bookplate all my life, I instantly recognized the scene when I came upon this snapshot of his desk from that time, obviously the basis for the self-expressive *ex libris*.

Much about his identity is revealed in the combination of preserved and invented detail that my father instructed CMB (Clara Mae Buchanan, one of his early loves) to engrave for his bookplate. Central to it are bookends carved in the figures of scholarly monks whose ancient system for transmitting knowledge is juxtaposed with the symbol of modern scientific inquiry, the microscope prominently in the foreground. Dueling pistols recall, with irony, the diversions of my father's Texan youth. The skull and lit candle are conventional *memento mori* symbols, signaling his absorbing interest in the cultural representation of death.

The caduceus above the central image (which I cannot identify: a religious icon, a portrait of a Renaissance prince, a pagan philosopher, or what?) is the traditional badge of my father's profession, but its symbolism was more personally meaningful to him than to many physicians. It is the staff of the god Hermes, several of whose properties dovetail with my father's preoccupations.

A trickster god, Hermes would have smiled on my father's artistic whimsies and delighted in the fantasy characters he invented to populate my childhood: Ign-Ign, Great Granny Grunt, Baby Dodo, Rabid Ant, Goggle-Eyed Slewfoot. A god with a sense of humor would have shrieked with delight, as we kids did, when Daddy dramatized our favorites, Chief Geezer and Inspector Upchuck, by hollering into the spittle-splashed horn in the center of the steering wheel as if it were a two-way radio. And because he was also the god of roads and protector of travelers, Hermes would, presumably, be the patron of modern-day car crazies such as my father. Further strengthening their accord, this god was an arborist and a scientist, but, at the same time, a devoted friend of art and literature.

This twofold association with art and science is reflected in the two snakes twined around Hermes' staff: they are Wisdom and Knowledge, prevented from devouring each other, kept in balance, by the power of the god.

It is significant that the only authors whose names appear in the book-plate are three who gloried in the duality that the caduceus demands: Goethe, a theoretical as well as hands-on naturalist and one of the progenitors of literary Romanticism; Milton, whose poetry swept up and bathed in the light of heaven the latest discoveries of the scientific revolution; and Sir William Osler, the great Johns Hopkins doctor whose works my father collected and who assimilated, as perhaps no other comparably distinguished physician ever has, the trickster aspect of Hermes. (Osler invented a pseudonym and corresponding alter ego to publish his prank "research papers" on subjects such as *penis captivus*, in respected medical journals.)

But the worlds of William Osler (1849–1919) and of my father did not easily accommodate the union of art and science. In my father's case, I believe that the painful necessity of sacrificing his literary and artistic impulses to his scientific vocation produced the emotionally inaccessible man that I knew. In a pensive 1938 journal entry written just before embarking on his *Wanderjahr* abroad, he came up with a striking metaphor for this denial of such a large part of himself. In it, he portrays himself as rowing toward medicine while the current pulls him artward:

Do you know how a boatman faces one direction, while rowing in another? I feel as he must: striving to obtain one goal (medicine), & looking longingly in another direction (travel & literature & art). Let's hope the current is not too strong & the stream straight.

Apparently the stream was straight, for after the last cultural fling of his *Wanderjahr*, he rowed forward into thirty-eight years of dedicated medical practice. But not, I posit, without the dark pain of longing and regret.

Setting aside this particularly existential (and speculative) source of anguish, just about the only time I saw a display of emotion in my father (I do not count his getting drunk at the news of his brother Collett's death as an emotion) was when his dog Tara, the one that pushed my mother out of the marital bed, lay dying of an inoperable cancer.

Tara loved the backseat of the family's blue Ford Falcon, in which she would travel with my father on non-Aston Martin-accessible house calls, her enormous head hanging out of the window, slobber trailing behind them in long, windborne skeins. As she sickened, she staggered with clear intention toward the car. Daddy gathered her, no doubt nearly his own weight, into his arms, much as years later Larry would lift Daddy's cancer-weakened body into his embrace.

With enormous tenderness Daddy carried her to the car, where he had prepared the seat with mounded-up blankets and pillows to cushion her bony body. Nobody was surprised the next morning to see my pajama-clad, muzzy-eyed father emerge from the back door of the Falcon, after somehow spending that night, and all those after, curled around her body on the narrow seat, comforting her as she lay dying.

His great affection for dogs seems to have originated in his Texas childhood, where he had any number of them—mutts and hunting dogs, and a pit bull named Ace that he adored.

At age twenty-seven, just before leaving on his solitary trip around the world, his journal records a difficult 2:00 a.m. parting in New Orleans from a girlfriend:

> Unable to appear at the Pontchartrain in such a shaken up state, I stopped at the Lee Circle Liquor Store and had about four Tom Collins and listened to Mildred Bailey sing on a recording "I Let a Song Go Out of my Heart" until I was sufficiently fortified to go home.

Admitting to distress or emotion, or whatever it was that required four strong drinks to remedy, is a rare event in the hundreds of pages of journals and letters that I found in the attic box. But, get him on the subject of Ace—now that was another matter. Almost as much journal space in July 1938 is devoted to saying good-bye to Ace as to his girlfriends, and the now-aged Ace appears in dozens of frames from the rolls of film he ran through his new Leica III.

> Went to see Ace in the afternoon: that black scoundrel of a dog is the most beautiful specimen of caninity I have ever seen . . . we were both overjoyed! . . .

Next morning (9th) received train and ship tickets. Went back out to see Ace.

"Overjoyed!" A hot word from my cool father.

Proust's narrator recounts how the family's cook, Françoise, exhibited a calculated cruelty toward those working under her in the Combray household while lavishing pity on the suffering of distant humanity—a pity which, the young narrator mordantly observes, would increase in direct proportion to the distance that separated the sufferers from herself. This kind of telescopic compassion is not an uncommon phenomenon, and has a close relative in the kindness one sees displayed toward pampered urban household pets, even as, a stone's throw away, homeless people sleep on benches.

Loving dogs seems to have been my father's telescopic way of getting around to loving us. In a certain sense, you can make the argument that it is pure and easy selfishness to love those most immediate to us—spouses, children, family—and that, by increasing the radius of our affections one dimension (in Daddy's case to his patients) or one species (his dogs) beyond the family circle, he was admirably stretching his love limits, which were, it is generally agreed, rather inelastic.

There's no question that he loved his mother and his dogs, but for us in his family, the abiding and soul-niggling question was: did he love his wife? His brother? His children?

One of his children, my brother Chris, has often wondered that and remembers, as do I, being cruelly teased by our father. In a letter Chris sent me, long after Daddy's death, he quoted a few lines from Graham Greene: "Childhood was the germ of all mistrust. You were cruelly joked upon and then you cruelly joked. You lost the remembrance of pain through inflicting it." To which Chris added: "We—us boys—were never taught that we could love and be loved or how to do it. We felt only the need. The son of a bitch."

I know what he means but I also know for a calcified fact that the man loved me (and the rest of his family). If you have any reason to doubt this, refer to Exhibit A at the end of this book, the simplest among several clever, labor-of-love letters he wrote me over the years; and to further dispel any lingering doubts, take a stab at Exhibit B. Then tell me he didn't love me (or, here's a late-breaking thought: perhaps he wanted me to love him?).

I was the longed-for baby daughter who came along nine years after the first son, Bob, and seven years after Chris. I came at a good time in my parents' lives, postwar (1951), with the medical practice established, and Boxerwood just finished, so named, of course, for the dozen or so boxer dogs my father had at that time.

All the same, I understand Chris's sentiments. Despite being in the birth-order and gender catbird seat, I felt very little emotional or affectionate love from either of my parents. We were not a family that touched, and there was little kissing; maybe a peck once I was tucked in bed. I don't think I ever heard the words "I love you" from any member of my family, but I don't recall missing them, either. Looking back on it, they would have seemed superfluous, even suspect.

But during one particularly emotional period in my life I felt that those words needed to be spoken, even if the sands were running out for the one to whom I wanted to say them. It was 1987. My father had been diagnosed with a malignant meningioma and was sick and weak from radiation. I steeled myself for the visit the night before, and in the morning I resolutely buckled myself into the car and drove to Boxerwood. Going in though the kitchen, I falsettoed a fakey "yoo-hoo," which he either didn't hear or pretended not to, and then I worked my way toward his study.

Daddy was there alone, going through his files (for a final time, as it turned out) and puttering about distractedly. Even sick, he stood with the posture of a powerful man who had never gone to fat. When he used to work shirtless in his gardens, he reminded me of the barrel-chested older Picasso I had seen in pictures. Now Daddy was in his maroon wool Brooks Brothers bathrobe, thin and moth-eaten in places, the same robe that clothed his body when it was shoved into the crematorium and which I would willingly march back through all the crowded years to roll him out of, if only I could have it.

His back was toward me, and, although I am sure I did not proceed in this manner, I retrospectively envision myself as an exaggerated cartoon cat-burglar, tiiiiippy-toeing toward my quarry, my anticipatory forefinger dangling before me.

The forefinger did in fact tap the maroon bathrobe, and its startled occupant turned toward me. His surprised expression suggested that, indeed, I was that predatory, black-goggled cartoon character, which didn't help the real me in blurting out the impossible four words I had rehearsed for the past twenty-four hours: "Daddy, I love you."

The surprised look passed from his unshaven face and it softened, almost in pity. He hesitated, then reached out and patted me on the shoulder and said, as if consoling a weeping patient, "There, there."

Even without overt demonstrations or verbal expressions of love from my father, I still believe there was love, of the deepest kind, in everything he did. I, like all who knew him, remember the sincere love he felt for his land and of course his dogs, but also for the practice of medicine and his patients. The thing that accounted for his cool remove, his air of solipsistic distraction, was, as my mother so trenchantly wrote, that he reserved his love hierarchically "for Ideas, for Art and then for People . . . and very much in that order."

"People" did not necessarily mean those in their limited social circle, but for sure it meant his patients. They knew he cared for them, and they were right. Hardly a night of my youth went by when I didn't hear the phone ring and my father stir in the bed that two sheets of drywall separated from mine (which raises some questions: what did I hear of their lovemaking? I remember nothing . . . or was there none?). He would reach over to the telephone's black Bakelite handle rubbed smooth by many a nighttime grasp, then there would be a brief murmur, more stirring, my mother's querulous voice, and before long the sound of a car engine clattering to life and heading out. Often he'd drive for miles and miles to address a problem as insignificant as a week-old hangnail or as momentous as a footling breech, and would return haggard and unshaven for breakfast.

Daddy somewhat resembled Dr. Ernest Guy Ceriani of W. Eugene Smith's famous "Country Doctor" photo essay and often had that same look of haunted exhaustion.

Like Dr. Ceriani's patients, Daddy's were the poorest in the rural county where we lived. Once the war was over (Daddy was the designated wartime doctor in Rockbridge County during World War II) and he had the time to take some pictures, he occasionally stopped by their homes with his Leica and, later, his large-format Linhof, to make their portraits— arguably an ethically compromised and problematic thing to do, but his sensitivity to the issue seems undeniable.

In the attic are several large envelopes of letters from patients that attest to the fact that he loved them and they loved him back. Where he would not show his own family the slightest bit of concern for any illness with a fever under 103 degrees, he would lavish attention on patients with a litany of specious complaints as long as your arm.

An especially neurasthenic patient wrote my father this letter, probably in the mid-1940s. She was thirty-two years old.

I get blind and drunk and sick and some days stay that way all day and if I don't vomit I nearly die. and nearly everything I eat makes gas on my stomach I have the indegestion sometimes until I get so weak and nervous I don't know where i'm at. and other times when I eat it don't make me sick at all but it seems like what I eat won't stay down I have to throw it back up and if I eat one bite to much it gives me the indegestion. I have to make water ever little while and it just burns me until I get so sore that nothing does me any good but washing in cold water. and I itchis so bad to, Is a place on me below just hurts like a beating some times it burns and hurts like a raw sore and other times it just thumps and hurts. and if I stoop on a walk much it hurts worse. I get sore across the lower part of my stomach. and feel so full by times like I am swelled. around my waiste and up my back by times feels like it is dead. I have the whites night bad to. by times I get numb all over and so hot. by times I just ache and hurt all over espacilly my breast and between my sholders. also take the sick headache. have the near-algia in my teeth and jaws. the least little thing just worries me nearly to death and I can't Keep from crying. my womb was inflammed about nine or ten years ago and I have been nervous ever sence. I stay so tired I don't care what I move or not and can't sleep at night. I get so weak down below it feels like ever thing in me is coming out, I stay blind and light headed . . .

He had a high proportion of female patients, or at least it seemed so to me. I think he showed them exceptional respect and was known for spending an unusual amount of time, even back then when an average appointment was a full thirty minutes, really listening to what they were saying. You can be sure this concerned mother heard back from him after he received this letter:

> Dr. Munger,
> Dear Sir;
>   I am writing to you
> about my son.
> He went to mowing
> Grass again and he
> has taken sick his
> Bowles has started
> running off again 5 and 6
> times a day like hog
> Brains.

My father's acceptance of human frailty and his tolerance and patience in his medical practice were almost godlike, or so it appeared to us, as we watched him dozens of times uncomplainingly lay down his linen napkin before taking even the first bite of a long-awaited holiday feast and gather up his medical bag to head to the OB floor for the night—and this without ever a disparaging comment or a rueful sigh.

But, all the same, I doubt it would surprise his patients to know that, yes, he just plain lost it one time.

It was the summer before his retirement on his sixty-fifth birthday, November 22, 1976, probably sometime around the bicentennial celebrations in July. As I recall it, some staggering drunk, fathead father of six revved up the roadster and packed his terrified family into it for a joyride. On the bridge over the bypass he lost control of the car and it flipped, smearing all of his un-seat-belted children along the road, and raining them over the sides of the bridge onto the windshields of the startled drivers below.

The ambulances brought them to the emergency room, where Daddy, the only doctor on duty that day, worked feverishly to save them, the unharmed husband raging in the waiting room. When the last of them, the wife, died under his desperate hands, Daddy went out into the hall and pressed his forehead against the cool plaster wall. The new widower found him there, and along with the powerful smell of whiskey came invective and accusations, most affectingly: "You little shit, you let her die on me."

That was the line my despairing father kept repeating when he came home, tired, pissed off, and looking more than ever like the exhausted Dr. Ceriani. It was the only time I ever heard him talk about a patient or his medical practice. Ever.

Sometimes I wonder if it was the diminutive that bothered him as much as anything. He was a "little shit" (the writer Tony Horwitz said that he was once greeted in a saloon in Tennessee with the words, "I shit out a turd this morning that was bigger than you"). Daddy might have been a shit at times, but he wasn't that little. At least not as little as the height on this 1928 passport says:

In addition to being off a digit on his birth date, I sure as hell hope it was incorrect as well about his height: five foot three at age seventeen? Hell, I'm an osteoporotic old woman and I still break five foot four. His next passport in 1936 pegs him as five foot eight and he looks about that next to my mother (five foot five), who was wearing heels for her wedding.

But, okay, five foot eight isn't all that tall, and there's this about him, too: he was oddly sensuous.

Here he is in September of 1926, at age fourteen, leaving Dallas to enter the seventh grade at Choate.

Isn't there something languidly insouciant in his hip-cocking posture? A coddled Dallas kid with a background of sunny privilege should be rigid with fear heading off by himself to the cold Northeast with all the steely sons of the robber barons.

Evidently, he found his own steeliness at Choate (which must have taken some doing, what with his father's death in his second year) because he almost immediately discovered a talent for wrestling. By his junior year, he was captain of the Choate wrestling team, which was so successful that they occasionally took on collegiate-level opponents.

Ultimately, wrestling in 1933 at Washington and Lee University, he won every match of the season not by points but by pinning his opponents to the mat. His W&L wrestling career culminated in the Southern Conference Championship of 1933, which he won despite having dislocated his shoulder (and which provided me with this arresting image now framed in my studio):

Still, despite the new steeliness and that athleticism, something about him, the full lips, his easy physical grace and his sinuousness,

combined with an aloof intellectualism, reserve, and hauteur,

suggests that my Mom had a tough row to hoe.
All that and, of course, his "death thing."

It's not as if she didn't have plenty of warning about that death thing. Surely she must have visited his apartment on Pinckney Street in Boston between her somewhat understated report of their first dinner together

> JULY 19
>
> 1939
>
> *Wednesday. Verging off hot today. Usual sort of day. Dinner + evening with Dr. Bob Klinger. World traveler — interesting gent.*

and the wedding three months and eight days later.

To be sure, my mother's first sightings of the "interesting gent" wouldn't have given her any inkling of what she would find on Pinckney Street. She was then an impoverished lab technician earning eighty dollars a month at Massachusetts General Hospital in the Ear, Nose, and Throat Department. She had graduated from Bennington College in 1937, thanks to Aunt Ethel's tuition payments, which had continued well past the death of Uncle Skip. But, despite having been accepted at Yale and Johns Hopkins medical schools, her lifelong dream of becoming a doctor had to be scuttled once the Gages' money stopped coming, so she took a job. (Summer jobs during her college years included a stint giving tennis lessons to young John Kennedy and changing Teddy's sheets at their summer home in Hyannis Port.) Perched on a stool by a window on an upper floor of the hospital, she painstakingly counted blood cells all day.

During her thirty-minute lunch break she would drink a Coca-Cola and idly gaze out the window at the traffic circle leading to the hospital entrance. Especially in those straitened times, it was impossible not to notice the chauffeured car that arrived punctually at noon and then returned its trim, white-coated passenger exactly one and a half hours later.

After months of voyeuristic conjecture, perhaps even fantasy, she was startled one Wednesday morning in July to find herself in the elevator with her employer, the renowned Harvard laryngologist Dr. Harris Mosher, and the spruce little doctor with the generous lunch hour. When the elevator stopped at her floor, they all exited and by the time the elevator returned the two professors to their offices, a dinner engagement for that night with the man she referred to as "the smoothie Southern doctor" was in my mother's date book.

He was a fast mover, my father. Twenty-eight days later, when stymied by my grandmother Jessie's sudden and somewhat hypocritical prudery in not allowing my mother and the brash doctor to sail up the Nile together without benefit of matrimony, he announced cavalierly, "Well, I guess I'll have to marry you, then."

And that was his proposal of marriage, after only three dates. Her diary reports that each of them was a dinner date and they were a week apart, during which time my mother also dated several other people, especially her main squeeze, the historian, future MacArthur Fellow, and Pulitzer Prize winner Carl Schorske. Each date with the smoothie Munger was reported, but without any emphasis or elaboration. Completely baffling.

The day after the proposal, which had come on August seventeenth, her diary reveals that she "put in a plea for time to think, but I have a certain feeling." The day after that she said yes, and, with what I suspect was relief, she reported, "his eyes made me sure."

Obviously, she was not put off by whatever she had seen of his domestic life on Pinckney Street. His decorating theme even then was Morbidity.

(Yes, those are fingers from a real mummified hand to the left of the unconcerned Buddha.)

If she had rifled through his drawers (as who wouldn't have, left alone while he mixed her a highball in the next room?), she would surely have noticed a similar theme running through the items from his youth that he chose to keep.

No report cards, yearbooks, letters, wrestling trophies, or dried boutonnières were preserved from his six years at Choate, just a 1930 literary magazine in which he published a pair of short stories. They both featured the same main character.

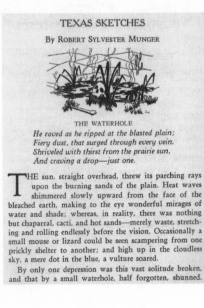

It was Death.

I suppose that even if she had discovered these things at 91 Pinckney Street, my mother was far too enraptured to have realized how big a part his fascination with death and life's evanescence played in this young man's life. I wonder if she noticed that even their honeymoon was structured not around what most red-blooded males would be looking forward to, but rather around a visit to the Orozco mural at Dartmouth College, and in particular the panel featuring a skeletal mother delivering stillborn Knowledge into the bony hands of a ghoulish academic.

After the wedding my father took but one picture of his new bride. But after this lone honeymoon picture, as you unspool the tightly rolled and crumbling 35 mm nitrate negatives, come image after image of the Orozco mural. It seems clear that Daddy chose the honeymoon destination as much because of his interest in Orozco's approach to the concept of Death as for the romantic possibilities of autumn-ablaze New Hampshire.

I'm guessing that his fascination with mortality began with the all-too-real death of his father when he was sixteen years old, but it was during his 1938–39 travels around the world that he married it with his blooming interest in art and literature, a marriage that lasted as long as that with my mother. Let's look back for a minute: remember my mother's first recorded impression of my father from her diary of July 19, 1939?

"World traveler—interesting gent."

20

World Traveler, Interesting Gent

Over the years, Larry and I have been asked how it is we have such a strong bond, and we respond that it was formed in the annealing crucible of impoverished travel. As newlyweds, he and I set out in 1971 to spend my junior year traveling from northern Denmark to Greece. We had earned enough in our first year of marriage for the plane tickets, but Gee-Gee, in a gesture reminiscent of Hattie's bequest to my father, slipped us fifty dollars for the road and my parents promised to send a hundred dollars each month to American Express as we went along. We carried two backpacks heavy with books and a 1950s white Samsonite overnight case lined in scarlet taffeta, which held my 5 × 7 inch view camera, the tripod for which was strapped beneath the lighter of the two backpacks.

If any backwater of disconsolateness exists that is blacker and lonelier than the one our travels sped us to, I do not want to see it. We knew no one, and were so broke by the end of each month that I remember eating cold *petit pois* out of a can in the Dickensian gloom of our clammy Paris hostel—imagine, in Paris, gastronomic capital of the world. We embraced on any number of sagging mattresses, always too short for his six-foot-four frame, and on third-class train and ferry rides. Taking turns carrying the white suitcase, we walked lonely northern European streets in the perpetual wintry twilight, while strangers brushed by us and entered their warmly lit homes. We made love frequently, if my journals are to be believed, and visited every museum and gallery within our reach, fervently looking at art as if it were the lodestone, the vinculum that would hold us together. In the end, I think it might have been.

FIRENZE S. M. NOVELLA

My father had set off on a similar, though better-funded and more ambitious, year of travel in July 1938, when he was twenty-six. Just out of Tulane Medical School, the boatman rested on his oars and let himself drift, for the last time, dreamily toward Art and Culture.

He had traveled to Europe three times before, and each trip had been dedicated, or so his journals suggest, to Art (in his mind, yes, with a capital A, and Culture with a capital C). It is clear that art was his lodestone, his vinculum, too. I expect that on his earlier trips his traveling companions, and especially his mother, Pan, were busy shopping while he methodically went from museum to cathedral to library, noting in detail his impressions, his art passion spilling over in fevered journal jottings. I've deciphered the secret language in bowls of spaghetti more easily than the writing in these notebook pages.

His journal presentation improves for the 1938 expedition, as if he understood the significance of this epic trip. In the saddlebag grip swung over his shoulder that was his only luggage, he carried a zippered calfskin notebook that he maintained, with reasonable legibility for a doctor, throughout the nine months and one day of his journey. I have it before me now, as vibrant as any new hour.

Companion reading to this journal is a collection of highly entertaining letters that he sent to Pan in her Melrose Hotel suite in Dallas. As they arrived, a secretary at the Magnolia Petroleum Company named Kate Frierson was pressed into service deciphering and typing the letters for Pan. When she was done, Miss Frierson wrote Pan that the letters were

> most interesting. . . . He shows splendid talent as a writer aside from his chosen profession. These compare very favorably with some diaries of very reputable travelers/writers . . . they are original, terse, with just enough humor.

One of the "reputable travelers/writers" whose epistolary style my father clearly favored was Flaubert, who wrote just as faithfully, and in as much detail, to his own adored mother while traveling through Egypt almost a century earlier. And Miss Frierson is right about his talent: Daddy's letters to Pan are witty and original, high-flown at moments, didactic at others, rife with assurances of thrift, rich in descriptive detail, and occasionally even emotional and excited, in a multi-exclamation-mark kind of way. Strange for my generally reserved father, I have to say.

The range of his observations is far-reaching: he describes the flora and fauna as well as the manners and customs in the localities visited; also architecture, costume, dialect, music, modes of transport, cuisine, drink, methods of summoning a waiter, how coffee is prepared and consumed, means of carrying babies, the behavior of beggars and prostitutes, the design of oars (interesting in light of his own oarsman metaphor) and techniques of rowing, the prevailing medical problems, and the available means of responding to them—this inquisitive onlooker visited every kind of hospital, clinic, medical school, and medicinal spa.

Throughout, his fascination with death is conspicuous, as when in Grindelwald, Switzerland, famed for its view of the north face of the Eiger, he notes the telescopes installed at all the hotels and cafes "thru which one can see the climbers fall, sometimes hanging for days before death, being watched by people below all the while."

⸺

He set out to go around the world, and he did it. His financial accounts are meticulous, and they report that when he boarded the ship *Manhattan* (from Manhattan, in fact), he had a budget of $1,460. (That was, incidentally, $335 more than Larry and I had for our own nine months of travel three decades later.)

When the *Manhattan* landed he immediately bought a black 350 cc BSA motorcycle in London, whose license, and affectionate nickname, was EYU97. Then, having never ridden a motorcycle in his life, he put the saddlebags on a rack above the back wheel and headed down Oxford Street during rush hour and straight on to Paris, where he began in earnest his Art *Wanderjahr*.

It is family legend that all he took with him in the saddlebags were the complete works of Plato, one change of underclothes, and his white tuxedo, but his journals reveal the predictable fallacy of familiar lore: in fact, my sartorially impeccable father crossed most of the globe indeed with Plato's complete works, but in a three-piece gray wool suit under a waterproof, Bogartian trenchcoat.

However, there is a grain of truth in the white-tuxedo legend: the one item this well-reared wayfarer considered absolutely necessary within his tight packing scheme was a pair of white kid gloves. And they got a real workout: his journals reveal that he attended any opera, play, orchestral performance, lecture, poetry reading, recital, or ballet on offer wherever he dismounted for the night.

He traveled in that three-piece suit the entire trip: through England, France, Belgium, Germany, Switzerland, Italy, Austria, Hungary, Yugo-slavia, Greece (the entire country, including Crete, several other islands, and the Peloponnese), Bulgaria, Turkey, Egypt, and thence (though at this point neatly stowing the suit in favor of khaki shorts and sandals) all the way to the Pacific, passing through Palestine, Lebanon, Syria, Iraq, Kuwait, Bahrain, India, Burma, Siam, Cambodia, and French Indo-China on his way to the port at Yokohama, Japan, from whence he sailed home.

Can you imagine wearing that three-piece wool suit to climb to the top of the pyramids?

That's what he did, obviously.

(A quick peek ahead in our narrative shows him still wearing it four months to the day after the pyramid climb, with the long trek across the Middle East and Asia behind him,

having just disembarked the *Heian Maru* in Vancouver.)

It must have been a pretty well made suit to look so good after the rocky territory he and EYU97 traversed. These appropriately dressed Greeks who helped him through a particularly difficult passage in the Peloponnesus surely wondered at his cufflinks and Windsor knot.

On the tonsorial front, however, he had slipped a little, as this picture taken in Athens the day before indicates, and was now somewhat scruffily bearded. There's something else, too . . . do you see it?

I do: there's a hint of distress in those very blue eyes.

It seems reasonable to suppose that the source of that distress would have been the fact that all of the countries he had just traversed were on the brink of war. On August 20, 1938, as Hitler was mobilizing his troops to invade Czechoslovakia, Daddy was blithely pointing his motorcycle into Nazi Germany from Antwerp (where, with a two-exclamation-point exultation, he made note in his journal of a genuine human skull in the Rubens' tomb that had been painted to resemble marble).

While in Germany, he laid up in ten cities, writing lyrical descriptions of cathedrals, of Bruno Walter's elegantly restrained orchestral direction, of the sublimity of Beethoven's original manuscript for his "Moonlight" Sonata, of the baths at Baden-Baden, the excellent performance of *The Barber of Seville*, and the pleasures of the autobahn. He composed eight pages of detailed, regressively spaghetti-ish notes on his opinions of the art at the various museums he visited.

But about what was really going on in Nazi Germany? Barely a word, save a remark on the good manners of the smartly dressed soldiers, and his aesthetic irritation at the ubiquitous posters of Hitler's "rather expression-less and certainly plain features." That's IT.

In a letter to Pan he wrote, a bit jokingly (I hope): "I did not even know there WAS a war scare until you mentioned it in your letter!" and goes on in the next sentence to quote something his Dallas friend Horace had written him:

> In a letter from him which I got yesterday Horace says "But, I know you, Bob, you'd choose to go in a museum and look at Egyptian mum-mies rather than look at a man who had just been shot to death by the Nazis."

His dedication to art and his fascination with images of death seem to have obscured with an almost willful blindness the real murders that were occurring around him.

But he was not blind to the beauty of the landscape through which he traveled. The Leica III that he used to photograph his old bulldog Ace back in Dallas had been stowed in the saddlebags and was well used on this trip. First and foremost he photographed death imagery,

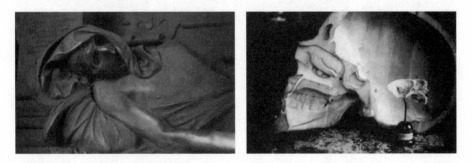

but he also made some better-than-average travel pictures. In fact, I think they're ravishing:

While most of his travel pictures were High Art only to the extent that his early artistic attempt with the gun and holster was High Art, all the

same, they give some idea as to the force of that strongly flowing current
of artistic sensibility against which he knew he was soon to be rowing.

As far as I can tell, his travels were entirely solitary until he reached Rangoon and teamed up with two other Americans for a viperous, tigery, machete-whacking hike from Burma into Siam. Apparently, he had been perfectly happy by himself, given over to his art and death passion, probably going through his travels in the same solitary way he went through the rest of his life, despite later having a wife and family with whom he could have shared his thoughts and never much did.

Not until Cairo did he finally part with his faithful companion, EYU97, after ferrying her around the Greek Isles, negotiating the rocky terrain of road-challenged Bulgaria and Turkey, and touring Egypt and Libya for nearly three weeks, his head protected from the wind and sun by native garb (over, of course, the three-piece suit).

Though he never seemed to miss the company of other humans, he took this parting hard. Just before he sold EYU97, he took her on one last midnight spin out of Cairo to the pyramids:

> The pyramids in the moonlight were cast in black relief, ponderous, mighty and mysterious as I drove back over the wide, totally deserted avenue, no construction or housing anywhere, into Cairo, trenchcoat flapping, the streetlights throwing my racing shadow eerily on the sands to the side of the road.

He memorialized their separation with a portrait the next day and laments in his journal (N.B. double exclamation marks): "Goodbye, EYU97!!"

Though he missed his two-wheeled companion, he described himself as "light as Shelley's skylark" as he resumed his travels with only his saddlebags, each half of which he reported to be the size of a woman's handbag, slung over his shoulder. He passed through Palestine, spent four days bogged down in the Syrian desert on his way to Baghdad,

and headed down the Euphrates to Basra, where he caught a boat for Bombay.

Once he reached the Far East, the culture, people, and art of these countries, especially Burma, are described in a rapture of aesthetic home-coming. Here he is—formerly a crass, car-racing, snake-killing, pistol-popping, booze-chugging Dallas kid now with a fevered desire for art, beauty, and the life of the mind—finally at peace and at home: at Angkor Wat in Cambodia.

He wrote in his journal, his handwriting looping extravagantly, about his solitary time among the ruins, his only human companion an occasional Buddhist priest in a saffron-hued gown:

> In my first view in the moonlight, it had been the immensity of the great temple that had taken my breath away. But in the daylight, it was the exquisite detail and carefully planned architecture—and the Apsarases! The demimondaines, those scantily clad, marvelous danc-ing girls with bulging breasts, narrow waists and sensuous hips—per-fect in beauty and potent in love—sent to earth to tempt the ascetic.

The spectacle was so amazing I could scarcely credit my eyesight, for here was a structure built a thousand years ago, so stupendous in its dimensions, in artistry, in purity, in magnificence, that surpasses anything you'll ever see in Greece, Rome, Egypt, Mexico or Central America.

And his is the voice of experience—he's been to all of them. He continues:

After many days of solitary exploration, on the last evening there I climbed slowly and wonderingly among the now familiar ruins. How was it possible for such a race as the Khmers to disappear so absolutely? How long did it take? Was there <u>no soul</u> left to see the ruthless jungle creep in and devour these magnificent structures?

Musing this, before I realized it, day had gone and twilight enveloped me. For some moments a hush fell over the land; there was not the faintest breeze to stir the jungle-tops. Sensuous roots of the banyan tree—like exploring fingers—found their way into every stone crevice—I could see, <u>feel</u> them . . .

From the shadows of the ruins arose an indescribable melancholy.
Loneliness, loneliness—in all this stupendous graveyard of man
and monument, I stood—the only living human being!

⸻

Reading those journals and letters, matching up the travel accounts with
the yellowed photographs, I find my father, filled with joie de vivre and
spirit and desire, on a dedicated quest to find the place of art in his life . . .
and the place of death in that art. The evidence, his joyous, art-inflected
accounts, indicate that, just as it would for Larry and me thirty years later,
art had firmly planted itself in his soul, with roots as deep and broad as
those of the banyan trees at Angkor Wat.

But he dutifully came back to America, picked up his oars, and resumed
rowing, against the current of desire, back toward science. Within a month
of his return, he reentered the practice of medicine, married my mother
six months later, and, his boat into the current, pressed forward.

⸻

For the next four decades he labored over his great masterwork, cajoling my mother from cave to cathedral, exploring the iconography of death in art. Lavishing his distinctive longhand on reams of yellow paper, he tried out various titles:

Keener it Cuts the Hay

The (graphic) pictorial representation of (personified) Death

The Personification of Death in Art

With a Crawl or a Pounce

With his Sickle Keen

The Personalization and Personification of Death in Art

Ten Thousand Doors

In his files are communications with nearly one hundred museums, galleries, and libraries, from Uganda to the Vatican, and more than 450 pictorial representations of death, in folders labeled:

Pagan

Norse

Peruvian and Indian

Middle Ages/Byzantine

Primitive and African

Greek

Etruscan and Roman

Medieval French

Jewish

Misc'l

Renaissance

Middle America/skeletons

Modern

Mexico/Middle America

Danse Macabre

Caricaturists and Realists

Indian

Trees

Physical death

Pagan, Slavic

Masks/Mexico

Babylon/Assyria

Oriental/Indian

Gravestone carvings

Attributes and symbols (sickles/scythes)

Abyssinian

Political cartoons

Egyptian

After his death, my exasperated and exhausted mother gathered it all up and stuffed it into two large boxes, which I have, page by crumbling page, finally sorted out. (Yes, that's Max under the table.)

Most of the writing is illegible, and the organization barely comprehensible. But the scholarship and dedication are crackerjack (one of his favorite words of approbation), although he might have paid more heed to his self-admonition, opposite, that he "steam up the lingo."

It saddens me that only occasionally do lines within the flaking pages remind me of the author of the charming journal entries of 1938–39, but this is one that does:

> By comparison, a skeleton is, by nature, chaste and uncorrupt, a batch of dry, rattly bones—quite incapable of the delicious merriment and the gamut of histrionics proffered by a cavorting, putrescent, flesh-flapping, hammy old corpse. . . .

Indeed, what is striking about this magnum opus is the lack of joy and wonder so evident in the journals and letters home from his Art *Wander-jahr.* He has made the trade-off, struck the deal that almost all of us sooner or later must strike between the thing we love and the thing we must do. Somewhere in the process, he lost the two-exclamation-mark art moment.

Except . . . except . . . he expressed hope for someone born in the next generation who could make art that married the concept of mortality with the redemptive force of beauty. He wrote these words the month I was conceived, August 1950:

We are perennially reminded that art is prophetic . . . and that some of our best modern works of art are those in which world- or self-dissolution is represented.

So perhaps it is not too much out of line to indulge in the prophesy and hope that there may arise a truly vital germ of creative art which will generate, in the midst of the constant threat of death, a will to endure, and which will: 1) lend strength and vitality to a more meaningful kind of life, and 2) emphasize and strengthen the life-conserving processes of civilization.

Am I suggesting here that I was born to redeem my father's lost artistic vision, the child destined to make the art that he was unable to make, to peer behind some of those ten thousand doors?

Maybe I am, and maybe I was. God knows I have tried.

21

The Cradle and the Grave

Even though I wanted to please my father more than anything, rebellion came naturally to me, beginning as a child. As reported earlier, my mother's journals from the 1950s are peppered with despairing accounts of frayed tempers and the hairbrush spankings she administered over my refusal to wear clothes, or, when she managed to get them on me, my refusal to change them until they were ragged. I remember those times, too: the powerlessness, the frustration and the furious agitation roiling within me, the strong desire to be left alone, Mowgli-wild, naked and dreadlocked. Especially I remember wanting to have things always my way.

Those difficult personality tendencies were exacerbated by the defiant temper of the 1960s, which coincided with the full noxious bloom of my adolescence and my banishment to Putney. But it was hard to rebel against my father, now distant geographically as well as emotionally; although I tried mightily, on some level I knew it was impossible. Even then, writing this doggerel prose poem in a 1969 journal, I admitted defeat. I wanted to be just like him and I wanted him to be proud of me.

It's obvious that he heavily influenced my nascent artistic aesthetic, but it was not through any direct means. He seldom discussed with me the deep artistic passions so evident in his youthful journals, and he was relatively close-mouthed about his lifelong, obsessive artistic endeavors, which ran the gamut from stained glass windows to Calder-like mobiles and hill-sprawling earth sculpture. If anything, for better or worse, what I learned directly from this distant, abstracted, art-making father was that whatever project he was working on at the time was more important to him than almost anything else, including, perhaps, even his family. My mother writes painfully about this indifference and neglect in her journal from 1956:

> I get the feeling that really I register only in a small part of Bob's life—that the creative world of his is the core of his being and I'm there to admire and comment and see that he has everything he needs. I get worked up over, say, the fact that he piddled around on his creations all day yesterday and yet couldn't do the Victrola fixing—or, even worse, didn't think of it, or, thinking of it, didn't do it—when I've begged for it so often.

He simply didn't have time to let us into his life; his passions were all that mattered. So, here it is again—my genetic roadways crowded with my Welsh grandfather's sentimentality genes, pushing earnestly along, and right behind them my father's pedal-to-the-metal, obsessive, death-inflected art-passion genes downshifting into passing gear.

As I worked my way to the bottom of the Daddy boxes in the attic, I found these pictures he had taken with the Leica outside New Orleans in 1939, some sixty years before my own Deep South work.

I could have taken any of these pictures. In fact, I *have* taken these pictures, almost every one of them, without the benefit of ever having seen them before. Recognizing them as my own pictures gave me a moment of woo-woo, hair-raising frisson followed by a vexatious pinch of resentment and resignation.

I began to see my artistic life—starting from my earliest pictures taken at age seventeen with that same Leica, right through to my own 2003 artistic exploration of death, published as *What Remains*—as the inevitable result of my silent father's clamorous influence.

The Leica had a Hektor lens with a wobbly focus knob and bad optical coating that caused a bit of flare that I rather liked (and still do). Handing it over to me, distractedly and with a hurried and insufficient explanation of how to load the film and focus, my father, like my high school English teacher Jeff Campbell portentously assigning me Faulkner, unknowingly performed his own decisive act of predestination.

It was the winter of my senior year at Putney School, the year of Faulkner, the year of Awakening. What I was awakening from was a fathomless sleep of ignorance, and by this I mean not just the ignorance of race relations I wrote about earlier. It was worse than that; I was a shallow, uninteresting, uninterest*ed*, and uninformed kid. My parents' lackadaisical style of parenting certainly made me independent, but it provided no structure or nurture for my creativity and intellect. I never had the art, dance, music, riding, tennis, and French lessons or the travel abroad that my own children, for instance, enjoyed: I languished in the limited Appalachian backwater of my own thoughts. And, for a girl living out in the country with not a lot to do or see, with not even a television, for Chrissake, those thoughts were anything but profound.

Except there were books, two in particular: *You Have Seen Their Faces* and *The Family of Man*, which I have still in their worn-out first editions (one cost a dollar, the other seventy-five cents). I know that the latter is controversial for its oversimplification, vulgar worldwide success, and naïve ideological posture, but I am not embarrassed to say that I am still moved by it. As a child, it captivated and enthralled me; I studied every picture, from the opening Wynn Bullock image of the naked child in the ferny forest, to W. Eugene Smith's "Walk to Paradise Garden" (a print of which I now own). It taught me the rudiments of sexual love, family and community life, of personal and social interactions, strife, and, perhaps most important, of empathic compassion for suffering.

In that last respect, *You Have Seen Their Faces* took over where *The Family of Man* left off. Margaret Bourke-White's photographs from the Depression are still among the most haunting in my photographic reservoir. Though back then I would need help with the captions, once read to me, the words spoken by the people in the pictures only compounded the crippling confusion and guilt that arose when I looked at the book. A rural Alabama resident said to the book's editor, Erskine Caldwell, "Of course I wouldn't let them plaster signs all over my house," adding, "but it's different with those shacks the niggers live in." Running her thick-nailed fingers under the lines, Gee-Gee read those words to me with not a particle of pissed-off in her voice, but something else: wretchedness and grief.

Until I could read on my own, I had to tease out whatever time Gee-Gee had in her work schedule to read to me. With calculation, I would watch as she ran water into a Coke bottle so well used that its green glass had grown milky. Once she had corked it with the funky tin sprinkler and wet the laundry, I knew there was at least one child's book's worth of reading before the uninterruptible ironing session. I could get my mother to read to me, too, if I caught her before she stretched out with the Georg Jensen ashtray on her stomach, a Kent cigarette in one hand, the *Atlantic* in the other, for her afternoon rest.

Best of all was when my father read to me. He would take me onto his lap before supper, his one deep golden cocktail beside him on the marble table, sometimes with a cherry at the bottom for me. We would open up the *Washington Post* to the funnies at the back and he'd read every single strip to me, even the ones, like *Brenda Starr*, that he thought were stupid. His favorites were *Pogo*, *Peanuts*, Al Capp's *Li'l Abner*, and *Barney Google* with the goo-goo-googly eyes, a line Daddy delighted in putting to music and singing at the top of his lungs as he rode on the sulky behind the Gravely mower. Our mutual favorite was *Prince Valiant*, which ran only on Sundays and was in color. Several times I wrote its author, Hal Foster, once asking if Prince Valiant had to wear underpants.

My childhood books, many with my name penciled laboriously on the front covers, are on the bookshelf in the attic: the A. A. Milne and Dr. Seuss books, *Charlotte's Web*, Richard Chase's *Jack Tales* and *Grandfather Tales*, Walter Farley's horse stories, *The Prisoner of Zenda*, *The Moonstone*, and a complete set of the Oz books in their 1908 first editions gloriously illustrated by John R. Neill.

Perhaps prematurely in my reading life, but premonitory as to my creative one, my father had given me a book called *Art Is Everywhere*, which has a chapter entitled "Are You a Camera?" It concludes by saying, "If you want to imitate a scene exactly as you see it, then use a camera!"

I should have taken that advice, but instead for many years I chose to imitate the scenes of my life by poorly reinterpreting them in my daily journal. The journals that remain after the annual from-the-bottom-up culling (and which I will most assuredly toss into the wood furnace before I take my own thirty Seconals) reveal that what I thought about was, chronologically: horses, then boys, followed closely by personal appearance and weight issues, popularity or lack thereof, and whether I was a slut. Cringing my way through the banality, cheesiness, and sheer peacockery of those early years, I almost welcome the high-flown ruminations of the post-Awakening, wannabe artistic soul, such as, for example, this windy contemplation of the importance of insecurity to the creative process (something to which I suppose I still subscribe):

> Can the artist produce under any motivation other than insecurity? . . . And is the end product, the tangible creation, made less valuable, less beautiful by the fact that it derives from a basic insecurity?
>
> . . . Sometimes I do wonder at my capabilities; at exactly what is innate and ready to be drawn upon within me. . . . How, for instance, did Picasso come about? Was it that he merely picked up a paintbrush before a saxophone? . . . Could he as easily have been a jazz player had he begun as such, or, despite the presence of his saxophone, would he have searched out his paintbrushes?
>
> So, is there any true path for me?
>
> . . . All I ask is, yes, to be happy—a simple, free and complete happiness and then the path will be decided in a wave.

That last sentence reminds me of the line that Oscar Wilde tossed out in response to a friend's anxious dinner invitation that had concluded with something like, "I don't know what I can possibly give you [to eat]!"

To which Wilde had breezily replied, "Oh, anything. Anything, no matter what. I have the simplest tastes. I am always satisfied with the best."

"Complete happiness" was all I asked; seems reasonable enough. Clearly I was not an artist who wanted to suffer.

But . . . all the same, I did. We all do. My particular suffering was often tied up with trying to please my distracted father, or, at the least, to get his attention. Remaining on nodding terms with the eighteen-year-old who wrote those journal pages is excruciating, but despite wincing at the rawness of my fear, my need, my ambition, and doubt, I also grudgingly recognize many of those things, still, in the person I am now.

Early in December 2000, when an armed convict came across the fields toward our house, I had already begun to think about the concept of death in relation to the land, as well as to photography and art. As that harrowing day played out, I confess to thinking that the timing of it had a perverse felicity, as if it were an apposite and propitious cosmic sign.

The morning he came, I was alone on the farm, our six greyhounds hanging out by the woodstoves while I spotted prints. I was listening to an audio book of *Moby-Dick* read by the late Frank Muller, which was drowned out, annoyingly, by the sound of a helicopter repeatedly passing over the farm. When the phone rang, I put down the spotting brush and my eyes readapted to distance; I could see the copter hovering close by, over the river.

Picking up the phone, I found Larry on the line from his office in town. He sounded odd. He asked me if anyone was with me, and said to answer carefully. Carefully? I said no, and he asked again if I was able to speak freely, and I said, with some impatience, "Sure, of course I am. What's up with you?"

He let out a sigh, and in a more normal voice told me that the sheriff had just called him and asked if I was home alone. Receiving the affirmative, he'd told Larry about an escapee headed toward the house and said I needed to lock the doors. This was a laughable concept in a house with nine (then unlockable) French doors. Sited on a raised plateau with long views and bounded on three sides by water, our house is protected almost entirely by geography, a classic stronghold. But Larry's imagination had gone to the worst case: the desperate man was already in and had a gun to my head.

My own imagination also went into horror-movie overdrive: terrified, I told Larry I was certain I was hearing movement in the living room. I quietly put down the phone and with exaggerated tiptoeing, managed a sightline.

Pie-Pie, the youngest greyhound, was stretching and changing sides by the stove.

Chagrined, I went back to the phone, and Larry explained the situation. A deputy had been sent to a residence on the other side of the county at four in the morning to arrest David Sensabaugh, who already had some minor sex offenses on his record, on four new felony charges. A few hysterical women were at the scene, one apparently rooting around in a shed for a gun, so the deputy cuffed Sensabaugh's hands behind his back and used the seat belt to strap him in the front seat of his idling cruiser.

While the deputy was distracted by the women screaming at him that he was a fat motherfucker and was going to pay, Sensabaugh pretzeled his handcuffed wrists down and under his feet. He undid the seat belt, scooted over to the driver's seat, and locked the doors. Gunning the car, he tore off into a field, plowed a few unnecessarily exuberant doughnuts into the frozen dirt, took out a fence, and, cutting through a neighbor's side yard, disappeared down the paved road. He went straight to a friend who hacksawed the handcuffs, then drove out our road, Route 39, ditched the car by the river, and set out on foot with the deputy's shotgun and two pistols.

The sheriff's department, joined by state police with dogs, was in howling pursuit of him by midmorning, but the fugitive knew the territory and mountain-goated down the cliffs above the Maury River. He crossed the icy river close to our cabin and spent some time there, drying himself before heading through the woods toward our house. His pursuers, stymied by the cliffs and the river, doubled back to their cars and took the road to the nearest bridge. They were at least fifteen minutes by car from our farm. As they set out, the circling helicopter pilot got a fix on Sensabaugh running toward the house and radioed Sheriff Day, who called Larry. Who called me.

After I hung up, I rushed to the windows and, seeing no one, was convinced, like Larry, that Sensabaugh had already gotten into the house. Slinking along the walls, going from room to room in an absurd pantomime of an imperiled (and unarmed) cop in a house search, I cursed those damn greyhounds and their complete lack of guard-dog protectiveness.

Finding no one, I roused the dogs and chased them outside. I made it to the garage, heart pounding, certain I'd find a suet-faced, overweight, weenie-wagging, knuckle-tattooed convict pointing a pistol at me from the driver's seat, but it was empty. I fired up the car and roared off the farm to the main road, where I nearly collided with the old Volvo station wagon wallowing around the last corner, Larry's frantic face pressed almost to the windshield.

Somewhat irrationally, I was obsessed with the dogs, certain that they would be shot when Sensabaugh approached the house and they ran, curious and friendly, in a pack toward him. I insisted on going back. When we got to the garage, Larry grabbed a shotgun and was about to make a tour of the house when we saw a scarecrow-like figure running awkwardly toward us along a fencerow, a pistol in his downward-pointing hand. We froze in indecision and fear.

At that cinematically perfect moment the helicopter reemerged from making a run along the river and banked down so close that we could see the anxious face of the pilot. With exaggerated arm motions we semaphored him toward the approaching figure. Right on cue, in a heroic Hollywood hurrah, a phalanx of speeding cop cars crested the hill, nearly going airborne, their wheels appearing elliptical with speed. They headed straight toward the copse of trees into which the fugitive had disappeared.

I had enough time after the deputies arrived to grab a little digital camera, and we stood on the porch, watching the men getting out of their cars and walking, with stunning nonchalance, toward the woods. They amiably hollered to Sensabaugh, who was then hiding behind a tree, to give up and come on back. He was having none of it, and the next thing we knew, the men were scrambling back to their opened car doors for cover as Sensabaugh opened fire. Dumbly we stood there watching as the firefight continued, until we realized that this was the real thing. *Incoming!*

We ducked behind the porch columns. After more rounds came a moment of silence. Then we heard the tinnily distinguishable pop of a lone pistol shot from within the trees. It was a shot to the head.

David Sensabaugh fell among the stumps and bracken of that untended copse, this man who had been the terrifying bogeyman in the closet, the Jack the Ripper, Hannibal Lecter, Perry Smith and Dick Hickock of my excitable imagination, bleeding out in the milky winter light.

In the end, it turned out he wasn't like any of those, and not overweight or weenie-wagging either, not even close. He was just a kid, my son's age, nineteen: skinny, wet, cold, scared, exhausted, confused, and defiant. And dead in my front field.

When it was over, after the medical examiner and ambulance teams had cleared out, we watched from the porch as Sensabaugh's weeping mother was led back to her car, and the trucks, television vans, and helicopter all took off. Then came a strange silence, a deep absence of something, and the farm grew still, as if beginning to heal itself.

I walked over to the place where he died. The underbrush was matted down, patches of blue and orange spray paint marked coordinates of some kind, yellow crime tape hung on the wild rose, and, at the base of a hickory tree, a dark pool of blood glistened on the frozen soil. I was tempted to touch its perfectly tensioned surface. Instead, as I stared, it shrank perceptibly, forming a brief meniscus before leveling off again, as if the earth had taken a delicate sip.

Death had left for me its imperishable mark on an ordinary copse of trees in my front yard. Never again would I look out of my kitchen window at that lone cedar on the prow of hickory forest in the same way as I had before. I would never be free of the memory of what happened there. But would a stranger, coming upon it, say, a century later, somehow sense the sad, lost secret of the place, the sanctity of this death-inflected soil?

22

Bearing Witness

I chose to play the role of that hypothetical stranger, but on different soil and much more than a century later, when I visited Civil War battlefields, looking for the answer to that very question: does the earth remember? Do these fields, upon which unspeakable carnage occurred, where unknowable numbers of bodies are buried, bear witness in some way?

And if they do, with what voice do they speak? Is there a numinous presence of death in these now placid battlefields, these places of stilled time?

Some years before I took these battlefield photographs, my friend Niall had sent me Wisława Szymborska's "Reality Demands." It's a haunting, wildflower-at-ground-zero of a poem that gazes unblinkingly as life goes on at the world's most blood-soaked battlefields. It reports "Music pours / from the yachts moored at Actium"

> *and couples dance on their sunlit decks . . .*
>
> *The grass is green*
> *on Maciejowice's fields,*
> *and studded with dew,*
> *as is usually the case with grass.*
>
> *Perhaps all fields are battlefields,*
> *All grounds are battlegrounds,*
> *those we remember*
> *and those that are forgotten . . .*

"There is so much Everything," Szymborska wrote, "that Nothing is hidden quite nicely." These lines, I decided, posed an artistic challenge that needed answering.

Five months after the shooting on our farm, in May 2001, I drove to the battlefield at Antietam and spent the night. Just past dawn, I pulled my rolling darkroom into a far corner of a field by the Burnside Bridge. The grasses were pendulous with dew, and it took a hot spring sun to lighten them into an airy undulation. I watched it happen. The fields began to ripple like satin cloth flapping in slow motion, as each stalk, exuberant with seed, swayed in easy unison with its neighbors. I looked across those oblivious fields, and thought Isaiah was right: *surely the people is grass.*

I wasn't alone in having these thoughts before the death-hallowed ground of Antietam. Indeed, I had plenty of company; by midmorning busloads of tourists stood reverently looking out across the landscape. I'm pretty sure their thoughts, too, were about the power of death to transform the perfectly ordinary fields before them, looking like every other field they had passed on the interstate, into something profoundly moving.

When I see an ordinary landscape like that, I also see the underpinnings of death; when the American prairies unfurl beneath my airplane window, or when I eagle-eye the trails as my horse gallops along them, I am reminded of the powdery bones shifting uneasily beneath all of it. And the skeletal bones of living humans, deep within a healthy body standing before me: I imagine them, too.

Among my father's collection of death iconography is a reproduction of a hanging scroll by the nineteenth-century Japanese painter Kawanabe Kyyōsai. In it, the eccentric fifteenth-century Zen monk Ikkyū dances with joyous abandon on the head of a skeletal courtesan, as a conga line of smaller skeletons, one holding the bare ribs of a fan, weaves around the pair. This same Ikkyū is known for his cautionary and unsentimental appraisal of earthly love: "Remember that under the skin you fondle lie the bones, waiting to reveal themselves."

In these lines, Ikkyū forms an unlikely cross-cultural kinship with Flaubert, a writer I highly esteem, as did my father. In an 1846 letter to his longtime mistress, Louise Colet, Flaubert echoes Ikkyū's observation:

I always sense the future; the antithesis of everything is always before my eyes. I have never seen a child without thinking that it would grow old, a cradle without thinking of a grave. The sight of a naked woman makes me imagine her skeleton.

What is wrong with us? Is this a sign of incipient madness? In Beckett's *Endgame*, the invalid Hamm tells his servant about visiting a friend in an insane asylum. Hamm, in an attempt to cheer the demented friend, drags him to the window and cries: "Look! There! All that rising corn! And there! Look! The sails of the herring fleet! All that loveliness!" The madman turns back to his corner. Where Hamm sees loveliness, the madman sees ruin.

As for me, I see both the beauty and the dark side of things; the loveliness of cornfields and full sails, but the ruin as well. And I see them at the same time, at once ecstatic at the beauty of things, and chary of that ecstasy. The Japanese have a phrase for this dual perception: *mono no aware*. It means "beauty tinged with sadness," for there cannot be any real beauty without the indolic whiff of decay. For me, living is the same thing as dying, and loving is the same thing as losing, and this does not make me a madwoman; I believe it can make me better at living, and better at loving, and, just possibly, better at seeing.

After two trips to Antietam, my diminutive greyhound Honey and I headed toward the thick cluster of Virginia battlefields in the Piedmont.

Leaving behind our serene Shenandoah Valley and crossing the Blue Ridge, we drove through increasing urban sprawl, catching glimpses of battlefield markers sandwiched between entrances to big-box stores. Entering the government-protected battlefield sites, I found the physical remains of the war immediately perceptible,

especially at the Spotsylvania Courthouse where the landscape bulged with earthworks so well preserved that they appeared serviceable for the next Civil War (which, given the present state of our politics, seems no longer so far-fetched). It was high noon when we got there and not a soul stirred. When Honey and I got out and walked around those rolling swells, one of us dislodged a lead Minié ball, deformed and dusted with white oxidation; the spoor, the spoils of war still surfacing, unbidden and irrepressible. Death owns these fields entirely. It sculpted this ravishing landscape and will hold the title to it for all time. The down payment, a deposit of fallen bodies, hopes, loves, joys, and fears, is now the dark matter of death's creation.

With the midafternoon heat, Honey and I retreated with the cameras into the woods, which were furiously thrumming with locusts and curiously sparse. The trees there seemed retarded in their growth, unconfident. Oaks were spindly; the Scotch pine poorly needled.

These had to be the great-grandbabies of the trees that stood during the Civil War, but still they seemed sickly, as if the hot metal embedded in their ancestors had weakened the saplings as they struggled up through that lead-poisoned soil.

In the late afternoon, my favorite time to photograph, we left the woods and went back out into the fields, empty now of tourists. Within the shadow of a luxuriant climbing grape that romped over a lone cedar, I set up the camera and Honey dug into the cool dirt for a place to sleep. The smell of that soil came up to me; the smell of ancient bloodshed, of bodies plowed under, all part of the land, part of the earth I was breathing, the creamy smell of the feminine force in the world. That force is Death, the dark, damp, implacable creator of life, the terrible mother who nourishes us and by whom we are, in time, consumed.

While Honey slept, I photographed in the waning light, the lumpen shapes of the vine-covered cedars looming monstrously over me. When finally it was too dark for pictures, I set up the tent at the top of a hill and scooped the remaining handful of ice from the cooler for a gin and tonic. Honey ate her supper, then curled next to me on the blanket while I stared down at a field nourished by the fallen.

As I watched, rising tendrils of ground fog pierced the gloaming, as if the spirits of the battlefield dead were drifting toward me. Those men, once vehemently real, are now vanished as utterly as I myself will be, these fields and distant mountains the final vision for their closing eyes, as they are for mine. The rich body of earth took them in its loamy embrace, acknowledging with each spring's luxuriant rebirth their dumb demands for remembrance.

The air was fragrant where I lay. It smelled of dirt and of grass, the eternal life of the dead. As wispy mist wrapped around the tent, I extinguished the lantern, and we bedded down for the night.

23

The Sublime End

I was in Sweden recently, where I discovered a particularly evolved attitude toward the disposal of dead bodies (and, of course, toward nudity, sex, war, gender issues, and so on). Having just researched the topic of whether it would be legal for my unembalmed, unincinerated, de-organed and de-eyeballed corpse to be simply placed in a hole dug in my pasture, I was intrigued to learn of a novel Swedish solution to human burial. In a country where cemetery space is at such a premium that older bodies are dug up and reburied more deeply so that second- and third-story tenants can be installed in the same plot, the practical Swedes have now developed a system for composting human remains.

They start by freezing the corpse in a vat of liquid nitrogen. Once solid, it is easily shattered into tiny frozen pieces, nugget-sized, by ultrasound waves or, somewhat less palatably, a hammer mill, a process likened by one proponent to that of making chipped beef. The nuggets are then freeze-dried and placed, with a starter of bacteria, in a biodegradable box to be buried as fertilizer for whatever plant you place above your still-serviceable "loved one." In my view, this is about as close as we're ever going to get to reincarnation: our very atoms coursing through the venous leaves of, for example, a long-lived oak.

It seems only right that we should set our species to the same immemorial task as any other compostable matter—the leaves piling up and rotting on the forest floor, or the kitchen scraps thrown every week onto the compost. The amount of resources expended in unnecessary funeral operations is absurd. Even cremation, long considered the simplest, least wasteful solution, uses a lot of power to produce temperatures sufficient to incinerate a human body (around 1,700 degrees). Cremation also releases volatilized mercury from dental fillings into the atmosphere, an arcane fact that concerns the Swedes.

So why not just let bodies decompose like any other compost, giving them, literally, a possibility for new life? The earth is well practiced in the business of efficient, ecologically sound burial: an average-sized human body, if buried in heavily soiled wood shavings from a horse stable and aerated every ten days, is disposed of in just over six weeks.

Now, you might reasonably ask, who on earth figured that out, and the answer is: a graduate student at the University of Tennessee's Anthropology Research Facility, popularly known as the Body Farm. The program endeavors to determine exactly how human bodies decompose, codifying stages of decay and the environmental and situational factors that affect it.

For years I tried to get permission to photograph there, writing the founder, a friendly and open-minded man named Dr. Bill Bass, who at first gave me permission but had to retract it after his board got wind of it. Then, in another instance of felicitous timing, Kathy Ryan at the *New York Times Magazine* asked me in the fall of 2001, not quite a year after the convict died on my farm, if I wanted to go to the Body Farm on assignment. Although commercial work is something I never do, I jumped at it. I was in.

Packing up my cameras and my wet-plate darkroom, I drove late at night to Knoxville, laying over at a seedy 1950s-era hotel on the airport strip that had a curtain-churning heater under the single-pane picture window in my room. At a frosty 7:00 a.m. the next morning I knocked on the office door of the wickedly handsome Murray Marks, my Forensics Department contact, who led me to the three-acre plot, its tall, wooden fence topped with razor wire, where bodies, donated or unclaimed, were laid out to decompose.

It was October, and, except for the dense smell of carrion, the overgrown and heavily treed hillside appeared to be just an unremarkable corner of scrubland not yet taken over by the parking lots lapping it on three sides. Murray unlocked the big gates, and I backed my Suburban into the opening, nearly filling it. As I climbed out, Murray was already walking back toward his car throwing out a casual wave and a "Good luck."

This was not what I expected.

I squeezed between the car and the fence and stepped into death's little garden plot. It was singularly quiet, save for the rustling of squirrels in the heavy leaf-fall and the droning of the HVAC at the nearby medical facility. The remaining leaves of the hickories were a brilliant yellow, and the pokeweed was empurpled at the stalk, with only a few leaves still green. There was not another living soul inside that fence with me. The only person I saw right away was a very tall dead man, lying on a level part of the landscape, dressed in mismatching reds, his long arms protruding from a sweatshirt that read HARVARD.

He was hugely swollen and his nostrils and ears were frothing with something gaseous. I now know it was bloat, a process of methane expansion that occurs, depending on the temperature, several days after death. It usually resolves without actual explosion, but looking at Harvard that morning I wasn't so sure he wouldn't pop at any minute. I felt pity for his distended midsection, jaundiced skin, and the cold-looking gap between the sweatpants and socks.

One thing about the helpless dead struck me right away: you want to fix them up, to press the sagging lips together, close the indiscreet legs, wipe the dripping butt, shutter the liquefying eyes. Surely if they had their druthers and knew they were going to be exposed to the scrutiny of strangers, they would have had their roots touched up or run a razor over their chin. Poor Harvard: six foot seven, he was too big for the clothes from Goodwill that the graduate student, probably doing research on the effects of clothing on decomposition, had bought for him. Several days of postmortem beard growth had roughened his cheeks, and his fingernails were dirty and long. He looked like a Dickensian down-and-out who had stumbled into Lewis Carroll's body-stretching fantasy by mistake.

I suppose it was the red that drew my eyes right away to Harvard, but in much the same way that light-struck eyes adjust to darkness, as I stood looking around me, my death-struck eyes now began to see bodies every-where—under the arching spirea branches, atop plywood boxes, beneath woven wire cages, drifted over with leaves, paired and in groups, many half-gnawed with missing parts, some nearly skeletal and some still zipped in body bags.

I walked up to a white body bag on the slope above Harvard, and, since Murray had told me I could open any of the bags, I gingerly unzipped it a bit. My heart lurched in its cavern as the gap revealed first the red hair and then the beautiful pale face of Gail Nardi, a reporter from the *Richmond Times Dispatch* who had interviewed me years before. I leapt away as if burned, and skittered back down the hill, heart pounding, reflexively swiping my hands against my pants.

Looking around to see if anyone had seen this animated little dance, I caught sight of a vulture in a locust tree, which cocked a defiant eye toward me and flapped down next to Gail. Yelling and waving my arms, I ran back toward her and he moved away on his pinkish legs but did not fly. I opened the bag a little further, revealing a pouchy white stomach. Maybe it wasn't Gail. This woman was way larger than I remember Gail, and why would Gail be here in Tennessee? I tried to remember what Gail looked like. Didn't she have green eyes? I lifted an eyelid: milky blue.

I freed her shoulders and, grabbing the sides of the bag, I pulled up, and she lazily rolled out, landing on her stomach. This definitely wasn't Gail. The legs were elephantine, out of proportion to her body.

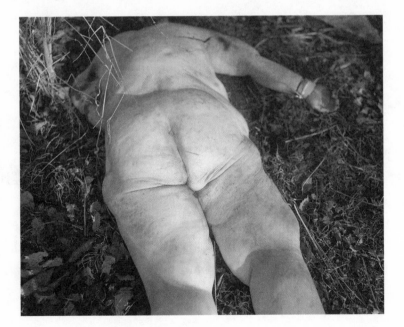

Relieved but still a bit shaken, I went back to the Suburban to get my cameras and set up the collodion chemicals. When I turned back to look at not-Gail, the vulture was next to her, pecking out the exposed eye, then working on the lips.

I made a wet-plate exposure of the bird, but the emulsion nearly slid off the glass in the cold. Blowing on my wet hands, I walked back to not-Gail and could hear the vulture grunting with his efforts. I shooed him away and saw that in just a matter of minutes he had rendered her face unrecognizable.

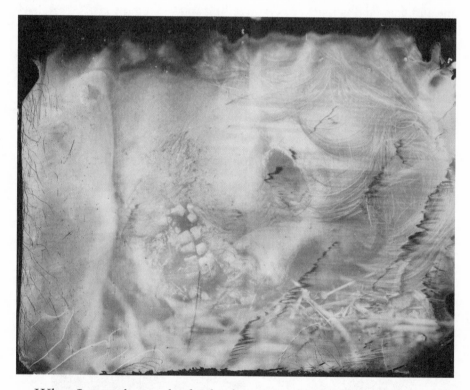

When I turned away, he fearlessly returned to her, hissing and occasionally spreading his huge wings. I thought, somewhat dubiously, of Robinson Jeffers's poem "The Vulture" in which he anticipates the "sublime end" of his body when it is eaten and becomes part of a carrion bird, a feathery, sharp-eyed life after death, "an enskyment."

Directly up the hill from not-Gail was White Mary, lying on her side, orange and brown liquids draining onto her white body bag, her skull sawed in half, presumably from an autopsy. She was wrapped in cloth as translucent and beautiful as any woven for the Pharaohs, the graceful drape of the reeking, saturated fabric accentuating her slender outline, the stickweed stems offering a rigid contrast to the line of her hip.

Except for White Mary, Harvard, and a few others, slender people were not much in evidence among the forty or so bodies in residence when I visited. Later, Murray told me that they had to buy a forklift to carry in the increasing numbers of the obese. And because the extra mass takes much longer for the maggots to reduce to bone and smear, they tie up the available parking places as they putrefy.

Pausing by a body and waiting until the rustling of the leaves quieted, I could hear the maggots noisily eating, a sound sometimes like the crackling of Rice Krispies in milk and other times, like raw hamburger being formed by hand into patties. The bulging skin roiled with their movements beneath it. In one instance recorded at the Body Farm, the industrious maggots reduced a man by forty pounds in just twenty-four hours, expanding themselves from the size (forgive the culinary comparisons) of an uncooked grain of rice to a plump macaroni.

Maggots had barely begun their work on Tunnel Man when I first saw him, although the vultures clearly had: they'd plucked his eyeballs from their sockets and torn the delicate skin around his ears. He was lying on his stomach, a diaper-like cloth still stuck on his pink buttocks, the red-berried branches of a common viburnum protectively arching over him.

Within a day, however, his bizarrely pink skin had begun to peel back, as if he had suffered a bad sunburn, revealing heavy pores of darker, less lifelike skin. His fingers appeared to be wearing little wrinkled finger rubbers, akin to those clerks use for counting money. The following day, after his body had been snuffled over by some animal, I grabbed his hand to move his outstretched arm back in place, and the whole top layer of skin came off in my palm as though I had removed his glove. By then, his face had blackened and maggots had begun spilling out of his nostrils and ears. Soon the eye sockets were a riot of turmoil, and wasps and yellow jackets were drowning in the spreading brown pond of goo beneath what used to be a face.

My tripod didn't go down far enough to photograph him straight on, so I took the 8 × 10 camera off and set it on the ground. I then stretched out flat behind it in the dirt so that I could look into the ground glass, trying not to think of whatever, *whomever*, it was I was lying on. Since the day was cloudy, the exposure was a long one. The furiously churning maggots over the necessary six-second exposure gave Tunnel Man a beautiful diaphanous veil over his ruined features.

I found him good company, Tunnel Man. He wasn't afraid of death, he was in no pain, and he had finally relinquished control. He was so much less painful to be around than, say, my then-living mother, lying on her back in the retirement home, tears leaking from her eyes, her face balled up with fear. In a sense, Tunnel Man had more life in him; life was feeding on him, the beetles and worms making inroads and leaving behind soil into which stray seeds would sink their fibrous roots.

Surely the people is grass.

We don't talk much about what happens when we die. Years ago, sex was the unmentionable thing; now it's death. This modern form of prudery encourages the spectacle of funerary pomp and the ironic sight of cemetery visitors picking wildflowers from the gravesites that hold literally more of the dead than the carved tombstone ever could. Although I've never been prone to that almost universal form of squeamishness, I have long been afflicted with the metaphysical question of death: what does remain? What becomes of us, of our being?

Remember that song by Laurie Anderson in which she says something about how when her father died it was as though a library burned to the ground? Where does the self actually go? All the accumulation of memory—the mist rising from the river and the birth of children and the flying tails of the Arabians in the field—and all the arcane formulas, the passwords, the poultice recipes, the Latin names of trees, the location of the safe deposit key, the complex skills to repair and build and grow and harvest—when someone dies, where does it all go?

Proust has his answer, and it's the one I take most comfort in—it ultimately resides in the loving and in the making and in the living of every present day. It's in my family, our farm, and in the pictures I've made and loved making. It's in this book. "What thou lovest well remains." That line, from Pound's Canto 81, is carved on the tombstone above the rank hole where we deposit our family's ashes.

> *What thou lovest well remains,*
> *the rest is dross*
> *What thou lov'st well shall not be reft from thee*
> *What thou lov'st well is thy true heritage . . .*

I went back to see Tunnel Man a few months later. He was skeletal, unrecognizable.

On one of my last days at the Body Farm, a female graduate student showed up around noontime and began futzing with the body she'd apparently been assigned—taking measurements and counting the carrion beetles and moth larvae. His skin was like mummified leather, a golden caramel color, as if it'd been basted with a buttery glaze and run under the broiler. Next to him was a nearly skeletonized woman haloed by an enormous grease stain, suggesting that she had likely decomposed during the hot weeks of September.

I was awfully glad to see another living being, having spent two days alone, or at least among some very uncommunicative company, so I went over and struck up a conversation with her. She seemed to have a corollary custodial assignment and, while I was chatting her up, she set about raking loose bones into a greasy pile. As she stuffed each body into its own gray plastic bag, a rack of ribs curled out of the top of one and sharp shinbones pierced the edges of another.

After a while, from outside the big gates, came the sound of an engine and two doors slamming. We went over to find an idling minivan, a sticker on its back window asserting that a middle-schooler was on the honor roll, and two men who looked to be in their late thirties, wearing baseball caps, standing uncertainly next to it.

They addressed me first, as the elder, but immediately realized their mistake when I blanched as they opened the hatchback, to reveal a body laid out amid the sports equipment. They then turned to the graduate student, who was busily putting on a pair of blue surgical gloves, and explained that they'd brought their friend Shelby to her, even though they had no idea why he wanted this for himself.

The men and I stood looking at the body, and one of them began to cry softly, his head pressed against the car, while the graduate student presented the other with the necessary paperwork on a clipboard. Shelby had been a tall man and was in good flesh, about the same age as his two friends. Except for the crudely sewn autopsy scar and his oddly deflated stomach cavity, he seemed perfectly healthy. He had a cloth covering his hips.

The grad student, like a dorm counselor checking in a freshman on the first day of school, glanced up from the clipboard and reported that the plot assigned to Shelby was at the top of the hill. We all glanced up in the direction of her gestures, then stood looking at this dead man, who must have weighed at least 200 pounds. After a beat, the crying friend rubbed his eyes and said, "Let's get on with it," and he and the other man began pulling Shelby out by the feet. The cloth pulled away and revealed a handsome phallus nested in pale pubic hair as the two men dragged the lower limbs out of the family minivan.

Grabbing an arm each, they pulled the corpse upright, the heavy head flopping on its stalk, front to back. Then each man draped an arm over his shoulder and began to haul Shelby along, his feet leaving a trail in the leaves. They got about ten steps and the crying man stopped, overcome.

The graduate student and I exchanged glances, and she suggested that she and I grab the legs and the two guys could carry the arms. We flipped him over and, with the woman and me in the lead, one of Shelby's legs in each of our arms, we lurched past White Mary, Tunnel Man, and several large oblong grease smears crosshatched with the impressions of rake tines. Both men were crying now, taking turns covering Shelby's flopping genitals with their baseball caps. The grad student and I pressed forward like two dray horses between the carriage shafts of Shelby's big legs.

Nothing is deader, or more ungainly, than a dead body. Dead weight is right. The pitch of the hill steepened, and the men were stumbling and sobbing behind us. Periodically Shelby's legs would be ripped out of our arms as one or the other of the men lost his grip, both emotionally and physically. Shelby's shoulder would sag heavily to the ground, the man supposed to be supporting it weeping against the chest sutures. Shelby had been allotted a berth alongside the fence at the very top of the hill and as we approached it the two friends, hooking a baseball cap on the bouncing testicles for the last time, lowered their end of Shelby and peeled off into the woods, leaving us holding the legs. Sighing, we reversed ends and each of us wrapped our arms around Shelby's clammy torso in an unsettlingly intimate embrace. At the count of three, we hefted him upright, his naked body pressed against us, and man-hauled him to his weedy little plot. At a second count of three, we both released and Shelby folded to the ground, his head making a sickening melon-y sound.

Panting, we stood looking down at him, crumpled inelegantly against some stickweed, and then we turned him onto his stomach, the preferred method for Body Farm decomposition. The grad student reached into her pants pocket and brought out a scalpel and made a quick slice in the back of the thigh, revealing a layer of fluffy fat and bright muscle.

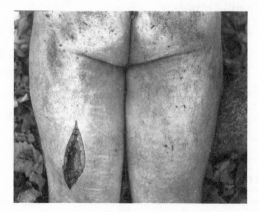

She was putting a sample of the still somewhat bloody flesh in a plastic bag just as the two friends emerged, red-faced and snot-nosed, from the underbrush. Since they seemed to have composed themselves, I asked them about Shelby. Who was he? How had he died?

They said he was a schoolteacher, the picture of health, and had died watching TV in the basement.

What? Died just like that? "What was the cause of death?" I asked, trying to keep the alarm I was feeling out of my voice.

"No clue," the friends said. There had been an autopsy that found absolutely nothing.

At this point I was on pretty good terms with dead bodies, inured to the putrefaction, the pus and particles of exploded tissue, the slime and lymph leakage from ruptured membranes. I had watched unperturbed as flies, just done laying their eggs in Tunnel Man, had lit on my arm as I focused my camera. I had returned at night to my room reeking of decomposition, the gag-making stench wafting up afresh from my film holders as I changed negatives in the motel bathroom. I had slipped on chunks of fatty adipocere and found hair stuck to the brake pedal of the Suburban as I drove home at night.

But nothing, none of this bothered me as much as realizing that I had pressed myself, as a lover would, against a man who had just died of completely unknown causes. His skin cells were now invisibly woven among the fibers of my shirt, and a rusty smear from the autopsy incision bloodied my forearm. I felt a little queasy. The first crying man placed his baseball cap, no longer needed as a fig leaf, back on his head, and we went down the hill.

Death as an artistic theme always produces a self-portrait, Joseph Brodsky once remarked, but this was coming just a little too close for me. I packed up for the day and drove back to the seedy airport strip, locating my motel by the bright lights of a liquor store that sold Everclear grain alcohol by the half gallon. I got in the shower and scrubbed down until I was as pink as Tunnel Man's back.

24

The X Above My Head

When my father casually handed me his travel-scarred Leica in January 1969, I knew almost nothing about photography except that I had occasionally been on the receiving end of the camera, modeling some at Putney for Jon Crary, my boyfriend at the time, now a distinguished art critic and academic. The Putney photographs reverberate still with the plucked string of actual memory, but not so the pictures from a decade earlier that my father took. I only "remember" him taking those pictures in the photo-adulterated way that the past becomes accessible to us. No transporting resonance floods my senses with the smells, temperature, textures, and emotions of that time. Those notes have faded, the string is stilled, the memories silent.

I have only the pictures. From them, I reconstruct full-blown, photo-detailed memories based on scraps of information I can pick out with a magnifying glass held over my father's contact sheets, memories constructed entirely of silver grain suspended in gelatin. They have no continuum; they float untethered from any recollection of the moments on either side of the fraction of a second during which my image was committed to film. I have no memory of the preparations for the trip to Goshen Pass, where he set me up to be photographed, pensive and (I'm guessing—or do I remember?) chilly in the morning light.

Nor do I remember the formal portrait session in the living room for which my hair had been carefully parted and combed, probably with some protest and doubtless by Gee-Gee, who had the patience of a stalagmite. Studying the many failures on the contact sheet, I suspect that I was not the most willing subject and understand why he was so proud of this picture, submitting it to contests and framing it for his office.

It has a limpid directness, and I happen to know how hard it is to get a peevish child to look with intent into a camera.

I wasn't peevish for the picture that Jon shot a decade later, although I see a similarity in the gimlet gaze, a gaze that knows how to respond, in a post-*Blow-Up* kind of way, to the suave seduction of the lens.

Breaking all the parietal rules, I had snuck Jon up to my attic room in Tower Dorm on that Wednesday afternoon in 1968, my seventeenth birthday. He shot the picture by the light of a dormer window just before we burrowed deep into the under-eave closet and washed down a bag of chocolate chip cookies with half a bottle of Scotch. After puking all night, I never again touched Scotch whisky. The memories that are conjured up by the photograph Jon took that day would have been disparaged by Proust as too shallow, limited to the single dimension of the visual, and, ultimately, voluntary. I think he has a point; the memory payoff from the picture is nothing compared to the pungent revelations provided me by all my other senses. Proust would call these involuntary memories, which reside within an impalpable and complex scaffolding of recollection. Unbidden, I have a vivid imaginative recall of the textures, tastes, and smells of that afternoon kneeling at the Tower Dorm toilet each time I accidentally mistake a whisky for a bourbon. These are memories that cannot be ripped apart and thrown in the woodstove like my journals or photographs; there's no burning up the layered memory trace of smell and taste.

⚬———⚬

Those few times on the other side of the lens and the pictures in *The Family of Man* and *You Have Seen Their Faces* were all I knew about photography when my father initiated the wobbly momentum that righted itself to become my artistic life. On my first day of taking pictures, with the Leica and a perplexing Weston light meter in hand, I did what I still do to this day: I headed out into the Rockbridge County countryside to find the good light.

And the subject matter?

Well, judging by the earliest pictures from the first rolls of film, I shot many of the same things I still focus on today: the landscape of the rural South, with its keen ache of loss and memory; relationships among people; the human form; and the ineffable beauty of decrepitude, of evanescence, of mortality.

(It should be noted that Robbie Goolrick, longtime family friend, probably has as much claim as I do to this picture of—l. to r.—his sister, Lindlay, me, and my Putney roommate, Kit, but we have agreed to share the credit.)

Most intriguing to me now as I look back through my earliest work is clear evidence of a precocious premonition of mortality, like this image from my twelfth roll of film late in 1969.

It was taken shortly before I left to work, as part of Bennington College's nonresident term, with the Frontier Nursing Service in one of the poorest pockets of lost America, Harlan County, Kentucky. My job was to muck out the stables and care for the mules and horses that carried us into the hollers of coal country, so remote and treacherous that no vehicle could reach them. Although our mounts were burdened with saddlebags, and we carried backpacks of medical supplies, I usually also carried my camera and occasionally photographed while the nurse worked.

Possibly I knew that taking pictures under these circumstances was a breach of some kind of nursing (and photo) morality, but I was so enthralled with the power of photography to convey a concept (never mind how ham-fistedly) that the altered end result was all that mattered to me. Was I Jim Lewis's asshole who makes lousy art? Does a picture this bad deserve Faulkner's moral pass? I fear not, but these complexities had not yet troubled my art-bewitched, embryonic photo-ethical sensibility.

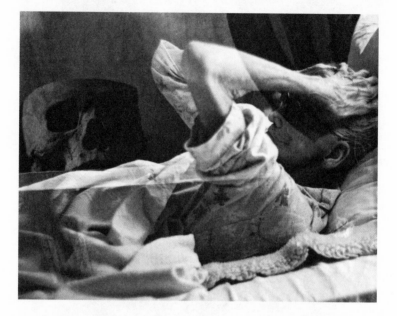

Clearly subtlety wasn't my long suit, but upon my return from Kentucky I toned down the corny skeletal symbols and pressed into service some Byronic drama to make my morbid point. Originality wasn't my long suit, either, in this post-Kentucky work. My father had recently purchased a set of prints of Duane Michals's Death Comes to the Old Lady, a sequence of five images of an old woman who, at the approach of a bourgeois-looking Death, wafts skyward in a blur. I had clearly taken careful note of it before beginning my own death-narrative series.

The first picture in The Dream Sequence is of a pensive young woman at breakfast, still in her nightgown, her robe hung over the chair. In it, she is daydreaming of (or remembering?) a predawn visit from her deadly doppelgänger. The first and last images of the sequence are crisp and sharply focused. Those in-between, depicting the dream state, are soft-focus. I achieved this effect by placing a stocking under the enlarger lens, a trick I had learned from my accomplished and influential photography teacher at Bennington College, Norman Seeff. My models were seventeen-year-old identical twins, Eve and Rhea Huntley.

In the girl's daydream, the doppelgänger gently awakens the sleeper, dresses her, and brushes her hair.

Lightly she plants the kiss of death on her neck, and, in a fashion similar to the old woman in Michals's piece, they are transported with some unearthly velocity toward what looks like a reasonably comfy version of the afterlife.

The daydreamer awakens, still feeling the freighted, phantasmal kiss on her neck.

This early artistic preoccupation with mortality might have been expected given my father's influence and the art and artifacts of death throughout the house, but still I am surprised, going through my old negatives, to find such clear evidence of it so early on. Now I realize that I misspoke in 2003 during the What Remains exhibition at the Corcoran Gallery of Art, when I repeatedly asserted that my photographic exploration of death had begun when my first greyhound, Eva, dropped dead. Clearly I hadn't taken a look at my old contact sheets, where it is abundantly evident. However, Eva's death definitely revived it, kicking it into high gear.

She died on Valentine's Day, 1999, five years to the day after I bought her from a man who had smashed her pelvis by slamming a stall door on her. She was pathetically needy, annoying, and stupid, and I adored her. A graceful creature, despite her injuries, she dropped dead doing what she loved best: running across the hoary fields one early morning at the farm. Larry carried her to the barn and laid her on a plank, where she froze solid.

Refusing to let anyone move her, I wept noisily and unpredictably, irritating everyone in the family. As I stood next to her rigid body, I grew curious about what would finally become of that head I had stroked, oh, ten thousand times, those paws she had so delicately crossed as she lay by my desk, their rock-hard nails emerging from downy white hairs.

Was it ghoulish to want to know? Was it maudlin to want to keep her, at least some part of her? Was it disrespectful to watch her intimate decomposition? I put these questions aside, picked up the phone, and called a friend who, bless his heart, didn't bat an eye at what I was asking him to do.

When he was done skinning her, he brought her back to me in two parts. He carried her body in a straining black plastic bag. Her skin he hooked by a forefinger over his shoulder, like a jacket carried by a politician seeking the rural vote at a county fair. I hung the pelt in the vestibule closet, where it gave me an enormous stomach lurch each time I went to hang a visitor's coat.

The black plastic bag I queasily handed over to Larry. He placed the pink, hairless carcass into a custom-fitted woven steel cage and buried it, marking the spot with a stake. When, months later, I shoveled and brushed aside the fragrant humus as carefully as any field archaeologist, I found what looked like a crude stick drawing of a sleeping dog. Her bones, punctuated by tufts of irreducible hair and small cubes of tofu-like fatty tissue, appeared like a constellation in a black sky. After bagging the larger bones, I reverently picked out the tiny pieces that remained: tailbones, teeth, and claws. Back on the floor in the studio, I reassembled her, head to tail, bone by bone, and set up my camera.

But neither this exploration of Eva's decomposition nor even my early Leica pictures mark the start of my fascination with death. Once again, my archival dig in the boxes of my attic revealed a strange truth.

In a Tupperware container pressed tightly against those "Daddy" and "Evans" boxes under the eaves is a Kodak-yellow X-ray film box from the 1950s, labeled by my father, somewhat deprecatingly with too-obvious quotation marks: Sally's "Art."

Packed inside, the larger papers folded multiple times, are my drawings and paintings from age three to about ten, their dates of execution noted in my father's unmistakable handwriting. My early work had two dominant themes: horses and death. The horse pictures you've seen, generic and uninteresting. But the death drawings are another thing altogether. Strikingly, all of them are of my father. I can only think that they were drawn as an inoculant against the pain of his eventual, inevitable death, certainly not as a wish for it.

This drawing is from 1958, when I was only seven years old. "That's you Dad," it says to the death-eyed, snaggle-toothed corpse.

Even at that early age, I feared my father's death almost pathologically.

My journals give evidence of that fear, with Daddy-death nightmares recounted in dense, dream-stupid detail. One such entry, from my summer in San Miguel, Mexico, in 1969, concludes:

> It frightens me: I have drempt [*sic*] in the past that daddy has died . . . I must come to realize that it <u>will</u> happen—it must assume the form of the lands, the lives, and of the ideas that he has loved. His death must become an integral part of my father and, thus, my past & future & self.

Those nightmares vividly depicted a variety of morbid scenarios, but none of them predicted with accuracy the nature of his actual death. However, a look in the yellow X-ray box reveals that, in fact, I had prophesied it eerily in a drawing that I made, according to the note on the back, on February 16, 1958.

In it, a motley parade of characters (a rabbit, a squirrel, a dog, birds, an angel, and a circus pig with acrobats atop) gathers around the couch where my sleeping father lies. All faces except one are smiling. The one that is not smiling is in a balloon behind the couch, a small figure flanked by two larger ones.

An "X" floats above her unhappy head. A chorus of cries rises to the heavens, around the apparently weeping cloud: "Wake up. Wake up Daddy. Wake up love."

One clear-sighted acrobat observes, "He won't wake up."

Thirty years later, on May 22, 1988, my sleeping father did not wake up, but it took him hours to die. Once he had, we figured out why: as we retraced his last steps, we found that the thirty Seconals he had taken were so old that their glass bottle did not list an expiration date and, never mind that, thirty pills, especially an expired thirty, were barely enough for a fatal dose. Stuck to the bottom of the bottle was one last pill that he must not have been able to choke down. I have it still. It is an incongruously cheerful, almost psychedelic orange.

That Sunday afternoon, after Ron and my father had said their good-byes, I had driven him back to the Roanoke airport to return to New York. Round-trip, it was a bit more than two hours. When I walked back in the door at Boxerwood, Daddy was deeply asleep on the couch, but not dead.

Standing helplessly before him, I probably resembled that small figure in the drawing with the down-turned arc of a frown, an "X" of misery, disbelief, and horror floating above my head.

I knew this was it, and I knew that we were not going to try to save him. My mother showed me a note that Daddy had left. Shakily written on the back of a sheet of his personalized medical prescription notepaper, it was brief and unemotional:

"Dear ones—family & friends I leave you in 'peace of mind' w/ much much love Please do not call First Aid"

Later we were to find a first effort at this note, written confidently in pen on the same prescription paper but ripped in half.

> Dear Ones ——
> I want my family
> + friends — my loved
> ones — to know
> that I'm leaving their
> company in a
> tranquil frame of
> mind.

There is something strange about the two. I have the clear sense that the first, the one in ink, was written at a different time than the second, perhaps the weekend before when he had originally planned his suicide for the convenience of the family. The second, in a shaky hand and in *crayon*, for Chrissake, was written, I am quite sure, after he'd swallowed the last bright orange pill, or the last but one.

Take a look at the picture of him on the couch again: what do we make of that little corner of protruding plastic? It gives evidence of the larger sheet that somebody had thought to put beneath him in case he lost control of his bladder.

Who did this? It could have been Daddy, so afraid of incontinence, but cynically, I thought: "Mama. She loves that sofa."

But when? Was she there when he took the thirty pills and lay down to die? Did she sensibly bustle about, fetching a dry-cleaning bag from a winter coat in the closet, patting it down on the cushions before he stretched out on them for the last time?

Or did my mother go to the grocery store and, when she finished unpacking the groceries, go into the living room and find him? Understanding the situation, did she realize the risk to the couch and shove it under him as he lay dying?

So many unknowns, and she's not here to ask.

However it came about, the couch was protected, and Daddy was dying. But slowly.

With resignation I pulled up a chair and sat beside him as he lay for the next several hours, his chest barely rising with weak inhalations. My brother Chris and our dear friend KB arrived. We took turns at the chair. I remember some "Hurry up and die" jocularity that now causes me regret. Gin and tonics were served, but still he didn't die. His respiration was slow and irregular and I grew dizzy as I tried to match my breaths to his. Occasional gaps in his breathing caused the room to go silent, until his depressed membranes feebly inflated again.

When the last breath lightly shuddered from him, his face almost immediately turned a waxen blue-gray and his muscles slackened as he sagged into lifelessness. As I watched, it appeared to me that he shrank by an almost quantifiable amount, seemingly more than the twenty-one grams vanishing at the moment of death (supposedly of the soul) that Dr. Duncan MacDougall had measured in 1907. For a second, his pale, almost ethereal form reminded me of the delicate mantle of the Coleman lantern at our cabin flaming out into a diaphanous blue ash.

He was facing at that moment whichever of the many death symbols had finally come to him after his fifty years of research—Thanatos, child of night, brother of sleep, and friend of the unhappy, or the Grim Reaper, with his sweeping scythe and galloping white horse, or the dark wing of the gleaming crow. He was at last in the embrace not just of the concept of death, in whose peculiar thrall he had been almost his entire life, but of Death itself.

I, personally, think it was the crow that fetched him away. He had always jokingly remarked (or at least I took it as a joke) that he expected to be reincarnated as a crow, and for a time he had kept one, Jim Crow, as a family pet.

In his later years, he had cultivated an enduring relationship with the Box-erwood crows, calling them to him by banging on a large aluminum pan. The sky would appear to darken above him after a few minutes of clangor, and he would then scatter moistened dog kibble to the seething black mass that landed around him. The crows eagerly anticipated this moment each day, and when they came to him they came for both kibble and compan-ionship, pecking at his shoes and pants legs. This gathering—a murder of crows—was not there to take him away, not then, anyway.

But I think they came back for him.

Here we are, family and friends, after the memorial walk around the gardens at Boxerwood that served as my father's public funeral. My mother is holding the box containing his ashes, and we are preparing to place it in the crypt. It's late afternoon on May 28, the Saturday after his death. I set up the view camera to take a memorial picture. Not so easy with that crowd.

The kids had changed out of their hot funeral finery and were ready for some play with the water hose. Ron Winston had flown back down and was impeccable as always. The rest of us were tired and sad and ready for a stiff drink. I had time for just one picture, and I asked our friend Hunter if she would push the shutter release once I had pulled the dark slide out and returned to the line-up. With an unconvincing "Say: Cheeze," she did, my old Goerz Dagor lens allowing a tenth of a second of light to hit the film, and that was that. I replaced the dark slide, we headed to the crypt with the ashes, and two days later I developed the sheet of film.

As I turned on the light, my eyes popped out on their stalks—what the hell is that wingspread white thing at our feet?

I have no photographic explanation for it. No mirror was in the grass at the tip of my brother Chris's sneaker reflecting the sunset, no errant light flashed or exploded and no chemical light, either. Simply inexplicable.

I am not a particularly credulous person. I don't believe in pictures of UFOs or the ectoplasm of spirit photography or in the existence of the dancing fairies Sir Arthur Conan Doyle endorsed. But when I look at this picture I come as close as I will ever get to the spiritual.

I find comforting the notion that the feathered light was the bright soul crow of my father taking flight. The picture captured his getaway, his enskyment, before the earth overtook the physical remains of that irreducibly complex, unknowable man. Now, on occasion, a crow pecks at my studio door until I come to see what's up. He stands there unafraid, clinging to the vinyl threshold with his strong claws, and cocks his shiny black head, his gleaming eye fixed on mine.

Postscript

EXHIBIT A

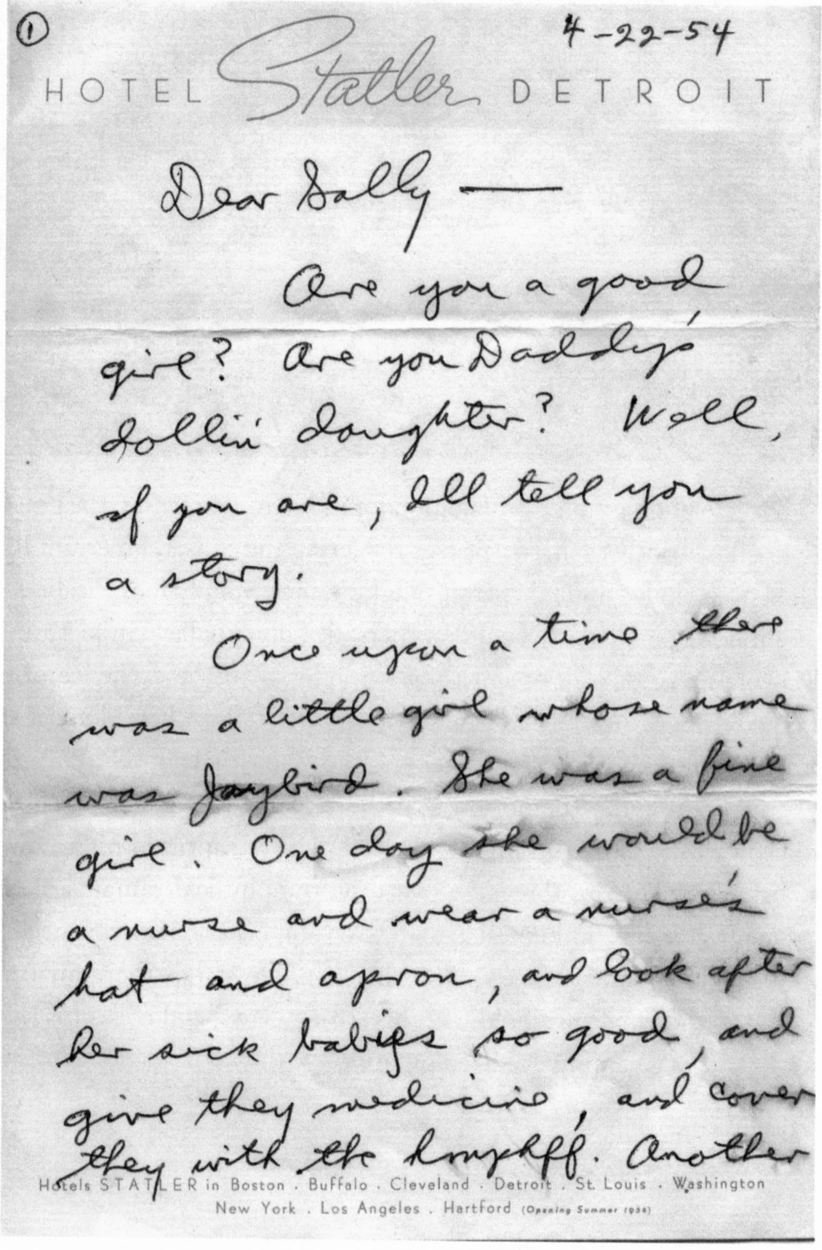

① 4-22-54

HOTEL *Statler* DETROIT

Dear Sally —

Are you a good girl? Are you Daddy's rollin' daughter? Well, if you are, I'll tell you a story.

Once upon a time there was a little girl whose name was Jaybird. She was a fine girl. One day she would be a nurse and wear a nurse's hat and apron, and look after her sick babies so good, and give they medicine, and cover they with the longkff. Another

Hotels STATLER in Boston . Buffalo . Cleveland . Detroit . St. Louis . Washington
New York . Los Angeles . Hartford (Opening Summer 1956)

day she would be a little doggie, and sniff about, and eat off the floor, and scratch herself. Sometimes she was even Susan Burke, a dearly beloved friend. And once long ago she was Santa Claus carrying a big pack of toys. But many, many times during the day she was just plain Jaybird busy at all sorts of things and a joy to her mommy as she went serenely about her housework.

Hotels STATLER in Boston . Buffalo . Cleveland . Detroit . St. Louis . Washington
New York . Los Angeles . Hartford (Opening Summer 1954)

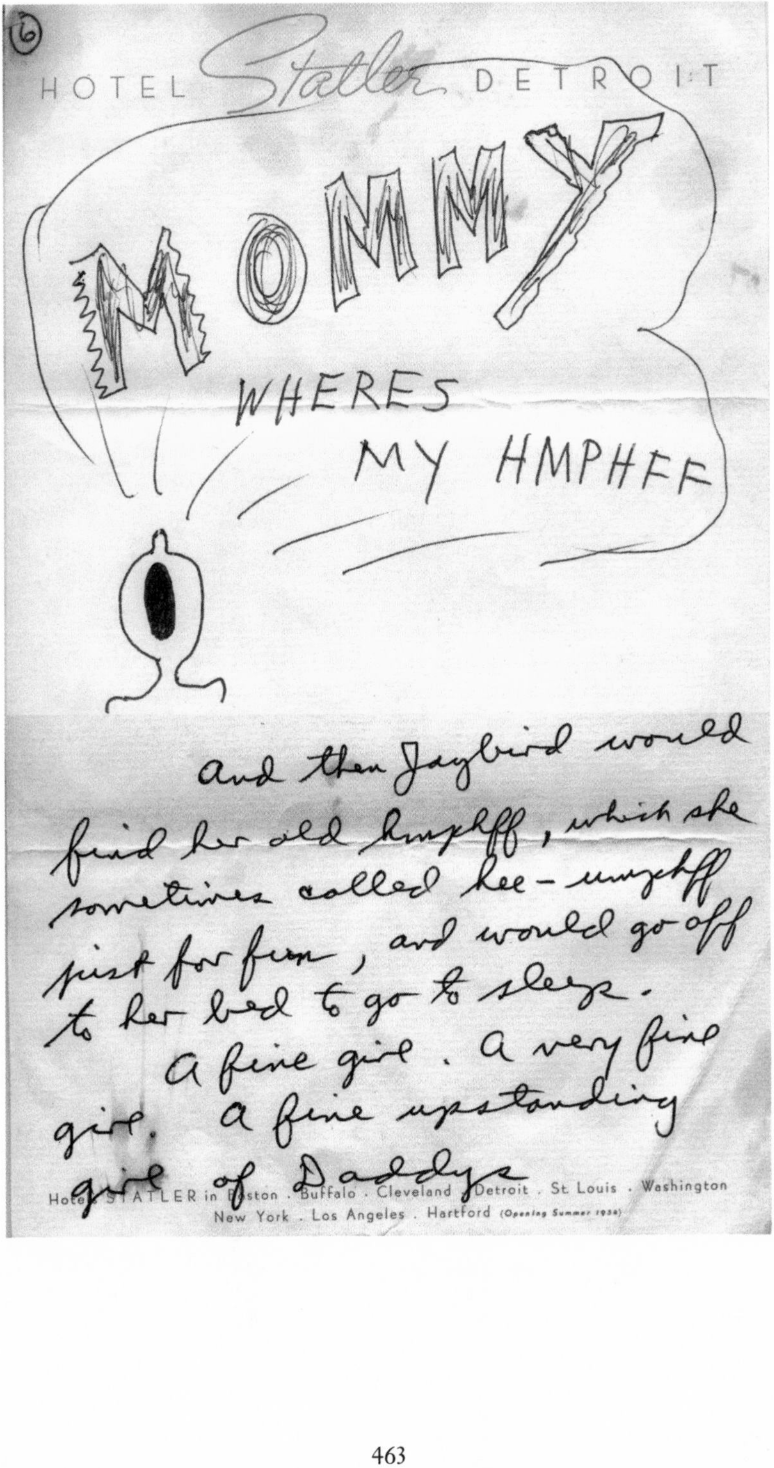

HOTEL *Statler* DETROIT

MOMMY

WHERES MY HMPHFF

And then Jaybird would find her old hmphff, which she sometimes called hee—umphff just for fun, and would go off to her bed to go to sleep.

A fine girl. A very fine girl. A fine upstanding girl of Daddys

HOTEL *Statler* DETROIT

(and mommye)

Lots of love to you,
Daddy

Hotels STATLER in Boston . Buffalo . Cleveland . Detroit . St. Louis . Washington
New York . Los Angeles . Hartford (Opening Summer 1954)

EXHIBIT B

Dear(A) Sally(B)

I(C) have(D) already(E) sent(F) ~~yrtt~~ your(G)

books(H).

love(I)

Daddy(J)

(A) From M.E. deere, beloved, precious; as found in

The cheapest of us is ten groats[1] too dear.

or

My heart's in the Highlands a-chasing the dear.

As used here, dear is merely poetic; but with buy, sell cost, etc., dear is still idiomatic. And between dear and expensive there are differences of nuance that deserve more respect than they get; e.g., an education at Putney at 3600 bucks is expensive but not dear. Needless to elaborate, this statement is subject to severe revision in individual instances.

(B) Sally as used here probably has no relation to Salii, an old Italian college of priests of Mars, but to mention the latter does have the appearance of erudition.[2] The chief business of the Salii fell in March, when they began a procession thru the city, each of them dressed in an embroidered tunic, a bronze breastplate and a peaked helmet, girt about with a sword, while trumpeters walked in front of them. Gad, what a sight! At the temple they danced the war-dance, from which they take their name of Salii or "dancers". ③

In abbrev. Sal [L. salt]. Salt; much used in chemistry, cooking, and wounds, sometimes apparently with doubtful efficacy as indicated by the words, cum grano salis

Sally, n., witticism, squib, quirk, pleasantry. Such as, "Dear quirk." (Hm, a good idea. Ed.).

Sally. To rush out, to make a sally (not this Sally!). Eg. They break the truce, and sally out by night ④   and,

A sally of youth; a sally of levity. Finally,

   Of all the girls that are so smart
     There's none like pretty Sally;
    She is the darling of my heart,
     And lives in our alley. ⑤

Ⓒ The ninth letter and third vowel of the English alphabet. I was first dotted in the fourteenth century ⑥ (I have a vague soupçon that this is not germane; let's try again):

The nominative case of the pronoun of

the first person; the word by which a speaker or writer denotes himself.

> What I am thou canst not be; but what thou art any one of the multitude may be.
>
> S. T. M. Bagley

In metaphysics, the conscious, thinking subject; the ego.

> Between you and I, this is a piece of false grammar[7] which, though often heard, is not sanctioned, like its opposite, It's me, Pussydog.

I, like we, is liable to be used with different meanings, for instance:

> Sometimes isolate into th night
> that my ice hurt, and iola go to
> an i-dr.
>
> Gizella Werbezerk-Piffel[8]

(D). Have. As here used, the possessor of the object(s) and the performer of the action are not necessarily the same. Dost thou remember King Henry V:

> Break thy mind to me in broken English; wilt thou have me?
>
> Shakespeare (authorship doubted).

And for elegance and sheer beauty the following lines by one of the truly prominent younger poets:

> Have a care
> Havelock
> Ellis
> Haversack
> Have a lot
> Take two.

Brown Bogus ⑨

And finally, Shakespeare's Romeo:

> My bounty is as boundless as the sea,
> My love as deep; the more I give to thee
> The more I have, for both are infinite.

Act II, Sc. 2, L.133.

(E) What can one say about Already, for God's sake?! Now if it were Always (I'll be loving you, allllllways ··· etc, etc), — that's a horse⑩ of a different color.

(F) Sent. Past tense and past participle of send. To cause to go or pass from one place to another. Also to send forth, as

> In faith I send thee forth.

Or as used in the past tense:

469

Noah sent fifth a dove.

Also :

Le corps d'un ennemi mort sent toujours bon.
(The body of a dead enemy always smells sweet).

Attributed to Chas IX of France

(G) What is yours is mine, and all mine is yours.

[M.E. yore, youre] absolute possessive.
But Satan now is wiser than of yore.

There is no doubt a natural temptation to substitute the wrong word; the simple possessive seems to pine at separation from its property, a phenomenon perhaps more suitable for the psychologist than for the philologist.

(H) Books Echtt. [A.S. from boc, bece, a beech-tree] (Tree! I'm glad you brought that up! On second thought, I'll make this the subject of another treatise sometime. Ed.) Book, tome, volume, omnibus, publication, inscription ⑪, treatise, codex, libretto, vade mecum, comic book.

470

Books, books, books

(ΣΣΜ) This verbal stroke of genius (if you will pardon the colloquialism) says everything there is to say about books.

① Love, from the A.S. lufu, lufe, love, — the strong yet tender emotion for whatever is considered most worthy of desire in any relation. Any work done or task performed with eager willingness, from the regard one has for the person for whom it is done. With a capital L, Love is the passion of love personified, especially Amor, Cupid, Eros ⑫, Aphrodite, Venus, Astarte, Kama, Freya — all deities of the first order unlike Bacchus who merely was invented by the ancients as an excuse for getting drunk.

The love song of J. Alfred Prufrock: I have measured out my life with coffee spoons.

In the room the women come and go
Talking of Michelangelo ⑬
                    T.S. Eliot ⑭

He who loves not wine, women, and song,
Remains a fool his whole life long.
                    Thorne Smith.

Love your neighbor, yet pull not down your hedge.
                    Trifie Prudentum.

> ①) Daddy. A diminutive form of an arachnid having a small body and eight very long legs ⑮ No known connection to Daedalus, the mythical greek representative of all handiwork, who made the labyrinth at Gnosus for the Minotaur ⑯

This letter was sent to me by my father just before my seventeenth birthday. Its main text, including salutation and sign-off, comprises just ten words. Each of the ten, however, has a footnote, often a long, chatty, quotation-filled footnote, depending from it. Further footnotes spring from the original footnotes and a bibliography is added for good measure, the whole apparatus swelling the letter to eleven handwritten pages.

The footnotes and bibliography combine whimsicality with scholarship, real sources with bogus ones, in a way that William Osler would have approved, and reveal the pleasure my father took in the genre established by Ambrose Bierce's *Devil's Dictionary* (1911). Indeed, upon revisiting the *Devil's Dictionary*, I find that my father borrowed liberally from it. For example, Daddy's definition of dance, "To leap about expressionless to the sound of tittering music, especially with your arms about someone else's property," closely echoes Bierce's: "To leap about to the sound of tittering music, preferably with your arms about your neighbor's wife or daughter."

One of the non-jokey definitions in my father's letter deals with love, "the strong yet tender emotion for whatever is considered most worthy of desire in any relation. Any work done or task performed with eager willingness, from the regard one has for the person for whom it is done. . . . "

Notice what just happened there: my father slid from a legitimate, dictionary-derived definition of love into a similarly straightforward definition of the phrase "labor of love," the sort of thing that in a conventional dictionary might appear farther down in the same entry, among the compounds and variations. No comment or explanation is offered for this digression, and the footnote continues as though what's written relates simply to love. Daddy seems to be completely unaware of folding the "labor of love" into the primary definition of love.

But is it too much of a stretch (Hermes, who gave his name to hermeneutics, is, after all, the god of interpretation) to suggest that this eliding of love into labor has some psychological significance? Perhaps hard work offered this man an outlet for the strong yet tender emotions that he had difficulty expressing otherwise.

TRANSLATION

April 6, 1968

> Dear🅐 Sally🅑
> I🅒 have🅓 already🅔 sent🅕 your🅖 books.🅗
> Love🅘
> Daddy🅙

🅐 **Dear** From M.E. <u>deere</u>, beloved, precious; as found in
The cheapest of us is ten groats❶ too dear.
Or
My heart's in the Highlands a-chasing the dear.

As used here, dear is merely poetic; but with <u>buy</u>, <u>sell cost</u>, etc., <u>dear</u> is still idiomatic. And between <u>dear</u> and <u>expensive</u> there are differences of nuance that deserve more respect than they get; e.g., an education at Putney at 3600 bucks is <u>expensive</u> but not <u>dear</u>. Needless to elaborate, this statement is subject to severe revision in individual instances.

❽ Sally as used here probably has no relation to Sâlîi, an old Italian college of priests of Mars, but to mention the latter does have the appearance of erudition.❷ The chief business of the Sâlîi fell in March, when they began a procession thru the city, each of them dressed in an embroidered tunic, a bronze breastplate and a peaked helmet, gird about with a sword, while trumpeters walked in front of them. God, what a sight! At the temples they danced the war-dance, from which they take their name of Salii or "dancers".❸

In abbrev. Sal [L. salt]. Salt; much used in chemistry, cooking, and wounds, sometimes apparently with doubtful efficacy as indicated by the words, *cum grano salis.*

Sally, n., witticism, squib, quirk, pleasantry. Such as, "Dear quirk." *(Hm, a good idea. Ed.)*

Sally. To rush out, to make a sally (not <u>this</u> Sally!). E.g. They break the truce, and sally out by night.❹   and,

A sally of youth; a salty of levity. Finally,

> Of all the girls that are so smart
> there's none like pretty Sally;
> She is the darling of my heart,
> and lives in our alley.❺

❻ I: The ninth letter and third vowel of the English alphabet. Ĭ was first dotted in the fourteenth century.❻ (I have a vague soupcon that this is not germane; let's try again):

The nominative case of the pronoun of the first person; the word by which a speaker or writer denotes himself.

What I am thou canst not be; but what thou art any one of the multitude may be.

S.T.M. Sagley

In metaphysics, the conscious, thinking subject; the ego.

Between you and I, this is a piece of false grammar❼ which, though often heard, is not sanctioned, like its opposite, *It's me, Pupdog!*.

I, like <u>we</u>, is liable to be used with different meanings, for instance:

Sometimes isolate into the night that my ice hurt,
and iota go to an i-dr.

Gizella Weberzerk-Piffel.❽

❶ **Have**. As here used, the possessor of the object(s) and the performer of the action are not necessarily the same. Dost thou remember King Henry V:

Break thy mind to me in broken English; wilt thou <u>have</u> me?

Shakespeare (authorship doubted).

And for elegance and sheer beauty the following lines by one of the truly prominent younger poets:

Have a care

Havelock

Ellis

Haversack

Have a lot

Take two

Brown Bogus❾

And finally, Shakespeare's Romeo:

My bounty is as boundless as the sea,

My love as deep; the more I give to thee

The more I <u>have</u>, for both are infinite.

Act II, Sc. 2, L. 133.

❺ What can one say about Already, for God's sake?! Now if it were <u>Always</u> (*I'll be loving you, Alllllways*--- etc, etc), -- that's a horse❿ of a different color.
❻ **Sent**. Past tense and past participle of <u>send</u>. To cause to go or pass from one place to another. Also to <u>send forth</u>, as

In faith I send thee forth.
Or as used in the past tense:
Noah sent fifth a dove.
Also:
Le corps d'un ennemi mort <u>sent</u> toujours bon.
(The body of a dead enemy always smells sweet).

Attributed to Chas IX of France

❻ What is <u>yours</u> is mine, and all mine is <u>yours</u>.

[M.E. yore, youre] absolute possessive. But Satan now is wiser than of yore.

There is no doubt a natural temptation to substitute the wrong word; the simple possessive seems to pine at separation from its property, a phenomenon perhaps more suitable for the psychologist than for the philologist.

❿ **Books**. Echttt. [A.S. from <u>boc</u>, <u>bece</u>, a beech-tree] (*Tree! I'm glad you brought that up! On second thought, I'll make this the subject of another treatise sometime. Ed.*). Book, tome, volume, omnibus, publication, inscription❶, treatise, codex, libretto, vade mecum, comic book.

Books, books, books

(E.E.M.) This verbal stroke of genius (if you will pardon the colloquialism) says everything there is to say about books.

❶**Love,** from the A.S. <u>lufu</u>, <u>lufe</u>, <u>love</u>, -- the strong yet tender emotion for whatever is considered most worthy of desire in any relation. Any work done or task performed with eager willingness, from the regard one has for the person for whom it is done. With a capital L, <u>Love</u> is the passion of love personified, especially Amor, Cupid, Eros❷, Aphrodite, Venus, Astarte, Karma, Freya -- all deities of the first order unlike Bacchus who merely was invented by the ancients as an excuse for getting drunk.

The love song of J. Alfred Prufrock:
I have measured out my life with coffee spoons.

In the room the women come and go
Talking of Michelangelo⓭

T.S. Eliot.⓮

He who loves not wine, women, and song,
Remains a fool his whole life long.

Thorne Smith.

Love your neighbor, yet pull not down your hedge.

Trixie Prudentum.

❶ **Daddy.** A diminutive form of an arachnid having a small body and eight very long legs.⓯ No known connection to Daedalus, the mythical Greek representative of all handiwork, who made the labyrinth of Gnosus for the Minotaur.⓰

Footnotes to the Footnotes

❶ *"groat"*: Obsolete; no longer used by the timid.

❷ *"erudition"*: Erudition has been defined as something squeezed out of a book into an empty skull.

❸ *"dancers"*: to dance, v.i. To leap about expressionless to the sound of tittering music, especially with your arms about someone else's property.

❹ *"They break the truce, and sally out by night"*: This refers to political and social events which, having occurred some time ago, need not to be dwelt upon by the modern student of world affairs.

❺ *". . . and lives in our alley"* These lines, of course, are subject to a criticism far too extensive for these brief notes, see Bibliography, and especially the analysis by Sir Sisyphus Ogle.

❻ *"I was first dotted in the fourteenth century"*: by a fly. It is observed by Carlton Bugbutt that the systems of punctuation in use by the various literary nations depended originally upon the social habits and general diet of the flies infesting the several countries.

❼ *"grammar"*: a system of pitfalls thoughtfully prepared for our use.

❽ *"Gizella Weberzerk-Piffel"*: As quoted by Bibette C[orney] Bunscomb in "The Beginning of Naturalism in Druidic Fiction." The remarkable dead-pan ending in the quoted lines contains an enigma that continues to baffle scholars such as Bunscomb.

❾ *"Brown Bogus"*: The merit of Bogus' intensely personal verse, long known to readers of the "little magazines", has now been acknowledged by a broader public.

❿ *"horse"*: cf. Chapter "Coloration in Horses' in Nautybird Curtsy's Horses, 1909, Misty Press, Chincoteague, Md. Among Miss Curtsy's many publications we may single out her large anthology All About Horses which was left tragically incomplete about halfway thru the author's original plan.

⓫ *"inscription"* = something profound written on another thing, such as *"Kilroy was here"*, penciled on the Washington Monument.

⓬ *"Eros"*: Not to be confused with Ralph Ginsberg.

⓭ *"Michelangelo"*: These lines suggest the futility of "arty" talk by dilettantes.

⓮ *"T.S. Eliot"*: See Prof. Hamfat's "The Plant-lore and Garden-craft of T.S. Eliot". Presently, Prof. Hamfat is at work on a monograph proving that T.S. Eliot was familiar with the writings of Shakespeare, and that his poems must be reinterpreted accordingly.

⓯ *"A diminutive form of an arachnid having a small body and eight very long legs."*: Unedible. The study of zoology is full of surprises.

⓰ *"Minotaur"*: The genus has a wide geographical distribution, being deplored wherever found.

Bibliography

J.C. Ramshackle. The Absolute Canons of Taste.
Gildersleeve and Rosencrantz. The Death-Wish in Figurative Painting of
      Neolithic Man.
C.W. Kit + H.K. Caboodle. Paradoxical Persona.
Schmelle Bussybottom. Die Poetischen Beiträge zum Bother.
Torquato Tasso. Epigrams.
Baumgart and Bagatteli. Imperial Symbols in Certain Parking Meters.
S.T.M. Sagley. Personal Communication.
Gregory Giglioni and Hugo Gass. Eruditorium Penitentiale.

Acknowledgments

This book received careful and loving attention from four dear friends: Ann Olson and John Pancake of Goshen Pass, Virginia; Niall MacKenzie of Vancouver, BC; and Michael Sand, my editor at Little, Brown.

Ann and John, bless them, shored up my shaky pins with strong drink and expensive cuts of blood-rare grilled meat, all the while reassuring me that yes, I could do this writing thing. Then they stood behind their promise to edit it all. When I'd go off on some wheezy polemic or fail to meet the Minimum Metaphorical Appropriateness Threshold, they'd gently offer alternatives, and always with unnecessary humility. They were generous with their time and skills, working not just from their home on the Maury River but also from posts as far-flung as Ukraine, Taiwan, Germany, France, and Burma. I offer my sincere thanks for their help.

In my palace of memory, meager though it may be, I have rooms— whole galleries—that are furnished entirely by Niall MacKenzie. His eidetic power of recall, his scholarship, arch wit, and gift of language have enlivened those rooms and, in turn, this book. I am grateful for his ability to help me place certain concepts in historical, social, and personal contexts that would otherwise have escaped me. He edited my lax punctuation to a freaking fare-thee-well, and I thank him for his forbearance. Working with Niall over the past two decades has been like having a history department, *Fowler's*, the *OED*, and Christopher Hitchens at his droll, hilarious best all rolled together and at my disposal.

Throughout the making of this book, and despite considerable vexation, Michael Sand remained as patient, smart, creative, witty, and kind as he has been since we first worked together in 1991. His sense of how this book should look and feel was pitch-perfect, and I don't think we had a single disagreement (okay, just that one). As with the two other books that preceded this one, he guided me through *Hold Still* with a light and deft hand, and I am grateful for his wisdom in doing so. This book is the richer for his intelligence, restraint, and just plain good-heartedness. If only I could run this paragraph by his editorial eye, as I did every other one in this book, it would be a lot better for it.

My brothers, Chris and Bob Munger, gave this book a good going-over, remembering things I had forgotten and forgetting things I thought I remembered, several times setting me straight on my "memory's truths." I especially thank Chris for his careful reading of the book and the time he spent with me on it.

At Little, Brown I'd like specifically to thank Reagan Arthur, Judy Clain, Nicole Dewey, and Garrett McGrath for believing in the book and being so supportive. Copyeditors Betsy Uhrig and Janet Byrne made many helpful suggestions, and Elisa Rivlin's exacting and sometimes witty legal advice probably saved my ass, though costing the book one supremely entertaining anecdote. I have been very lucky to have Laura Lindgren design a few of my books, and this one is as beautiful as all the others. Mario Pulice absolutely nailed the cover on the first try.

Several people helped me with the technical aspects of this book, foremost among them my wonderful assistant and friend, Caitlin Mann (no relation, sadly), who scanned hundreds of pictures, letters, and crumbling scraps of paper. She also taught this Luddite enough that I am now able to manage on the computer without her, something I had thought impossible. Also helpful were Amy Atticks, Lydia Gorham, Gaia Raimondo, Lizzie Cuthbertson, and Flannery McDonnell.

I am very grateful to my dear friends and family members who left their busy lives, many traveling some distance, to come to the Massey Lectures at Harvard: Steve Albahari, Jamie Lee Curtis, Michael Godfrey, Robbie Goolrick, Edwynn Houk and Julie Castellano, Melissa Harris, Peter Jones and Charlotte Frieze, Jessie and Virginia Mann with Liz Ligouri and Eyal Einik, Emily Matthews and Rob Sokolow, Arno and Sandy Minkkinen, Hunter Mohring and Karen Bailey, Bob Munger and Jill Nooney, Rob Munger, John Ravenal, Bev Reynolds, Betsy Schneider, Putri Tan, Mame Warren and Henry Harris, Cathy Waterman, and John and Carol Wood. That they came meant more to me than they could ever know.

I appreciate the time spent with Gee-Gee's only remaining child, ninety-year-old Constance Harris, and her daughter Pat Broadneaux. Their keen humor and observations enriched my understanding of Gee-Gee, and the images they allowed me to use from their family albums add meaningfully to the book.

For their Munger archive help, I thank Jim Baggett, John and Margaret Harper, Alan Heldman, George Jenkins, Mary Marcoux, Margaret Martin, Bob Montgomery, Carolyn Satterfield, and my adored Birmingham family: Edgar, Margot, Edge, and Katharine Marx.

The following helped me with this book in various ways, and I am grateful:

Geoffrey Brock, Steve Cantor, Nicola Del Roscio, Simone Dinnerstein, Bill and Linda Dunlap, Huger Foote, John Habich, Paul Hendrickson, Jon Humburg, Bob Keefe, Rhea Kosovic, Sarah Kennel, Ken Lanning, Sanford Levinson, Jim Lewis, Steve Lydenberg, Janet Malcolm, John Edwin Mason, Seth McCormick-Goodhart, Sammy Moore, Kit Morris, Lynn Nesbit, Ted Orland, Ann Patchett, Ann Ponzio, Kim Rushing and family, Kathy Ryan, Henry Simpson, Andrew Solomon, Anne Southworth, John Stauffer, Michael Steger, Butch Straub, Calvin Tomkins, Catharine Tomlins, and Dodie Kazanjian, Jeffrey Toobin, Lisa Tracy, Mame Warren, Robert Wilson, my friends at Gagosian and Houk Galleries, and the many people who allowed me the use of their pictures or words.

And with deepest love I thank my immediate family: Larry, Emmett, Jessie, and Virginia.

Photo Credits

Page 10: Copyright Becky Pearman Photography

Page 13: William Gillies (The Portrait Group)

Page 50: Norman Seeff

Pages 52 and 53: Coleman Blake

Page 66: Cy Twombly, photo courtesy Nicola Del Roscio and The Cy Twombly Foundation

Page 68: Cy Twombly, photo courtesy Nicola Del Roscio and The Cy Twombly Foundation

Page 72: Nicola Del Roscio and The Cy Twombly Foundation

Page 75: Courtesy The News-Gazette, Lexington, VA

Page 76: Courtesy Washington and Lee University

Page 77: Steve Szabo, photo courtesy estate of Steve Szabo, © Estate of Steve Szabo

Page 78: Beth Trabue Gorman

Page 84: Cy Twombly, photo courtesy Nicola Del Roscio and The Cy Twombly Foundation

Page 113: *Damaged Child, Shacktown* courtesy Library of Congress Prints and Photographs Division, Washington, DC, Farm Security Administration / Office of War Information

Page 135: Courtesy The New York Times Magazine; special thanks to Kathy Ryan for making this possible

Page 145: Cover image courtesy *Aperture, The Body in Question* (*Aperture;* 121: Fall 1990); special thanks to Melissa Harris for making this possible

Page 162: John Gunner

Page 171: Permission for the use of this image was generously given by Alan W. Heldman

Page 182: P. S. Ryden, Syracuse, NY

Page 199: Courtesy The News-Gazette, Lexington, VA

Page 219: Courtesy Michael Miley Collection, Special Collections and Archives, Washington and Lee University

Page 221: Kim Rushing, courtesy Kim Rushing

Page 229: Kim Rushing, courtesy Kim Rushing

Page 231: Kim Rushing, courtesy Kim Rushing

Page 236: Maude Clay, courtesy Maude Clay

Page 251: Courtesy Pat Broadneaux and Constance Harris

Page 257: Courtesy Pat Broadneaux and Constance Harris

Page 258: Courtesy Pat Broadneaux and Constance Harris

Page 301: Courtesy The Cy Twombly Foundation and Robert Rauschenberg Foundation, Cy Twombly, Untitled, Xerox on paper, 6 x 9 inches (original photograph by Robert Rauschenberg, c. 1952)

Page 313: Courtesy the Birmingham Public Library Archives

Page 314: Courtesy the Birmingham Public Library Archives

Page 315: Patent courtesy the Birmingham Public Library Archives

Page 320: Both courtesy the Birmingham Public Library Archives

Page 321: Courtesy the Birmingham Public Library Archives

Page 329 (upper): Courtesy the Birmingham Public Library Archives

Page 331: Permission for the use of this image was generously given by Alan W. Heldman

Page 357: Caitlin Mann, courtesy Caitlin Mann

Page 367: Photographs by W. Eugene Smith, Collection Center for Creative Photography, University of Arizona, © The Heirs of W. Eugene Smith

Page 398: Ted Orland, courtesy Ted Orland

Page 415: Michael S. Williamson, courtesy Michael S. Williamson

Page 437: Jonathan Crary, courtesy Jonathan Crary